PERFORMANCE
FORDS

PERFORMANCE
FORDS

GRAHAM ROBSON

First published in 2004

A catalogue record for this book is available from the British Library

ISBN 1 84425 027 X

Library of Congress catalog card no. 2003113466

Published by Haynes Publishing, Sparkford, Yeovil, Somerset, BA22 7JJ, UK

Tel: 01963 442030 Fax: 01963 440001
Int. tel: +44 1963 442030 Int. fax: +44 1963 440001
E-mail: sales@haynes.co.uk
Web site: www.haynes.co.uk

Haynes North America, Inc.,
861 Lawrence Drive, Newbury Park,
California 91320, USA

Printed and bound in England by J. H. Haynes & Co. Ltd, Sparkford

Contents

Building an image

Victories made all the toil worthwhile – this being Didier Auriol on the way to winning the 1988 Tour de Corse in his 'works' Sierra RS Cosworth.

Performance Fords in Europe? Quite simply, until 1962, there were none. Ford cars might already have won the Monte Carlo Rally, and the British Saloon Car Championship, but this was down to driver experience rather than brute power. How could there be any performance Fords, when the small cars had used side-valve engines until 1959, and the larger models were heavy and under-powered?

But that was then, and this is now. By the 1970s, and ever after that, Ford not only built and sold more road cars than almost any other car maker, but it was selling fast and exciting models as well. Not only were there millions of Fords on the roads, but rallies and races were full of them – and winning ones, too.

The breakthrough came in 1962. Not only was this the year in which that dynamic personality, Walter Hayes, joined the company, charged with transforming its image, but it was also the year in which Ford set out to develop a worldwide high-performance image. It was a programme that started slowly, and there certainly wasn't a 'five-year plan', but racing, rallying and the launch of specialised new cars soon built up a momentum of their own. It was not until the 1970s that a more coherent strategy began to emerge.

First in the USA, then in Britain, and later in Europe – before long the world of motoring knew what performance Fords were all about. In 1964, Ford-

USA built its first Le Mans car (the GT40), three years later the first Cosworth-designed Formula One engine appeared, and from 1968 there was the Escort Twin-Cam. After that there was the Capri RS2600 in Germany, then the first 16-valve engines arrived – and after that the sky was the limit.

High hopes

Let's be quite clear about this. Without Walter Hayes, there might never have been any performance Fords in Europe, and without the flamboyant success of the original Lotus-Cortina this strategy could so easily have been a flop. Walter, though, had two major advantages – not only was he new to the business, but his chairman, Sir Patrick Hennessy, gave him a free hand.

It was Walter who forged the links with Colin Chapman of Lotus, Walter who somehow found some money to set up a new Motorsport Centre at Boreham, and Walter who acted as an honest broker to bring Lotus, Cosworth and Ford together in 1965.

Although the original Lotus-Cortina was an unreliable indulgence, the Cortina GT was a fast-selling and durable success, so it wasn't long before the sales force fell into line and backed the new strategy. Slowly, but profitably, the business of marketing performance Fords built up. After that, even if Hayes and sales chief Terry Beckett had recommended selling pink-painted tricycles, and the public had liked what it was offered, the dealer chain would have been happy too.

Until 1970, although there seemed to be no settled strategy, more and more higher-performance derivatives began to appear. The Cortina GT was a successful road car which Boreham turned into a great rally car, the Corsair 2000E was the best of a mediocre V4 engined bunch, the Escort Twin-Cam was a Boreham invention that somehow sneaked into production, and the Capri was almost a 'born again' Mustang.

At this point, though, the Rallye Sport programme was invented and with it came the idea of building special cars in a special place. Although this venture was short-lived, it helped to produce an on-going high-performance culture within Ford. Bob Howe, who was Ford's original AVO employee, started work on this idea in August 1968 and recalled: 'J25 – the Twin-Cam – was causing considerable disruption at Halewood. Alex Trotman (he would become Ford's worldwide chairman in the late 1990s) was then running product planning, and told me that the next Escort motorsport car, with BDA engine, couldn't be built there. Alex told me to find a new place, outside the company as we knew it.'

After looking round most of Essex it seems, Bob settled on a Ford-owned building at Aveley, which had just been vacated by another department. To make it suitable for building cars, the total investment in tools, assembly lines and facilities was little more than £600,000.

Well before the end of the year – November 1969 – approval had been granted for a new business-within-a-business to be developed. The Advanced Vehicle Operation (AVO), as it was dubbed, had several objectives, principally to design, develop and build: '. . . a range of low-volume, unique derivatives, for sale by Ford Rallye Sport dealers throughout Europe . . . to project an image of Ford as a technical innovator . . . to support the Ford competition effort in Europe by providing vehicle derivatives in appropriate volume . . .'

Ray Horrocks, a marketing specialist, became the new department's

Sir Patrick Hennessy was Ford-UK's long-serving chairman, who authorised a move into high-performance cars in 1962.

Although the Model T made Ford rich and famous, this was the 'Tin Lizzie' image which had to be changed in the second half of the 20th century.

manager. Several other important personalities joined the small team. Dick Boxall moved down from Halewood to control the building of the AVO plant, Stuart Turner arrived at Boreham as competitions manager, which released Henry Taylor to look after the development of the high-performance engines. Rod Mansfield, later to set up Special Vehicle Engineering in the 1980s, arrived as the fifth employee, to work on design and development.

In the original scheme of things, it might have been possible to build 13 cars a day, but by the early 1970s that capacity had been pushed up to about 30 a day – say, 7,000 cars a year – all on a single five-day week, and an eight hour shift. The first car – an Escort RS1600 – was driven off the line by F1 Champion Graham Hill, with Ray Horrocks alongside him, on 2 November 1970.

What to build – and when?

There was never any lack of ideas about new high-performance models. After Ford's 'works' team won the *Daily Mirror* World Cup Rally in 1970, the idea of building a cheap-and-cheerful car called the Escort Mexico matured. In six months AVO had it in production alongside the RS1600.

Surviving documents, dated 1969 and 1970, suggest that AVO could not survive merely by making cars to support the Motorsport department ('homologation specials', in other words, would not keep the place full). The team were originally considering building cars with 16-valve 1.6-litre BDA engines, and an OHC conversion of the Essex V6 3-litre engine, which Holbay was developing.

These were proposed for the following models at first:

Escort-BDA   (later it would be called the Escort RS1600)
Capri-BDA   (this was previewed, but never put on sale)
Capri-3-litre OHC
Cortina MkIII-BDA
Cortina MkIII-3-litre OHC

By mid-1970, the strategy had changed dramatically, for the 2.6-litre Capri RS2600 had been developed for Ford-Cologne to use in motor racing, in the European Touring Car Championship. The OHC V6 project was fading away, and there was talk of turbocharging the 'Essex' V6 instead. Four-wheel-drive, as already previewed on the rallycross Capris, was also fashionable.

At the same time, the team was considering other projects – such as 3-litre Essex-engined Cortinas (Ford-South Africa would eventually build those), an RS2600-engined Ford Taunus for Ford-Germany, four-wheel-drive Cortina IIIs and Ford-USA V8 engined Capris among them.

The team also proposed setting up a 'customising department', but this was swamped by the Special Build facility, where cars already prepared to race-car and rally-car specification were built in special bays, even before being delivered to their customers.

'The arrival of the Mexico, almost by accident, was really the salvation of AVO,' Bob Howe recalls, 'because the RS1600 really didn't sell as well as we had hoped. We expected to sell 1,000 RS1600s a year – in my enthusiasm I thought that was an ongoing demand – but at £1,495 in 1971 it was an expensive car, almost as much as a Zodiac, and demand soon fell away. The assembly lines at AVO weren't flat out until 1972.'

Other proposals all fell by the wayside, and the team had its work cut out in developing the RS1600, the Mexico and – for 1973 – the Pinto-engined RS2000. Then the onset of the Energy Crisis in October 1973, and the huge rise in petrol prices which followed, hit AVO's prospects very hard indeed. After Ford's sales dropped, and the mainstream Escort factories found themselves with spare capacity, the whispering campaign against AVO began ('Stuart Turner's plaything' – as I once heard it described). The decision to close AVO at the end of 1974 came as a shock.

After the closure announcement, design work on the new Escort RS MkII models – RS1800, RS Mexico and RS2000 – carried on. Even so, by the first weeks of 1975 the AVO assembly lines had emptied, the slings were empty, and the plant was progressively mothballed. It was finally dismantled in the early 1980s. No trace now remains.

Fruits of victory – this being a posed shot of the trophies won by the 'works' rally team in 1963.

Racing and rallying all helped to push forward the same sporting image. This was one of the famous Zakspeed Escort RS1600s, at the Nürburgring in 1974.

New direction

Although the 'performance Ford' programme did not disappear in the late 1970s, it marked time, changed emphasis, and waited for the motoring outlook to brighten up. Although MkII RS model development was completed by the surviving staff at AVO, assembly of those cars was centred at the dedicated Escort assembly plant at Saarlouis, on the German/French border. Soon after this, the last remaining AVO engineers dispersed, and reassigned to other jobs.

Sometimes a good idea did not make it to the showrooms. When conceived in 1980, the Escort RS1700T showed great promise, but lack of four-wheel-drive meant that it was cancelled in 1983 before deliveries could begin.

By the end of the 1970s, in any case, Ford had concluded that it needed to develop a different type of 'performance Ford' – not 'RS' but 'XR'. This time, it was hoped, the emphasis would not be on Rallye Sport, but on ExtRa performance, with more emphasis on equipment and image, rather than on a motorsport heritage. Because the new-fangled XR types would not be built with motorsport so obviously in mind, Ford hoped there might be more sales.

From the beginning, XR derivatives of three forthcoming 1980s models were planned – an XR2 version of the Fiesta, an XR3 version of the front-wheel-drive Escort, and an XR4 version of the forthcoming Sierra.

This explains why the first higher-performance front-wheel-drive Escort, the XR3, was developed by mainstream engineers within Ford-of-Europe, and it also explains why the car, which went on sale in October 1980, was by no means as capable as AVO would have made it.

Fortunately for Ford, ex-AVO engineer Rod Mansfield had not lost his enthusiasm, or his influence. In February 1980 his phone rang: 'It was Gerhard Hartwig, chief engineer of vehicle engineering,' Rod recalls, 'asking me to found Special Vehicle Engineering. I thought for about three milli-seconds, and said "Yes, please!" . . .'

In fact, it was product planner Mike Moreton who had sparked off the change somewhat earlier: 'When AVO closed down, I took what was left of AVO with me, then wrote a Strategy Paper on Specialist Vehicles in Ford-of-Europe, pointing out that specialist cars could certainly be built at Saarlouis, but they needed to be backed by a specialist engineering activity . . .'

Starting with no more than a dozen engineers, Mansfield rapidly built up SVE to more than 50, before it slimmed down again at the turn of the century. There was never any difficulty in attracting engineers. 'Once they heard about SVE, I got a stream of applications to join . . .' said Mansfield.

Money, in the form of operating budgets, was always tight, as was time – because Sales and Marketing was crying out for fast, smart and sexy derivatives. Original SVE products, therefore, were cheap and cheerful – both the Capri 2.8i and the Fiesta XR2 went from 'Good Idea' status to the assembly lines in no more than a year – and in each case SVE had a flying start.

Conceived way back in AVO days in the mid-1970s ('This was the obvious successor to the Capri RS2600', Mike Moreton recalls), the Capri 2.8i was mainly a packaging job, while the XR2 was little more than a careful amalgam of USA-spec Fiesta engineering and Fiesta Supersport styling.

But it got the show on the road, and immediately brought SVE to the motoring world's attention. Although these were, indeed, 'specials', they didn't look that way. All the cars from SVE were as well-detailed as any other new models coming from this major corporation, and that was one of SVE's strengths.

Big ambitions

Within a year, SVE was looking further into Ford's future, not initiating projects, but taking on those which the dealers wanted to sell, and which 'mainstream' Engineering found too cumbersome. It wasn't long before SVE made a speciality of such activities – where administrative corners had to be cut, where favours had to be called in, and where deals had to be done, they were supreme. It was no wonder that this was also the period in which the 'RS' badge was dug out of retirement, and once again became important in Ford's line-up.

This was where Mansfield shone. Distrusted by some of his 'mainstream' colleagues because of his high-profile public reputation, he was the figurehead who built up SVE as a 'can-do' organisation. There are those who said that he made a speciality of missing deadlines, but there are many more who admit that his enthusiastic team was superbly qualified.

But they couldn't do everything. With its head down on important cars like the Escort XR3i and the original Escort Cabriolet, SVE was really too busy to take on Stuart Turner's two new 'homologation specials' in 1983 and 1984 – the Escort RS Turbo and the Sierra RS Cosworth – but it did so anyway! It was typical of Mansfield that he therefore parleyed even more staff out of his bosses – then persuaded Stuart Turner to loan him three Motor-sport staff from Boreham – Terry Bradley, John Griffiths and Bill Meade – to make up the shortfall.

For you and I, these were the cars which sealed the SVE and RS reputation for all time – the RS Turbo for packing so much performance into a civilised package, and the flamboyantly high-winged

Selling the project! Stuart Turner and Mike Moreton showing off the very first RS200 to top management in March 1984.

The RS200 was never likely to be profitable, but it has become legendary among all Ford enthusiasts.

Sierra for, well, everything! Before SVE, nobody had been able to harness 132bhp to front-wheel-drive, and certainly no-one else at Dunton would even consider 150mph Sierras. The RS Turbo, incidentally, was another remarkable project, which raced from 'Good Idea' to 'Job 1' status in a mere 18 months.

This, though, was quite overshadowed by SVE's work on four-wheel-drive cars – not only the Sierra Cosworth 4x4 and the Escort RS Cosworth, but the Sierra XR4x4, the closely related Granada, and several variations on the theme. No rival except Audi tried as hard to influence the public's taste, and no team could have been as puzzled by the slow sales of all these types.

It was the enthusiastic Bob Lutz, chairman, Ford-of-Europe, who urged Ford along the way to 4x4 cars, as Rod Mansfield confirmed: 'He loved cars. He made engineers go crazy, because he always wanted another derivative. He very much wanted Ford to go 4x4 . . .'

SVE's first 4x4 Sierra was originally only meant to be a show car, but even before the end of 1982 Lutz's brief had changed to: 'Make a production car out of your ideas . . .' Not even SVE could do this in less than two years, but the wait was worth it. It proved, if proof was needed, that this incredibly talented team could tackle anything, and get it right.

Not that every four-wheel-drive car they developed came to the market. Among several cancelled, and never even admitted to by Ford, was the Escort XR3i/RS Turbo 4x4 of the late 1980s, which was a very 'hot' programme for a limited period. You don't believe it? Neither did I, until I

Sheer machismo on rubber – the Sierra RS500 Cosworth was built only in 1987, but then dominated motor racing for several years after that. It made money for the factory too!

E501 NWN

visited Boreham one day, and was shown a series of complex and empty castings which had finally been abandoned by the engineers.

There was more. If John Wheeler had ever convinced his bosses that the second version of the stillborn Escort RS1700T should be a four-wheel-drive machine, it would certainly have been engineered by SVE at Dunton. And if Ford's product planners had agreed that 4x4 should ever be matched to automatic transmission Scorpios (prototypes were built – not easy in view of the bulk of the automatic box), SVE would have finalised those ideas too.

Peak activity

As far as the public was concerned, SVE was at the height of its fame in the late 1980s/early 1990s. First they became justly famous for developing, and taming, the rear-drive Sierra RS Cosworths, but they also made the four-wheel-drive version into a supreme road car (and an oh-so-nearly-successful World Championship rally car). Next (and, in my opinion, a master stroke) was the way that John Wheeler was transferred from Boreham to SVE, the whole team then turning his brilliant idea into the wonderful Escort RS Cosworth model.

Make no mistake about this – it was SVE who shook down the complex body engineering (Cosworth 4x4 – plus Escort cabin was an extremely difficult challenge), who finalised, oversaw, and monitored that conversion of the body shell manufacturing facility at Karmann, and who made the road car such a soft riding, well-equipped and sexy machine.

But there was more at this time. First, there was the design of the short-lived Fiesta RS Turbo. An XR2i with the Escort RS Turbo engine? No, not at all, for a great deal of work was needed to match the power train to the smaller car. Then, in a great hurry, work was completed on the still-to-be-launched front-wheel-drive RS2000, which had been designed by 'mainstream' Engineering, but whose handling in prototype form was so disappointing that SVE had to be brought in at the last minute to do a rescue job.

Oh, and at the same time, there were new-generation Escort cabriolets (some with power-operated soft-tops for the first time), diesel-engined Granadas (no, don't mock), and other derivatives.

Then SVE seemed to go off the boil – not that they had forgotten how to deliver, but that for a time Ford management seemed to lose heart in 'their' sort of machines. Which may explain why they were allowed to make only one prototype rear-drive RS2000 (with a 16-valve RS2000 engine and an MT75 gearbox), and a very similar Escort RS Cosworth-based rear-drive car fitted with a silky-smooth Cosworth V6 24-valve unit instead.

The rebirth, very deservedly too, came when SVE then got the job of designing and developing the Fiesta-based Puma, although by this time it was taking longer to get such cars on to the market. Work started in 1994, but it was not until February 1997 that we first set eyes on it.

Like all its spiritual predecessors, the Puma was a much better car than it originally promised to be, for it had excellent handling and storming performance, yet with few unique components except for the sleek, swoopy, 2+2-seater body style. Even though SVE wasn't allowed to lower the ride height ('Legislation!' was the excuse I got when I complained . . .), this was the best-handling and best-steering Fiesta-based car of all time.

Two well-known Ford characters – Mike Moreton (left) and John Wheeler, with the original 'mule' for the Escort RS Cosworth, which was built in 1988. It might look like an Escort RS Turbo to you, but under the skin there was a shortened Sierra Cosworth 4x4 platform . . .

Strategy changes

In the mid-1990s, Ford's attitude to the marketing of high-performance models had changed direction – yet by 2000 it had reversed on to an original path. The first change, in a reaction to ever-tightening legislation and the rapacious attitude of insurance companies, was to abandon the 'RS' and the specialised-model theme completely. The second change, which began to emerge in 2000/01, was to get back into that market once again!

In 1995/96 not one, but four different high-performance Escorts all disappeared – XR3i, RS2000, RS2000 4x4 and RS Cosworth – with low sales, new noise regulations, high insurance costs, and a change in public demand all variously being blamed. Although the Puma arrived soon afterwards, there was then an ominous lull.

For a time, Ford stated that it would develop a series of 'ST' badged models (ST = Special Tuning), but cars like the Mondeo ST24 soon proved the point that these were to be 'warm hatch' rather than 'hot hatch' types. Salvation, however, was at hand. Richard Parry-Jones became the technical chief, who was not only a closet motorsport freak, but he was also absolutely determined to raise Ford's standard of roadholding and handling.

It helped that, in 1998, Ford finally took control of Cosworth Racing, recalling vividly just how resourceful that company had always been in producing great road car engines as well as out-and-out competition units, and decided to do the same again in the 21st century.

At this time, Ford's bosses, too, concluded that they did, after all, need to be represented at the flamboyant end of the market. As Parry-Jones rose smoothly through the heirarchy, he generated enthusiasm, took disciples with him, and somehow the 'performance Ford' ethos was mysteriously reborn. As the new century opened, it gradually became clear that Ford would reintroduce not one, but maybe even three new levels of faster-than-standard types. The lowest level would be the ST models, the sporty-but-still practical types would carry the RS badge, and it was even rumoured that the legendary 'Cosworth' badge might also re-appear on selected top-of-the-range models.

The first evidence of this came when Richard Parry-Jones's successor in Europe, Martin Leach, previewed, then presided over the much-delayed launch of the Focus RS in 2002. By that time it was already clear that other RS, and maybe Cosworth-badged performance Fords would follow.

As Ford proudly reached its centenary in 2003, several new performance Fords were known to be in development. The story was by no means complete – and Ford enthusiasts hope that it will never be so.

Projects like Supervan were a pure indulgence, and were never sold to the public, but Ford's clientele loved to see the engineers 'thinking aloud'. Supervan 3 of 1995 had a 650bhp Cosworth F1 engine mounted amidships, and drove the rear wheels.

Acknowledgements

A book like this can't be written quickly. In my case it has taken 40 years, for you could say that I first became interested in 1963, when I rallied in one of the very first Cortina GTs. Since that time I have enjoyed lengthy experience of almost every one of the cars listed, and have personally owned about half of them.

Over the years, too, I have enjoyed long conversations and interviews with Ford characters as diverse as Walter Hayes and Peter Ashcroft, Sir Terence Beckett and Brian Hart, Rod Mansfield and Stuart Turner, John Wheeler and Martin Leach, Colin Chapman and Henry Taylor, Bob Howe and Keith Duckworth, Mike Moreton and Ray Horrocks. If you then add on the talks I have had with other 'performance Ford' personalities, the list is almost endless. Each and every one added something to the stories I have to tell.

I owe very special thanks to everyone at Ford's Photographic Department in Essex, who have now been helping me with illustrations for my Ford-related projects for almost 30 years. The work which started with research into the 'works' Escorts of the 1970s is still on-going today. In this, and in helping me with other aspects of Ford's heritage, I owe special thanks to Tom Malcolm, Jim Fowler and Dave Hill.

Quite simply, this job could not have been done without their help – and I thank them all.

Graham Robson, Bridport, October 2003

World rallying was the peak of the Ford publicity and marketing iceberg. Colin McRae (left) and Nicky Grist with the first of the Focus WRCs, which won so many World rallies from 1999.

Cortina GT MkI

1963–1966

The Cortina GT of 1963–1966 was the original performance Ford, and donated some of its chassis engineering to the Lotus-Cortina. From late 1964, it had a wide-mouth grille, and through-flow ventilation in the cabin – for the day, a great advance.

Motorsport

Originally seen as an 'interim' car, to be used until the Lotus-Cortina came on stream, the Cortina GT won many events on its own merits. First used in 1963, it became an outright rally winner, and a successful 'class' car in motor racing.

Boreham worked hard to add to the GT's strength, and homologation specification. 'Works' rally cars won the East African Safari and the French Alpine events in 1964, plus many class and category wins up to 1966. Success in his own GT caused Ford to sign up Roger Clark, who became a fixture in the team. In 1963 alone, the GT won the British Saloon Car Race Championship, and the prestigious 12-hour Marlboro saloon car race in the USA.

The very first of the 'Performance Fords' was the original Cortina GT, a simply engineered up-grade of the Cortina which went on to sell in huge numbers, and to win countless rallies and races around the world. Not only was it the first type of car to be prepared at the brand-new Boreham Motorsport Centre, but it was the essential base from which the Lotus-Cortina was evolved, a car which had an even more glittering reputation.

Ford originally designed the Cortina as a family car to fill a yawning gap between the small Anglia and large Zephyr/Zodiac ranges, the emphasis being on a spacious cabin, with a lightweight body shell, low running costs and low selling price. This was the car which featured the characteristic 'Ban-the-Bomb' tail lamp style, and it immediately became the best-selling Ford of all time – and headed the UK's charts for month after month.

At first there was no plan to make a sporting version. Engineer Fred Hart and the new Public Affairs Director Walter Hayes then got together and encouraged the birth of a Cortina 'secret weapon'. A 1.5-litre version of the engine, which had already proven to be bomb-proof in Formula Junior racing, was power-tuned by Cosworth (this was its first official contract with

The original Cortina GT was easily recognised by those famous 'Ban the Bomb' tail lamps, and of course, by the 'GT' badges on the rear wings.

Ford), while the transmission, suspension and braking were all improved to suit. The GT was given front-wheel disc brakes when most other cars in its class still used drums. The new 78bhp car was introduced in March 1963. At £749 (two-door) or £767 (four-door) it was a real performance bargain.

The same engine/gearbox combination was used in a Capri GT, but this was not a success. It was also used in the Corsair GT, but this model was too heavy and too 'transatlantic' to be a 'Performance Ford' either.

In the original models, the zestful performance, the slick gearchanging, and the eager character were all well-liked, although the awful choice of intermediate gear ratios, and the rather basic trim were not. (It was based on the 'De Luxe', not the 'Super' version of this range.) There were no radial-ply tyres on this car, and there was too much painted metal in the cabin, but no-one seemed to mind. Before long, up to 3,000 GTs were being built every month.

I actually owned two such cars from new, which were thrashed unmercifully, and which never let me down. Like many customers, I found the all-day 80mph cruising speed and the possibility of 28–30mpg fuel economy quite beguiling – for by mid-1960s standards, this was difficult to beat.

In the next three years the specification was changed persistently, although there was never any need to make changes to the engine, which was both robust and amazingly tuneable. In October 1963 there was a new fascia, with a built-in rev counter (earlier cars had used an instrument 'pod' on the steering column).

Only one year later the entire Cortina range (which included the GT and the closely related Lotus-Cortina) was given a 'mid-life' facelift. Mechanically, this involved adding twin trailing radius-arms to locate the GT's rear axle more accurately (this system would be adopted on Lotus-Cortinas from mid-1965 too), but the most visible change was yet another new fascia style, which included swivelling 'eye-ball' fresh air vents on either side. This, together with chrome air outlets on the rear quarter pillars, and a full-width front grille, made the 'MkI½' GT visually quite distinctive.

Before MkI production ended in the summer of 1966 (the re-styled MkII was on the way), no fewer than 78,947 GTs had been built, and the 'Performance Ford' image had been well-and-truly established.

The first Cortina GT had its rev-counter on a pod on the steering column, with extra dials on the centre console.

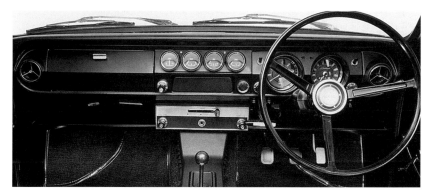

From late 1964, the Cortina GT received a restyled fascia, complete with 'swivelling eyeball' face-level vents on each side of the display.

Specification

Cortina GT MkI

ENGINE

Type:	Ford Kent overhead-valve four-cylinder
Capacity:	1,499cc
Bore/stroke:	80.97 x 72.8mm
Compression ratio:	9.0:1
Max power:	78bhp at 5,200rpm
Max torque:	97lb ft at 3,600rpm
Cylinders:	four, in-line, longitudinally mounted
Cylinder head:	cast iron
Block:	cast iron
Valve gear:	two valves per cylinder, operated by single camshaft, pushrods and rockers
Fuelling:	one downdraught dual-choke Weber carburettor
Installation:	front-mounted, longitudinal

TRANSMISSION

Type:	front-engine, rear-wheel-drive
Gearbox:	four-speed manual

SUSPENSION/STEERING

Front:	independent by coil springs, MacPherson struts, anti-roll bar and telescopic dampers
Rear:	beam axle, with half-elliptic leaf springs, (radius arms from late 1964), telescopic dampers

STEERING

Type:	recirculating ball, no power assistance
Lock-to-lock:	4.2 turns

BRAKES

Front:	9.5in (241mm) solid discs
Rear:	9.0 x 1.75in (229 x 44.5mm) drums
System:	hydraulic, no servo assistance

WHEELS & TYRES

Wheels:	steel disc, 4.0J x 13in
Tyres:	5.60-13in cross-ply

BODY/CHASSIS

Type:	pressed-steel monocoque, two-door or four-door saloon
Weight:	1,750lb (794kg)

PERFORMANCE

Max speed:	94mph (151kph)
0–60mph:	13.9sec
Standing-start ¼-mile:	18.7sec

PRICE at LAUNCH

£749 (two-door saloon) in 1963

Lotus-Cortina MkI

1963–1966

The Lotus-Cortina MkI was built from 1963 to 1966, and was Ford's first-ever twin-cam-powered model.

Many years ago, when so-called 'classic owners' couldn't be bothered to learn all about their cars, the original Lotus-Cortinas sometimes got a bad press. Go-faster fanatics tended to look at Escort Twin-Cams, see that they were smaller and lighter, and chose them instead. That tide turned some time ago. Lotus-Cortinas – particularly MkIs – are now extremely desirable machines.

It is important that these cars should be preserved, understood and loved, for when the original model was unveiled in 1963, it was the very first Ford 'homologation special' – indeed the first very Performance Ford of them all. Everyone of you out there who owns a hot Escort, Capri, Fiesta or whatever, should know that Ford's sporting and performance heritage was born at Cheshunt more than 40 years ago.

Hayes + Chapman = Dynamite

This story really started in 1962 when Fleet Street newspaper editor Walter Hayes arrived at Ford, to take over the Public Affairs department. This job included overseeing Ford's activities in motorsport, which was still a rather lack-lustre affair. Within months of his appointment, Hayes got the go ahead to start planning a bigger programme, including a new race-winning saloon.

Getting together with Colin Chapman of Lotus, Hayes worked out a brilliant scheme for a new homologation special. With the help of Keith Duckworth at Cosworth, Lotus was already developing its own new twin-cam engine. This was actually based on the rugged bottom end of the Ford pushrod engine already being fitted to Anglia models, and to Formula Junior

18

cars, while Ford was about to reveal the ultra-light Cortina, of which a more powerful Cortina GT was planned.

The Hayes-Chapman 'master plan' was for Lotus to completely re-engineer the brand-new Cortina GT model, not only by slotting in the new Lotus-Ford twin-cam engine, but to use as many light alloy body panels and castings as possible, and to accept a new Lotus-developed rear suspension system. Not only that, but the cars – at least 1,000 of them, to ensure Group 2 homologation – would be assembled at the Lotus factory in Cheshunt, to the north of London.

In later years, incidentally, when the new model had established its own legend, both Hayes and Chapman claimed to have had the original bright idea . . .

To be rushed through against a near-impossible timetable, the Lotus-Cortina (or the 'Cortina-developed-by-Lotus' as Ford insisted on calling it for a time) would be previewed in January 1963 and put on sale as rapidly as possible, with homologation being rushed through so that the 'works' teams could start beating the 3.8-litre Jaguars in motor racing!

MkI development – complete redesign needed

The first Lotus-Cortina was about as different from the 'base' Cortina as possible – although experience (often bitter, and troublesome) on production cars, meant that they became progressively less and less special as the months and years passed by. Starting around the basis of a Cortina GT two-door body shell, Lotus added its own 105bhp twin-cam engine, backed it by the close-ratio Elan gearbox (which used a Cortina casing, in any case), and specified transmission assemblies with light alloy clutch bell housing and rear axle nose piece castings instead of steel.

The rear suspension was completely revised. Not only were the Cortina's leaf springs discarded – they were replaced by combined coil spring/damper units which occupied the same space as the standard car's dampers – but there was

Every Lotus-Cortina MkI production car was white with characteristic green stripes and the panel across the tail. These cars were much faster, lighter and lower than the Cortina GT.

The original Lotus-Cortina had 5.5in-rim width wheels, which was thought to be very daring in the early 1960s.

Lotus-Cortinas became famous race and rally cars. This was Sir John Whitmore's legendary 1965 European Touring Car Championship winner.

substantial tubular stiffening inside the shell to strengthen the shell mountings for these springs. The beam rear axle was then located by a combination of twin trailing radius arms and what was called an 'A-frame' which effectively tied the body shell to the axle nose piece. Other special touches, which were immediately obvious when one opened the boot, were the wide-rim steel spare wheel bolted to the boot floor instead of tucked to one side, and the electrical battery which also lived in that area (because of the bulk of the twin-cam engine, it could no longer be fitted in the engine bay).

Add to this the lower and stiffened suspension, the 5.5in steel wheel rims, the new fascia and the aluminium doors, bonnet and boot lid panels, the standard colour scheme of Ford white with Lotus green flashes on the sides and across the tail, and the Lotus badges (even though this was officially a Ford!), and here was a distinctive machine. There were no alternative colour schemes – although some owners had their cars resprayed after delivery.

Series production, in numbers, did not begin until the middle of 1963 (Ford's own Cortina GT, after all, did not go on sale until March of that year), yet as soon as it was homologated in September 1963 the Lotus-Cortina started winning in saloon car races. On the track, however, and especially on the road, there were many teething problems, most of them connected with that special rear suspension, and with Lotus's own incredibly casual attitude to build quality.

The crux of the suspension problems was that the combined shock/spring mountings gave the shell a hard time in areas for which high stresses had not originally been expected. This often resulted in body shell kinks appearing in that area until Lotus beefed up the stiffening arrangements. More serious was the tendency of the A-frame to cause high stresses at the mounting point on the axle casing. After a period of use and repeated stress and vibration, bolts fixing the banjo casing to the rest of the axle tended to loosen off and this let out all the oil. Unless the owner kept a very careful eye on this assembly, the first indication that something was wrong was when the axle became noisy – after which a breakage was inevitable.

Motorsport success

Once the initial teething troubles had been sorted out – and mechanics had learned how to keep the fragile rear suspension in one piece – the original Lotus-Cortinas soon built up a phenomenal record in motor racing. The leaf-spring rear suspension installation was adopted as soon as possible (in mid 1965), when it also became a great rally car.

In motor racing, Jim Clark won the British Saloon Car Championship in 1964 and Sir John Whitmore won the 1965 European Touring Car Championship. Lotus-Cortinas were also dominant in Britain in 1965 and 1966, and in Europe in 1964 and 1966, although quirks in the regulations denied them of outright success.

'Works' Lotus-Cortinas won the Acropolis and RAC rallies of 1966, the Swedish Rally of 1967, plus the 1965 Welsh Rally.

In the first two years of assembly therefore, many changes and palliatives were forced through, some of them never publicised. Some engines did not develop full power, so Special Equipment versions were also made available, these having 115bhp engines; these were surprisingly little known at the time.

From July 1964 a two-piece propeller shaft (with a centre 'steady' bearing under the floor) took over from the one-piece, most of the light-alloy panels and castings were abandoned in favour of pressed steel and cast iron, and a wider set of gearbox ratios was fitted. Then, from October 1964, the latest 'Aeroflow' type of body shell was standardised, with full-width grille, a new-type fascia and through-flow ventilation.

Next, in June 1965, came the most important change. The A-frame suspension was abandoned in favour of the Cortina GT's leaf spring and radius arm set-up, which track tests by heroes like Jack Sears and Vic Elford showed to be surprisingly effective. Finally, from October 1965, yet another set of gearbox ratios was used, these being from the Corsair 2000E. This, incidentally, was the first time at which left-hand-drive versions of this model were officially built.

Because the Cortina was about to be restyled, the last of 3,301 MkIs was produced at Cheshunt in the autumn of 1966, after which there was a six-month gap with no Lotus-Cortinas on the market. Then, in March 1967, Ford announced the Lotus-Cortina MkII, a very different car which it proposed to build at Dagenham, among other MkII-shape Cortinas, rather than at Lotus, whose build quality had often dismayed Ford, to put it politely.

Early Lotus-Cortinas had a simple fascia/instrument display . . .

. . . but a much more comprehensive display was fitted from late 1964.

Specification	
Lotus-Cortina MkI	
ENGINE	
Type:	Lotus-Ford, twin-cam
Capacity:	1,558cc
Bore/stroke:	82.55 x 72.8mm
Compression ratio:	9.5:1
Max power:	105bhp at 5,500rpm
Max torque:	108lb ft at 4.000rpm
Cylinders:	four, in-line, longitudinally mounted
Cylinder head:	cast aluminium
Block:	cast iron
Valve gear:	two valves per cylinder, twin chain-driven overhead camshafts, bucket tappets
Fuelling:	twin dual-choke Weber Type 40 DCOE carburettors
TRANSMISSION	
Type:	front-engine, rear-wheel-drive
Gearbox:	four-speed manual
SUSPENSION	
Front:	independent by coil springs, MacPherson struts, anti-roll bar and telescopic dampers
Rear:	beam axle, with (original cars) combined coil spring/telescopic damper units, A-bracket and radius arms. From June 1965, half-elliptic leaf springs, radius-arms and telescopic dampers
STEERING	
Type:	recirculating ball
Lock-to-lock:	3.0 turns
BRAKES	
Front (disc):	9.5in (241mm)
Rear (drum):	9.0 x 1.75in (229 x 44.4mm)
System:	hydraulic, with vacuum servo assistance
WHEELS & TYRES	
Wheels:	steel disc wheels, 5.5Jx13in
Tyres:	6.00-13in cross-ply
BODY/CHASSIS	
Type:	pressed-steel monocoque, two-door saloon
Weight:	1,820lb (825kg)
PERFORMANCE	
Max speed:	106mph (170kph) approx
0–60mph:	9.9sec
PRICE at LAUNCH	
£1,100 in 1963	

GT40

1964–1969

Ford designed the GT40 as a race winning two-seater, but a few road cars were also produced. The shape was so perfect that the reborn car of 2003 was almost identical.

Ford's greatest sporting icon was designed with one great aim in life – that it should win the Le Mans 24 Hours race. If it should beat Ferrari on the way, so much the better. This, though, is not a simple story. The original GT40 was not a success; the Fords which first won at Le Mans were very different, and the GT40s which took the final victories for the type at Le Mans in 1968 and 1969 were privately owned.

The miracle was that the project was successful at all, for its history is a real muddle. Financed from the USA, conceived and designed in England, then re-engineered in Detroit, here was a classic case of 'management by committee' – and, as usual, some of that committee did not really know what they were doing.

Ford has never enjoyed putting anything on sale that cannot turn in a profit. Amazingly, they did so with the GT40, which was put into limited production in the UK. It must be one of very few Ford models (the RS200 was another) guaranteed to make the company's accountants feel weak at the knees.

After Ford-USA had tried, and failed, to buy Ferrari in 1963, the reaction was to set up an in-house operation to beat the Italians at their own game (and win the Le Mans race). Although the basic idea, and the mid-engined style, came from Detroit, much of the engineering was from Eric Broadley's British Lola operation (and, later, Len Bailey). John Wyer was hired from Aston Martin to run the British end of the operation and to set up workshops and a factory at Slough.

The first prototypes were unsuccessful. Their aluminium-blocked V8 engines and Italian Colotti gearboxes were fragile, their aerodynamic

performance was frighteningly unstable, and they were unreliable. It was not until 1965, with robust new AC Cobra-style V8s, and a German ZF transmission, that they became competitive.

To make the GT40 eligible for Group 4 sports car racing, at least 50 near-identical cars had to be made. This was achieved – and, in the end, many more followed – by building the cars in Slough, from parts and sub-assemblies almost entirely bought in from specialists. The only major Ford-manufactured item was the big, 4.7-litre V8, which was similar in many ways to that which had already been used in the AC Cobra.

Cars which went on sale could either be used for sports car racing, or (for rich men, who could find suitable roads) on the open road. Even in the first two years, when the accent was purely on motorsport, a surprising percentage became 'road' cars – I can well remember collecting a road-registered GT40 in central London, driving it away in rush hour traffic, then blasting up the M1 motorway to my home near Coventry. It is the only car I can recall which never needed a horn, or flashing headlamps to persuade other traffic to move out of the way!

Even so, the ground clearance was adequate, the ride was surprisingly supple, and it was easy to start after an overnight snooze in the open air. The only major problems were that it attracted police car attention like honey attracts bees, and there was no way of arriving any-where, unannounced.

Like all race-winning sports cars of its day, the GT40 (that title came from its height, in inches, by the way) was a two-seater coupé with its engine behind the cabin, driving the rear wheels. To reduce costs, and to make it possible to manufacture the car in numbers, it was based around a steel monocoque, with glass-fibre body panels. Although door 'glass' ended in the usual position (parallel to the top of the windscreen), the door frames themselves swept in across the roof, almost but not quite meeting in the centre of the roof. This made entry and exit from the

On the GT40, hot air which had passed through the water radiators was exhausted through vents in the bonnet panel.

wrap-around seats a little easier – but it also made the doors difficult to manufacture, and to keep sealed at high-speed.

The engine was variously rated according to usage – well over 370bhp was available for racing with four dual-choke Weber carburettors, but as little as 300bhp (with a single Mustang-type Holley carb) was sometimes specified for road-going types – and the road cars had synchromesh on all forward gears of the ZF transmission. The rest of the chassis – all-independent suspension, rack-and-pinion steering, which was heavy at low speeds, and centre-lock wire-spoke wheels – was conventional: racing-type tyres were always fitted, even on road cars.

Because this was really a racing car which had to be sold in numbers, there were many compromises, while the hope that customers would drive the cars on the road imposed others. Although the cabin was adequately large for two passengers, there was nowhere to put luggage: on late-model 'pure-road' cars, attempts to add stowage boxes in the tail close to the silencers meant that everything got very hot!

Ventilation and creature comforts were poor, for except on a very few, much-modified cars, there was no way of getting fresh air into the interior without permanently opening one or both side windows (which only had pivoting Perspex panels in the middle of fixed plastic panes). Interior noise was high – and exhilirating.

Amazingly, though, a GT40 in road-car tune was quite flexible in traffic (but the cooling system could not cope with serious traffic jams), although it was best not to use any gear higher than third (of five) until the de-limited sign was passed. It helped to wear casual clothing, to carry almost no belongings – a briefcase and a toothbrush was quite enough to fill up the passenger's footwell – and to take regular doses of Valium to keep one's nervous system in check!

Although the first car was finished in April 1964, and raced at Le Mans a few weeks later, deliveries to private owners did not begin until August 1965. The rush to finish 50 'production' cars occupied 1965 and 1966, but assembly carried on thereafter, in small numbers. JW Automotive (John Willment's finance was behind this) took over the operation from Ford Advanced Vehicles in 1967, and sold the last few cars in 1969. Even then, the story was not quite over, as three tubs remained, with unallocated chassis numbers – these eventually being built up, with full approval from Ford, by the resourceful Brian Wingfield in the mid-1990s!

To be brutally honest, the GT40 was not a good road car, and it certainly was never meant to be used as one. No normal Ford dealer would have been able to deal with its day-to-day vagaries, and the idea of asking for

Proving that the road-car version of the GT40 was practical, Ford provided comfortable bucket seats, carpets and side windows which pivoted to provide ventilation.

comprehensive insurance is almost laughable. Even so, 35 of the original production run were initially delivered in 'road-car' spec, and a further seven civilised MkIIIs – the real road versions – were to follow.

If you include prototypes, specials (such as the open-top race cars, the much-modified JWA 'Mirages', and the 12 honeycomb-chassis'd MkIVs which raced in 1967, no fewer than 130 genuine factory-built or factory-blessed cars of this type were manufactured. Although many were crashed in motor races, and any number of them corroded badly in the 1970s when they were no longer fashionable to collectors, almost all of them have survived, been restored or, sometimes dubiously, recreated.

The story, however, does not end at that point. During the 1980s Peter Thorp's Safir company bought the rights to build another run of cars. Having updated the design in some ways (he used alloy fuel tanks, alloy wheels, better brakes and suspension, for instance), he then made a further 40 cars before the end of the 1990s.

Then there were the pastiches, or look-alikes (it would be wrong to call them replicas because they were not exact recreations). Starting in the 1970s, companies as diverse as KVA, Sbarro, ERA Replica Automobiles (of the USA), DJ Sports Cars and GT Developments all produced cars looking exactly right, but with tubular chassis of their own designs, and sometimes with different engines (notably the light-alloy Rover V8 power plant). Many more of these types were – and continue to be – made, which means that customers can enjoy the thrill of driving a so-called GT40 which looks right, even if almost every true side of the lineage had been lost.

Cortina GT MkII

1966–1970

Although the Cortina GT MkII of 1966–1970 had a completely different, more rounded body style, it used the same basic body platform and running gear as the original GT which founded this pedigree. The MkII version had wider front and rear wheel tracks, but was otherwise nearly identical at first.

The new body style, for which two-door and four-door styles were available, added a more capacious cabin, and the weight had crept up a little, but the GT's essential character remained. Mechanically, the same MkI-style 78bhp engine was used at first, but after only a matter of months a much better set of internal gear ratios (these were usually known as the 'Corsair 2000E' ratios, because they were typical of that particular car) were adopted. Wider rim wheels and radial ply tyres had become optional. All this, and up-rated trim and fascia appointments meant that the MkII began to sell even faster than the earlier type.

In October 1967, after only one year in production, the MkII was given a new, larger and more powerful version of the engine, this being the first usage of the famous 'Bowl-in-Piston' or cross-flow version of the Kent engine. Now of 1,599cc (with a longer cylinder stroke), and with a torquey 88bhp, this was the engine family which would power so many Fords in the next twenty years.

Although radial-ply tyres were standardised at this time, the rear suspension radius arms would shortly be deleted from the specification (except for some export markets). An estate car version of this car became available during 1968 as a special order.

From late 1968 there was a further upgrade. On the one hand, the GT had yet another change to the fascia style and there was the option of reclining front seats (two-door models only), the handbrake was finally located on a restyled centre console (instead of being an 'umbrella handle' under the dash), and there was a new type of gearbox linkage, the single-rail type.

By 1968 more than 3,500 GTs were being built every month. By the time production ended, in mid-1970, no fewer than 62,592 two-door and 54,538 four-door saloons had been sold.

The Cortina MkII was the first car to use the Kent cross-flow engine, in 1967, and was available in two-door or four-door styles.

Specification

Cortina GT MkII
(1,499cc at first, 1,599cc from late 1967 – 1.6-litre differences in brackets.)

ENGINE

Type:	Ford Kent overhead-valve four-cylinder
Capacity:	1,499cc [1,599cc]
Bore/stroke:	80.97 x 72.8mm [80.97 x 77.62mm]
Compression ratio:	9.0:1
Max power:	78bhp at 5,200rpm [88bhp at 5,400rpm]
Max torque:	97lb ft at 3,600rpm [96lb ft at 3,600rpm]
Cylinders:	four, in-line, longitudinally mounted
Cylinder head:	cast iron
Block:	cast iron
Valve gear:	two valves per cylinder, single camshaft, pushrods and rockers
Fuelling:	one downdraught dual-choke Weber carburettor
Installation:	front-mounted, longitudinal

TRANSMISSION

Type:	front-engine, rear-wheel-drive
Gearbox:	four-speed manual

SUSPENSION

Front:	independent by coil springs, MacPherson struts, anti-roll bar and telescopic dampers
Rear:	beam axle, with half-elliptic leaf springs, radius arms (no radius arms from 1968 on), telescopic dampers

STEERING

Type:	recirculating ball, no power assistance
Lock-to-lock:	4.2 turns

BRAKES

Front:	9.62in (244mm) solid discs
Rear:	9.0 x 1.75in (229 x 44.5mm) drums
System:	hydraulic, no servo assistance

WHEELS & TYRES

Wheels:	steel disc, 4.0J x 13in [4.5J x 13in]
Tyres:	5.60-13in cross-ply [165-13in radial-ply]

BODY/CHASSIS

Type:	pressed-steel monocoque, two-door or four-door saloon or (special order) five-door estate car style
Weight:	1,955lb (887kg) [1,994lb (905kg)]

PERFORMANCE
(1968/70 1.6-litre model)

Max speed:	98mph (158kph) approx
0–60mph:	13.1sec
Standing-start ¼-mile:	18.8sec

PRICE at LAUNCH

£810 in 1966
£865 in late 1967 (1.6-litre model)

The secret of the Cortina 1600E was the way that it combined Cortina GT running gear, Lotus Cortina suspension, and a special decoration package.

Specification

Cortina 1600E

ENGINE
Type:	Ford Kent overhead-valve four-cylinder
Capacity:	1,599cc
Bore/stroke:	80.97 x 77.62mm
Compression ratio:	9.0:1
Max power:	88bhp at 5,400rpm
Max torque:	96lb ft at 3,600rpm
Cylinders:	four, in-line, longitudinally mounted
Cylinder head:	cast iron
Block:	cast iron
Valve gear:	two valves per cylinder, camshaft, pushrods and rockers
Fuelling:	one downdraught dual-choke Weber carburettor
Installation:	front-mounted, longitudinal

TRANSMISSION
Type:	front-engine, rear-wheel-drive
Gearbox:	four-speed manual

SUSPENSION
Front:	independent by coil springs, MacPherson struts, anti-roll bar and telescopic dampers
Rear:	beam axle, with half-elliptic leaf springs, radius arms, telescopic dampers

STEERING
Type:	recirculating ball, no power assistance
Lock-to-lock:	4.2 turns

BRAKES
Front:	9.62in (244mm) solid discs
Rear:	9.0 x 1.75in (229 x 44.5mm) drums
System:	hydraulic, no servo assistance

WHEELS & TYRES
Wheels:	sculpted steel disc wheels, 5.5J x 13in
Tyres:	165-13in radial-ply

BODY/CHASSIS
Type:	pressed-steel monocoque, two-door or four-door saloon style
Weight:	2,065lb (937kg)

PERFORMANCE
Max speed:	98mph (158kph) approx
0–60mph:	13.1sec
Standing-start 1/4-mile:	18.8sec

PRICE at LAUNCH
£982 in 1967

Cortina 1600E

1967–1970

Although 1600E development was completed in a matter of weeks, and the budget was non-existent, it became an extraordinarily successful 'niche' model. In three years, no fewer than 57,524 four-door and 2,563 (export only) two-door saloons were produced.

Walter Hayes once told me that he spent £400 with Hoopers, the coachbuilders, to do a leather and wood interior for the Cortina GT – which was the essence of the 1600E. In fact, a little more than this was involved, for elements of the Lotus-Cortina MkII were included as well.

The 1600E catered for a growing niche in the market place, where 'E' stood for 'Executive', this being a type of car which might be sold to (or supplied to, by a company) a driver with higher aspirations than a Cortina GT. For the 1600E, Ford evolved an intriguing amalgam of features, which worked surprisingly well.

The basis of this car was the Cortina GT MkII, for the engine, transmission and chassis features were always shared. For the 1600E, however, the spring/damper settings of the Lotus-Cortina MkII were adopted (this lowered the car, and made it stiffer), while a set of the then-fashionable Rostyle steel wheels, with 5.5in wide rims, were standardised.

The real advance, though, was in the cabin, which was treated to special high-grade carpets, wood trim on the fascia and door cappings, plushily trimmed leather-look-alike seats, and an aluminium spoked steering wheel. Front seats reclined, and there was a special range of exterior colours (including metallic purple and gold shades).

Here, for £982, was a car which looked as distinctive as a Lotus-Cortina, and handled like one too, but which was as simple, fast and reliable as a Cortina GT. Almost without realising it, Ford had fallen on an unbeatable 'Unique Selling Proposition' which they sometimes managed to repeat, with other models, in years to come.

Although the 1600E always tracked the changes of the contemporary GT MkII, it also retained its rear suspension radius arms. For 1969, at mid-range facelift time, the price leapt to £1,073, but demand stayed buoyant. In 1970 the publicity coup of lending a fleet of 1600Es to every member of the England football World Cup squad worked wonders.

Corsair 2000E

1967–1970

This Ford publicity shot emphasises the gloss the company tried to apply to the 2000E. In fact, it was a near-100mph car.

Although early Corsairs were not liked (their styling was 'transatlantic' to say the least), they matured in later years. One particular version, the 2000E, was an agreeable amalgam of performance and equipment. Although not ultra-rapid, it deserves its inclusion as a 'performance Ford'.

The original Corsair of 1963 was devised as a replacement for the unsuccessful Consul Classic, and took shape around a longer-wheelbase derivative of the Cortina platform and running gear. Most of the extra cabin space was concentrated in the rear compartment. Accordingly it was longer, heavier and not quite as fast (although there was a Cortina GT-engined version). The style, by the Ford-USA personality Roy Brown, had a sharp

Wall-to-wall wood veneer on the fascia of the Corsair 2000E.

Motorsport

Although the Corsair was never intended to be a competition car, Ford used it several times for long-distance driving 'stunts'. The 2000E's claim to fame was when Eric Jackson and Ken Chambers 'raced' a Union Castle liner, the *Windsor Castle*, from Cape Town to Southampton in May 1967. By the judicious use of aircraft to lift the car over inhospitable stretches of Africa, the Corsair could have won the race, but in the end Ford settled for an honourable draw.

nose which was influenced by the Thunderbird of the early 1960s. It was, however, more roomy than the Cortina, although heavier, and had a definite marketing appeal.

Two years later the Corsair was the first British Ford to receive a new 60° V4 engine: this was a close relative of the still-to-come V6 Essex engine which was to power so many future models. The four-cylinder versions had a counter-rotating balancer shaft, but in their original specification were still not very smooth, or powerful.

The 2000E version, launched in January 1970, was an altogether better car and qualifies as a 'Performance Ford'. It was the second of the Ford 'E' (for 'Executive') models (the Zodiac had been first), and would soon be joined by the Cortina 1600E type, whose marketing thrust was the same. In the 1970s there would also be 'E-type' Capris and Escorts.

Ford wanted to use this engine in the Capri (which was still to come), and sought to power-tune it. In the Corsair 2000E the engine was much improved, for it had a twin-choke Weber carburettor and a new camshaft profile, which boosted peak output to 97bhp, and this was matched to the latest gearbox, which had a nicely chosen set of internal ratios. This unit soon became known as the '2000E' box, even though it was used in many other Fords of the 1960s and 1970s.

At the same time, the interior was much improved, with reclining seats, a walnut fascia panel, and cut-pile nylon carpets. A rev counter, a remote-control gearchange and Aeroflow ventilation were all standard. There was a vinyl roof cover and the exterior detailing was made distinctive with a new-type grille and with rubber-faced overriders.

Cortina GT-type suspension had always been standard, but for the 2000E wide-rim wheels and radial-ply tyres were added: radius arms were retained at the rear. Although Ford had no plans to make a motorsport car out of the 2000E, it was nevertheless a quick (if not sensationally fast) car, and could almost reach 100mph in favourable conditions. My personal memories are of a car which seemed to be as fast, but quieter in operation, than the Cortina GTs which I had owned a few years earlier.

Originally built at Halewood (on assembly lines parallel to those of the original Escort), and from 1969 at Dagenham, the 2000E was always a very successful model. Individual 2000E figures do not survive, but in less than three years no fewer than 331,095 Corsairs of all types were built.

Specification	
Corsair 2000E	
ENGINE	
Type:	Ford Essex V4-cylinder
Capacity:	1,996cc
Bore/stroke:	93.7 x 72.40mm
Compression ratio:	8.9:1
Max power:	97bhp at 5,000rpm
Max torque:	113.5lb ft at 3,000rpm
Cylinders:	four, in 60° vee, longitudinally mounted
Cylinder heads:	cast iron
Block:	cast iron
Valve gear:	two valves per cylinder, camshaft, pushrods and rockers
Fuelling:	one downdraught dual-choke Weber carburettor
Installation:	front-mounted, longitudinal
TRANSMISSION	
Type:	front-engine, rear-wheel-drive
Gearbox:	four-speed manual
SUSPENSION	
Front:	independent by coil springs, MacPherson struts, anti-roll bar and telescopic dampers
Rear:	beam axle, with half-elliptic leaf springs, radius arms, telescopic dampers
STEERING	
Type:	recirculating ball, no power assistance
Lock-to-lock:	4.8 turns
BRAKES	
Front:	9.62in (244mm) solid discs
Rear:	9.0 x 1.75in (229 x 44.5mm) drums
System:	hydraulic, with vacuum servo assistance
WHEELS & TYRES	
Wheels:	steel disc, 4.5J x 13in
Tyres:	165-13in radial-ply
BODY/CHASSIS	
Type:	pressed-steel monocoque, four-door saloon style
Weight:	2,254lb (1,023kg)
PERFORMANCE	
Max speed:	97mph (156kph) approx
0–60mph:	13.5sec
Standing-start ¼-mile:	18.8sec
PRICE at LAUNCH	
£1,008 in 1967	

At the end of the much-publicised 'Race against the Liner' from Cape Town to Southampton, Eric Jackson (left) and Ken Chambers (right) agreed to call a draw with the captain of the *Windsor Castle*.

Lotus-Cortina MkII

1967–1970

The Lotus-Cortina MkII carried the same body style as other Cortina MkIIs, and was always assembled at Dagenham.

The Lotus twin-cam engine was a neat fit, without too much crowding, in the engine bay of the Lotus-Cortina MkII.

Having driven lots of Lotus-Cortinas, not only when they were in production, but in later years when they had become 'classics', I have never quite understood why the MkII has always tended to be 'talked down'. Maybe it was all to do with the glamorous motorsport image of the earlier type, for in almost every way other than in outright straight-line speed, the smoother-styled MkII was a better car than the MkI. Not only was it better-built and better-equipped, but it had a more roomy cabin and it was more reliable.

Ford made sure of all that by deciding to assemble the restyled car at Dagenham, in and among all the other Cortinas. Although Lotus had churned out a satisfying number of MkIs, they had never done it with an eye to Ford quality standards, so Ford was determined to change all that. When the new model was being planned, Lotus in any case, was in the throes of moving to a new factory, one hundred miles away, in Norfolk, and might even have been relieved to abandon Lotus-Cortina assembly.

There wasn't any doubt, though, that some of the sporty and unique character had gone missing in the move back to Dagenham. What was really a twin-cam-engined Cortina GT MkII, somehow, lacked the charisma of the more special MkI – even if you knew that the back axle wasn't going to let you down, and that you could usually count on getting to the end of your journeys, short or long.

The motorsport connection between the Lotus-Cortina and Ford's single-seater race programmes was always clear. The single-seater alongside the MkII was a Cosworth FVA-engined Formula 2 car.

In developing the new model Ford, in fact, carried on the civilising process which they had already applied to the final MkIs. The new Lotus-Cortina MkII, which was introduced in March 1967 (some months after MkI production had ended – so the market place was screaming for new supplies when it appeared), shared the same rounded, two-door, style of the new-style Cortina GT. It had the same basic mechanical layout, fascia style (which included Aeroflow face-level ventilation), and the leaf-spring/radius-arm rear suspension layout which had served so well on 1965–1966 MkIs.

Although many new MkIIs were painted in the familiar white, because this was to be a Dagenham-assembled model it could be ordered in a whole range of monochrome colours. The 'speed stripe' was not available at that stage, but if the customer demanded this, a contrasting colour could then be sprayed on to the flanks and the tail panel, in the Ford dealer's paint shop.

This time the Lotus twin-cam engine was in Special Equipment guise, quoted by Lotus at 115bhp, but by Ford as 109bhp (net). As with the last of the MkIs, there was the '2000E' type of gearbox, but the axle ratio was higher this time – 3.77:1 instead of 3.90:1.

Like the original models, the suspension was lowered and stiffened, with 5.5in wide-rim steel wheels; this time 165-13in radial-ply tyres were standard. The spare wheel was mounted upright in the boot, but the battery still had its own tray on the boot floor.

The result was a more civilised car than the original type, a real flagship for the Cortina MkII range. Because Ford had no long-term motorsport plans for the new type, weight reduction and specialisation were no longer necessary. Sales figures show that their altered marketing approach was correct.

Far more MkIIs were made than MkIs – Ford quotes 4,032 examples. Although this model was in production until July 1970, the steam really went out of the programme after only a year (when the smaller and faster Escort Twin-Cam went on sale), for many enthusiasts turned to the Escort instead. Only 194 Lotus-Cortinas were built in the final year, 1970.

In those three years, important MkII development changes were limited to a new fascia/instrument panel layout from October 1968 (all other Cortinas had the change at the same time), and there was a new type of 'single-rail' remote-control gearshift control from that point. Officially, too, the car's name was changed to Cortina Twin-Cam from 1968, although the clientele never adopted that title.

Temperament . . . or reliability?

So, which type do you prefer? Classic car values suggest that the MkII is the poor relation, yet there are more of them available, some in remarkably good condition. Do you have the patience to put up with the well-charted vagaries of a MkI example, and to put up with the fragility of the aluminium panels in earlier types?

On the other hand, would you rather go almost as quickly in a MkII, remembering that, in 1967, *Motor* magazine testers suggested that: 'Anyone in the market for a £1,000 saloon who doesn't buy a Lotus-Cortina must be mad . . .'!

Specification	
Lotus-Cortina MkII	
ENGINE	
Type:	Lotus-Ford, twin-cam
Capacity:	1,558cc
Bore/stroke:	82.55mm x 72.8mm
Compression ratio:	9.5:1
Max power:	109bhp at 6,000rpm
Max torque:	106lb ft at 4,500rpm
Cylinders:	four, in line, longitudinally mounted
Cylinder head:	cast aluminium
Block:	cast iron
Valve gear:	two valves per cylinder, twin chain-driven overhead camshafts, bucket tappets
Fuelling:	twin dual-choke Weber Type 40 DCOE carburettors
Installation:	front-mounted, longitudinal
TRANSMISSION	
Type:	front-engine, rear-wheel-drive
Gearbox:	four-speed manual
SUSPENSION	
Front:	independent by coil springs, MacPherson struts, anti-roll bar and telescopic dampers
Rear:	beam axle, with half-elliptic leaf springs, radius-arms and telescopic dampers
STEERING	
Type:	recirculating ball
Lock-to-lock:	4.3 turns
BRAKES	
Front:	9.62in (244mm) discs
Rear:	9.0 x 1.75in (229 x 44.4mm) drums
System:	hydraulic, with vacuum servo assistance
WHEELS & TYRES	
Wheels:	steel disc, 5.5J x 13in
Tyres:	165-13 radial-ply
BODY/CHASSIS	
Type:	pressed-steel monocoque, two-door saloon
Weight:	2,025lb (963kg)
PERFORMANCE	
Max speed:	104mph (167kph) approx
0–60mph:	11.0sec
PRICE at LAUNCH	
£1,068 in 1967	

Escort Twin-Cam

1968–1971

One of the very first Escort twin-cam prototypes, pictured at Boreham in 1967. The Rostyle wheels were not adopted on production cars.

Motorsport

The Twin-Cam was a successful, but short-lived competition car, for it was superseded by the RS1600 in 1971. In 1968, 'works' cars won a flurry of major rallies (Roger Clark was the star driver), while Frank Gardner won the British Saloon Car Championship, and sister cars won races in Europe too.

Because it was strong, simple and easy to handle, the Twin-Cam could also win in rallycross (where it was immediately a TV star) – in fact it was competitive wherever it was eligible. Although fitted with different (Kent pushrod) engines, it was most famous of all for dominating the London–Mexico World Cup Rally of 1970 – this model giving rise to the Escort Mexico model which followed.

You've heard the legends. You've seen the tall stories. You've listened to the rumours. Can you believe them? Here they are:

Henry Taylor and Bill Meade invented the Escort Twin-Cam.

The first lash-up was built in a weekend at Boreham.

Ford Motorsport designed the car.

When the car went into production there were no drawings.

The code name – J25 – meant January 25th 1967 – when the plans were laid.

It's all true. The race and rally-winning Twin-Cam – was developed on a whim, evolved on a shoestring, and built with the minimum of facilities. The Twin-Cam, for sure, was designed before AVO was invented – but without it there might never have been an AVO operation. It was the car which inspired Ford sporting ambitions, and it also inspired the dynasty of RS1600, Mexico and RS2000.

Twin-Cam origins

Early in 1967 Bill Meade, Boreham's *de facto* motorsport engineer, was heavily involved in work on the latest rallying Lotus-Cortinas when he started to notice prototypes of a humble little saloon driving past his office window. According to legend – we are assured this is true – one day Bill stopped, buttonholed his team manager Henry Taylor, and said: 'Blimey, one of those things would go like hell with a Twin-Cam engine in it!'

It took more than a year for Meade's comment to become reality – even at Ford in the 1960s, miracles took a little time – but that single sentence was always the essence of the new car – it was an Escort shell with a Twin-Cam engine in it.

Planning, testing, crashing . . .

One Sunday morning in January 1967, Henry Taylor got together with product planner Bob Howe to prepare a management submission. Public Affairs chief Walter Hayes knew what was going on, but did not interfere: he would start lobbying later.

The rally team needed a new world-class competition car, and to meet the rules 1,000 road cars would have to be built. The concept was simple enough. The new Escort would be lighter, smaller and stronger than the Cortina. Why not graft the Lotus-Cortina's running gear into an Escort body shell?

Taylor and Howe managed to 'borrow' a prototype Escort body-chassis unit, in plastic, from the technical centre at Dunton. Meade and his mechanics then proved that it could be done: 'We stopped all normal work on a Friday afternoon in March 1967 when the "car" arrived in a truck,' Meade once told me. 'We shut the workshop doors, started there and then, and spent all weekend, mocking up a new car.'

Somehow the Lotus-Cortina engine, gearbox, struts and rear axle, all found a home. The engine had to be skewed, to gain clearance between carburettors and inner wheelarch, the battery had to go into the boot, while the 165-13in tyres only just fitted inside the arches! There were no drawings, no photographs, but just a few measurements, notes and sketches.

Months later, Taylor's engineers built a running prototype on the basis of a 1300GT shell. Hayes gained approval to put the car into production in 1968, and Boreham completed the development. After just six months, in January 1968, an early road car made its debut at the Escort launch in Morocco. So far, so good – but how on earth were the 1,000 cars to be built?

Twin-Cam – building the first cars

The new Escort was built at Halewood, near Liverpool. Reluctantly, management then agreed to assemble the cars, with strengthened Type 49

It was a miracle that the Lotus-Cortina twin-cam engine could be persuaded to fit in the Escort's engine bay – which had never been designed to accept it. The engine had to be skewed to the left to make this possible.

body shells, at first on normal tracks, then diverting them to a special area, where engines, gearboxes and axles would be added. To keep it simple, the strategy was that every production Twin-Cam would be painted white, with black trim, and every car would have right-hand-drive.

Even so, Halewood could not begin assembly – even in small quantities – until Spring 1968. Taylor, though, wanted to get the car homologated before the season began, by May 1968, (but could he convince the FIA that 1,000 cars had been built, even when fewer than 100 actually existed? He thought he could – and, in the end, he did!). It was agreed to assemble the first 25 cars at Boreham.

Most of those cars were delivered to favoured motorsport teams like Alan Mann Racing, and to overseas teams, although Boreham kept the majority for its own use. Selling for £1,123 in the UK – that was exactly the same price as the MkII Lotus-Cortina, by the way – the Twin-Cam was sure to sell well, just as soon as cars could be delivered.

Early Escort Twin-Cams were fitted with rectangular headlamps – superseded by circular lamps during 1969. The Rostyle wheels on this car were not standard.

The first motorsport appearance was in rallycross, at Croft, in January 1968, Group 3 homologation (500 cars built – so they said, would you believe it!) was achieved on 1 March 1968, and Ove Andersson drove a car in the San Remo Rally later that month. Roger Clark notched up the first big rallying win – Circuit of Ireland – at Easter – and Group 2 homologation (1,000 cars built, or so Ford said) was finally achieved on 1 May 1968.

The famous 'Twin Cam' badge made its first appearance on the Escort in 1968. It would soon find a home on the Lotus-Cortina as well.

Twin-Cam on the market

Twin-Cam assembly built up very slowly indeed, but Taylor had no qualms about getting early homologation. He knew that 1,000 would be built as soon as they could be sold – and he didn't care for the minutiae of regulations. In 1968, 302 were built, and 479 in 1969 – at the peak, a rate of 60–65 cars were produced every month. Almost all were sold in the UK.

It looked so invisible, at first. Except that the humble, rounded, white two-door saloons had 13in wheels with fat tyres, front quarter bumpers, and discreet little 'Twin Cam' badges, they were almost impossible to pick from their smaller-engined brethren. Much rubbish was written about 'flared wheelarches' to clear those tyres, but even after all these years I still don't think this was very significant.

Later, Ford spent little time on modifying the Twin-Cam. Except that the original cars were sold with rectangular headlamps, while those built after July 1969 had 7in circular headlamps, there were virtually no other development changes. If anyone complained about the total lack of colour choice they were politely told that there was no alternative. Even so, a few late-model cars were coloured other than white.

Twin-Cam on the road

When the Twin-Cam was a current model, I often enjoyed driving one. To me, keen, impressionable, and captivated by the car's character, every time

Specification

Escort Twin-Cam

ENGINE

Type:	Lotus-Ford Twin-Cam
Capacity:	1,558cc
Bore/stroke:	82.55 x 72.8mm
Compression ratio:	9.5:1
Max power:	106bhp at 6,000rpm
Max torque:	107lb ft at 4,500rpm
Cylinders:	four, in-line, longitudinally mounted
Cylinder head:	cast aluminium
Block:	cast iron
Valve gear:	two valves per cylinder, twin chain-driven overhead camshafts, bucket tappets
Fuelling:	twin horizontal dual-choke Weber Type 40 DCOE carburettors
Installation:	front-mounted, longitudinal

TRANSMISSION

Type:	front-engine, rear-wheel-drive
Gearbox:	four-speed manual

SUSPENSION

Front:	independent by coil springs, MacPherson struts, anti-roll bar and telescopic dampers
Rear:	live (beam) axle, with half-elliptic leaf springs, radius-arms and telescopic dampers

STEERING

Type:	rack-and-pinion
Lock-to-lock:	3.0 turns

BRAKES

Front:	9.62in (244mm) discs
Rear:	9.0 x 1.75in (229 x 44.5mm) drums
System:	hydraulic

WHEELS & TYRES

Wheels:	steel disc, 5.5J x 13in
Tyres:	165-13in radial-ply

BODY/CHASSIS

Type:	pressed-steel monocoque, in two-door saloon style
Weight:	1,730lb (785kg)

PERFORMANCE

Max speed:	113mph (182kph) approx
Acceleration:	0–60mph in 9.9sec

PRICE at LAUNCH
£1,163 in 1968

was like the first time, and my adrenaline raced. Compared with any other Ford of the day – even the 3.0-litre Capri – there was that extrovert rush off the line to reach exciting cruising speeds. There was the immensely eager way the steering turned the chassis in to any corner (Boreham's mechanics had seen to that). There was also the quite unmistakeable engine noise, and high-pedigree thrash of valve gear which easily penetrated the bulkhead.

A Twin-Cam was at its best on country roads, or being rushed up and over the mountains – any road, in fact, where the 106bhp engine's torque, and the agile handling, could dominate the drive. Put it on a motorway, on the other hand, and it was really out of its element, because it was a low-geared car which didn't always like to run straight in cross-winds.

With its 110mph-plus top speed, and its sub-10 second 0–60mph acceleration potential, it was an outstanding little machine, one which inspired the birth and development of AVO. The new organisation, on the other hand, was looking forward, not back, and had little time for the Twin-Cam. Even at the end of 1969, when the Twin-Cam was still in its prime, its successor, the Escort RS1600 had already been designed, and there was never any intention of transferring Twin-Cam assembly from Halewood to South Ockendon.

No matter. More than a thousand cars were built, and when it faded away in April 1971, its character lived on in the RS1600. Quite simply, it is remembered as the First, and the most Famous.

Boreham mechanic Mick Jones testing one of the prototype Twin-Cams at Boreham, in 1967.

Escort RS1600

1970–1974

The story of the RS1600 begins, of course, with its magnificent engine, which had four valves per cylinder, and belt-driven camshafts. It was a real trend-setter.

The Cosworth-designed BDA was an ambitious conversion of Ford's rugged Kent pushrod engine, rated at 120bhp/1.6-litre. Neatly packaged, it fitted the same space as the Twin-Cam. Because there were virtually no other changes, I always consider the RS1600 as a re-engined Escort Twin Cam.

Early cars were built at Halewood, but from November 1970 they were assembled at the new AVO plant at Aveley. AVO-built cars could be standard, could have many extras fitted, or could be fitted with motorsport parts. Many brand-new RS1600s were immediately torn apart, to be converted into competition cars: private owners created hundreds more from parts, or by re-engining Twin-Cams.

Most development changes occurred in 1972. Dellorto carburettors replaced Webers from the spring of 1972, while an aluminium cylinder block took over from cast iron in the autumn. At the same time as the new block arrived, equipment was upgraded with full carpeting, sports road wheels, and four-way hazard warning flashers. The slightly modified floor-pan, and more upright rear damper positioning (intended for MkII Escorts), were phased in towards the end of 1973 – but very few of this type of RS1600 were ever manufactured.

Ford manufactured far fewer RS1600s than originally forecast – only 1,139 fully built. Of these, only about 200 late-model cars had the alloy block/ trim upgrades spec. One reason for low sales was the relatively high price, the other being that their general appeal was limited. 'Real' cars, as opposed to conversions, should have RS1600 badges on the front wings, and 'RS' or 'RS1600' badges on the boot lid. All should have round-headlamp noses, quarter bumpers, and the same fascia layout as current Escort GTs.

The only way to pick an RS1600 from the Twin-Cam was by reading the badges on the flanks and tail. All RS1600s had circular headlamps.

Motorsport

'Works' RS1600s won rallies as prestigious as the East African Safari, the Finnish 1000 Lakes and the RAC, while in racing the peak came in 1974 when a Zakspeed car won the European Touring Car Championship outright. Although engines were expensive to tune and to maintain, hundreds of private owners won thousands of events, at all levels, until the late 1970s.

Specification

Escort RS1600

ENGINE

Type:	Cosworth-Ford BDA
Capacity:	1,599cc
Bore/stroke:	80.97 x 77.62mm
Compression ratio:	10.0:1
Max power:	120bhp at 6,500rpm
Max torque:	112lb ft at 4.000rpm
Cylinders:	four, in-line, longitudinally mounted
Cylinder head:	cast aluminium
Block:	cast iron (cast aluminium from late 1972)
Valve gear:	four valves per cylinder, twin belt-driven overhead camshafts
Fuelling:	twin dual-choke Weber Type 40 DCOE carburettors (twin Dellorto carburettors from April 1972)
Installation:	front-mounted, longitudinal

TRANSMISSION

Type:	front-engine, rear-wheel-drive
Gearbox:	four-speed manual
Final drive:	3.77:1 17.8mph/1,000rpm in top gear

SUSPENSION

Front:	independent by coil springs, MacPherson struts, anti-roll bar and telescopic dampers
Rear:	live (beam) axle, with half-elliptic leaf springs, radius-arms and telescopic dampers

STEERING

Type:	rack-and-pinion
Lock-to-lock:	3.0 turns

BRAKES

Front:	9.62in (244mm) discs
Rear:	9.0 x 1.75in (229 x 44.5mm) drums
System:	hydraulic

WHEELS & TYRES

Wheels:	steel disc, 5.5J x 13in
Tyres:	165-13in radial-ply

BODY/CHASSIS

Type:	pressed-steel monocoque, in two-door saloon style
Weight:	1,920lb (870kg)

PERFORMANCE

Max speed:	113mph (182kph) approx
Acceleration:	0–60mph in 8.9sec

PRICE at LAUNCH
£1,447 in 1970

The Mexico was launched at the end of 1970. Most had this extrovert striping scheme.

Motorsport

Although the Mexico was inspired by the 'works' cars which won the World Cup Rally of 1970, it was never intended for 'international' competition.

Mexico race and rally one-make championships were held for many years, in many countries.

Specification

Escort Mexico (MkI)

ENGINE

Type:	Ford Kent
Capacity:	1,599cc
Bore/stroke:	80.97 x 77.62mm
Compression ratio:	9.0:1
Max power:	86bhp at 5,500rpm
Max torque:	92lb ft at 4,000rpm
Cylinders:	four, in-line, longitudinally mounted
Cylinder head:	cast iron
Block:	cast iron
Valve gear:	two valves per cylinder, single camshaft, pushrods and rockers
Fuel and ignition:	single downdraught compound dual-choke Weber 32 DFM carburettor
Installation:	front-mounted, longitudinal

TRANSMISSION

Type:	front-engine, rear-wheel-drive
Gearbox:	Ford Type 3, four-speed manual

SUSPENSION

Front:	independent by coil springs, MacPherson struts, anti-roll bar, and telescopic dampers
Rear:	live axle, by half-elliptic leaf springs, radius arms and telescopic dampers

STEERING

Type:	rack-and-pinion
Lock-to-lock:	3.5 turns

BRAKES

Front:	9.62in (244mm) solid discs
Rear:	9.0 x 1.75in (229 x 44.4mm) drums
System:	hydraulic, with vacuum servo assistance

WHEELS & TYRES

Wheels:	pressed steel disc, 5.5J x 13in
Tyres:	165-13 radial-ply

BODY/CHASSIS

Type:	pressed-steel monocoque, based on conventional Escort, in three-door saloon style
Weight:	1,965lb (981kg)

PERFORMANCE

Max speed:	100mph (160kph) approx
Acceleration:	0–60mph in 10.7sec

PRICE at LAUNCH

£1,150 in December 1970

Escort Mexico MkI

1970–1975

If you have never driven a MkI Mexico before, let me give you a word of advice. Look at its character and its image before you look at its performance figures. Look at its reputation, its behaviour, and the exuberant way it can be driven, before you start taking 0–60mph times. Don't, in fact, expect too much from the stop-watch.

When launched in 1970, this was a great performance bargain, the only push-rod engined Escort which could approach 100mph, but a quarter of a century later it is certainly not remembered as one of the fastest of performance Fords. It was a skilful amalgam of Escort RS1600 engineering with a 1.6-litre Kent engine, always built at the AVO plant in Essex. The drive train – engine, gearbox and back axle – was the same as many mass-produced Ford models.

Original Mexicos were available in a white, Maize (yellow) and Sunset (red), but more colours were added later. Then came a choice of decoration – flamboyant side striping with 'Mexico' picked out in a panel on the doors, allied to similar stripes on the roof and across the boot lid was standard, but this could be deleted if required. Compared with the Twin-Cam/RS1600, there were De Luxe instead of GT-type seats, rubber floor mats instead of carpet – and a big options list.

There were two significant specification upgrades:

October 1972: RS1600-type interior trim, including floor carpets, a new in-line brake servo, the battery repositioned in the engine bay, the vertical spare wheel mounting adopted, and sculpted 'sports' road wheels standardised.

Autumn 1973: New floor-pan (intended for MkII Escorts), complete with revised (more vertical) rear damper location.

A total of 10,352 Mexicos was produced – 3,414 in 1972 – which compares with only 5,334 RS2000 MkIs, and 1,139 RS1600s.

The Mexico was much the most numerous of all Escorts built at AVO, and a surprising number have survived.

Escort RS2000 MkI

1973 and 1974

The RS2000, launched in 1973, used a 2-litre Pinto engine.

Most of us who drove RS2000s think it was the most accomplished AVO package of all. If only there had been time to build and sell more, AVO might have been profitable. If only . . .

For the first two and a half years of AVO's existence at Aveley, the RS1600 and the Mexico were the only two performance Escorts on the market. By 1972, however, another model was needed to fill up the production line. The principal demand came from Germany, where dealers wanted to be able to market a car which was almost as fast as an RS1600, but one which was considerably more civilised, and with a simpler engine.

The solution was to create an Escort which would fall neatly between the Mexico and the RS1600. AVO was looking for a 110mph top speed, but from an Escort with a more relaxed, easy-going, character. Fortunately a new engine was available – the overhead-cam Pinto design – which was specified. A new car, dubbed 'RS2000', higher geared, more civilised, and somehow more 'Executive' than 'Rallye Sport', soon evolved.

The Escort RS2000's interior was trimmed and equipped even better than the RS1600, and intended for fast road use.

For the first time on an RS, the engine was mounted exactly 'north–south'. Behind the engine was a new German-sourced gearbox, the Type E. Further development (and different ratios) would make this box ideal for use in the MkII RS models of the late 1970s. Other detail changes included a firmer front, and softer

Motorsport

The RS2000 was competitive only as a Group 1 ('showroom') car in international rallying, where its most notable successes were victory in the 1974 and 1975 Tour of Britain events – by Roger Clark and Tony Pond retrospectively.

Although it had only 100bhp, compared with 120bhp for the RS1600, the RS2000 was a fast road car, which also handled very well.

Specification

Escort RS2000 MkI

ENGINE

Type:	Ford Pinto
Capacity:	1,993cc
Bore/stroke:	90.82 x 76.95mm
Compression ratio (nominal):	9.2:1
Max power:	100bhp at 5,750rpm
Max torque:	108lb ft at 3,500rpm
Cylinders:	four, in-line, longitudinally mounted
Cylinder head:	cast iron
Block:	cast iron
Valve gear:	two valves per cylinder, belt-driven single overhead camshaft, fingers and rockers
Fuelling:	Weber 32/36 downdraught carburettor
Installation:	front-mounted, longitudinal

TRANSMISSION

Type:	front-engine, rear-wheel-drive
Gearbox:	four-speed manual

SUSPENSION

Front:	independent by coil springs, MacPherson struts, anti-roll bar, telescopic dampers
Rear:	live (beam) axle, with half-elliptic leaf springs, radius arms, telescopic dampers

STEERING

Type:	rack-and-pinion
Lock-to-lock:	3.5 turns

BRAKES

Front:	9.62in (244mm) discs
Rear:	8.0 x 1.5in (203.2 x 38.1mm) drums
System:	hydraulic with vacuum servo assistance

WHEELS & TYRES

Wheels:	steel disc, optional cast alloy disc, 5.5J x 13in
Tyres:	165-13in radial-ply

BODY/CHASSIS

Type:	pressed-steel monocoque, in two-door saloon style
Weight:	1,975lb (898kg)

PERFORMANCE

Max speed:	108mph (119kph) approx
Acceleration:	0–60mph in 9.0sec

PRICE at LAUNCH
£1,442 in Autumn 1973

rear springs than other types, smaller rear brakes, and a new four-spoke cast-alloy wheel option.

It was quite easy to 'pick' an RS2000 from its stable mates. Externally, the cars were equipped with colour-contrasting stripes along the flanks, bonnets and boot lids. Inside, the ambience was 'executive' rather than 'sporting'. All cars had nicely shaped reclining front seats, while many had an optional centre console, complete with a clock and provision for a radio installation.

The new car was unveiled in July 1973. All initial production was in left-hand-drive cars, and a quantity were also assembled at the Saarlouis factory in Germany. Right-hand-drive deliveries began in October – just in time for the Arab-Israeli 'Yom Kippur' war, and the Energy Crisis which followed, to cripple all new car sales. The RS2000 was priced at £1,586, when the Mexico cost £1,348 and the RS1600 £1,864.

Almost immediately there was one important chassis change, which came in November 1973 when all Escorts were given a new type of monocoque platform, with more vertical rear dampers and turret mountings.

What we did not know at the time either, was that all production of Escort MkI types was to cease before the end of 1974. This meant that the original-shape RS2000 was only in production for about 18 months – in fact it was by far the most numerous car built at the AVO plant in that time. Unsold cars at the end of 1974 were not actually registered until 1975.

No fewer than 5,334 RS2000s were produced, of which 3,759 were actually sold to British customers. There's no doubt that this short-lived car did exactly what was expected of it. Those who knew, or who were prepared to find out, discovered that the RS2000 was a pleasantly fast car, too, as these comparisons show:

Model	Top speed (mph)	0–60mph (sec)	Standing-start $\frac{1}{4}$-mile (sec)
Mexico	99	10.7	18.0
RS2000	108	9.0	17.1
RS1600	113	8.9	16.7

The RS2000, in other words, was almost as rapid as the RS1600 (the 16-valve car was only 2.2 seconds ahead in passing 100mph from rest), yet it was using a totally fuss-free, mass-production engine which was widely understood by every Ford dealer's mechanics. To this day, it is still an under-estimated car, for the later MkII version still takes the highlights.

Capri 3-litre MkI

1969–1974

The first Capri 3000GT was introduced late in 1969. All Capris shared the same style, but there was a big choice of engines, trim and equipment packages.

When the Capri was launched in 1969, Ford advertised it as 'The Car You Always Promised Yourself'. Unashamedly moulded around the form and success of the Ford-USA Mustang, the Capri offered something for everyone. Not only was it a sporty-looking coupé with saloon car service and insurance costs, but several engines were available.

Sales took off like a rocket (it may have helped that Ford dealers were able to park a Capri outside most railway stations on launch-day!), for this was a formula which worked well. One could fool the neighbours into thinking that this was a sports car, even though your bank manager didn't mind too much. By the time the last-ever Capri was built in 1986, nearly 1.9 million of all types had been assembled.

All British-type original-shape Capris were assembled at the Halewood plant on Merseyside (they shared space with the mass-market Escort), and came in 1.3, 1.6, 2.0 and 3.0-litre varieties. All of them had the same totally recognisable style – long-bonnet, short rear deck, close-coupled four-seater

This was the original fascia/instrument layout of the Capri.

coupé cabin (OK, I'll admit it, the rear seat was comfortable for children, but not for adults) – and at first all had rectangular headlamps. Ford also thoroughly confused the customer by offering up X, L and R dress-up packs, these referring to seating improvements, an exterior dress-up pack, and wider-rim wheels, plus other so-called 'rally' items: these had to be fitted to the cars when they were being assembled, not by dealers.

Some Capris (like the 'base' 1.3-litre type) were very slow, but the 3-litre, launched late in 1969, made up for all that. Even though the aerodynamic shape was poor (but we didn't think about such things in those days), the first 3-litre cars could still nudge 115mph. In any case, it wasn't the performance figures, but the Capri 3-litre's character, which made such an impression. Although it wasn't the smoothest car in the world (and, for sure, the early-spec cars had a very hard ride), it always felt fast, always felt brawny, and was always happy to oversteer if the driver felt like it.

To those in the know, a 3-litre was always recognisable by the use of the bonnet-bulge front style (which was not, at that time, applied to any other model of UK-built Capri). Most of them were ordered with the complete XLR pack (which included Rostyle wheels, of course), which made them very well-specified, yet still a lot cheaper than their so-called opposition.

Longer in the wheelbase than the current Cortina, but with the same basic type of suspension, the fastest of the Capris somehow found space for the Essex V6 engine, and its related gearbox, from the Zodiac, both of them virtually unmodified. Although that engine only produced 128bhp at first, it was lusty and almost unbreakable. It was only when power-tuners got their hands on it that they realised the block was not all that strong, and the cylinder head breathing was not easy to improve.

Early 3-litres were all 3000GTs, priced at £1,341, although many of them also had the XLR dress-up pack included, which lifted the price to £1,427. Within months, however, a more glossy 3000E type (E = Executive, as with the Cortina 1600E and the Corsair 2000E) was added to the range. Although it was not meant as a competition car, Ford encouraged its sporting, trendy, image by organising one-make 'celebrity races' where characters like Bernie Ecclestone and Frank Williams raced 3-litre Capris against current F1 and saloon car drivers in identical cars.

This Capri 3000GT has the XLR dress-up package, which originally included the black-painted bonnet.

Original-specification cars suffered from a poor choice of internal gearbox ratios (second gear was much too low) and a rather asthmatic engine, but in the next few years a whole series of changes brought real improvements. From October 1971, the engine was revised, so that peak power moved up to 138bhp (at 5,000rpm instead of 4,750rpm), while the gearbox ratios were altered (there was a higher second gear) and allied to a higher-geared final drive ratio.

Although these changes were not radical, somehow they seemed to have transformed the performance, for the top speed was now at least 120mph, and the 0–60mph time had dropped by two seconds. Not only that, but the car felt more

relaxed at motorway cruising speeds, and was even a little more economical. No wonder it sold so well.

There was more to come from this versatile range. From October 1972 (only three years after the first of the 3-litres had gone on sale), Ford-UK brought in a major facelift, inside and outside the cabin. Significantly, the 3000E was dropped in favour of a new top-of-the-line type badged 3000GXL. The latest cars came with the four-headlamp nose which had already been seen on some Ford-of-Germany Capris, while there were new sports-type wheels of what were called the sculpted-steel variety.

Inside the cabin, there was a much-revised fascia/instrument panel (it would eventually be carried over, in all details, to the MkII Capri which followed), plushier and better-shaped seats, and further sound-deadening to make this a quieter car. Under the skin, engine and gearbox carried on as before, although at the rear the axle radius arms had been dropped in favour of an anti-roll bar. In addition there was an automatic transmission option (but this was rarely taken up on UK-market cars).

Slowly, but definitely, as the years passed by, the 3-litre became less of a sports car, and more of a well-trimmed coupé, but the clientele didn't seem to mind. The last derivatives, after all, were faster, better-equipped, and softer-riding than ever.

At the very end of the run, in November 1973, Ford-UK produced the more specialised RS3100 version, but a major revision was already on the way. Nearly 900,000 Capri Is were produced. The Capri II of 1974 was a different type of coupé.

The Capri 3000E of 1970 had an even higher combination of trim and equipment than the 3000GT, but the same mechanical package.

Specification

Capri 3-litre (MkI)
(Up-rated spec from late 1971 in brackets.)

ENGINE

Type:	Ford-UK Essex
Capacity:	2,994cc
Bore/stroke:	93.7 x 72.4mm
Compression ratio:	8.9:1 [9.0:1]
Max power:	128bhp at 4,750rpm [138bhp at 5,000rpm]
Max torque:	173lb ft at 3,000rpm [174lb ft at 3,000rpm]
Cylinders:	six, in 60° vee, longitudinally mounted
Cylinder heads:	cast iron
Block:	cast iron
Valve gear:	two valves per cylinder, single camshaft, pushrods and rockers
Fuelling:	Weber downdraught dual-choke 38/38 EGAS carburettor
Installation:	front-mounted, longitudinal

TRANSMISSION

Type:	front-engine, rear-wheel-drive
Gearbox:	four-speed manual

(Optional three-speed Borg Warner [Ford C3 from 1972] automatic transmission)

SUSPENSION

Front:	independent by MacPherson struts, lower track control arms, coil springs, anti-roll bar and telescopic dampers
Rear:	live (beam) axle, half-elliptic leaf springs, radius arms [until 1972], anti-roll bar [from 1972] and telescopic dampers

STEERING

Type:	rack-and-pinion
Lock-to-lock:	3.3 turns

BRAKES

Front:	9.63in (244.6mm) discs
Rear:	9.0 x 2.25in (57.15mm) drums
System:	hydraulic, with vacuum servo assistance

WHEELS & TYRES

Wheels:	sculpted steel discs (Rostyle on original models), with four-stud fixing, 5.0J x 13in
Tyres:	185/70HR-13in

BODY

Type:	two-door four-seater coupé monocoque
Weight:	2,380lb (1,080kg)

PERFORMANCE

Max speed:	113mph (182kph) [122mph (196kph)]
Acceleration:	0–60mph in 10.3sec [8.4sec]
Standing start ¼-mile:	17.6sec [16.2 sec]

PRICE at LAUNCH

3000GT: £1,372 in October 1969

The very first 'works' Capri entry in motorsport came in the 1969 Lyon-Charbonnieres Rally, with a 2.3-litre V6 engine. Jean-François Piot and Jean Todt took seventh place.

Motorsport

Because of the glamour attached to the later RS2600, everyone forgets that the 2300GT/RS, as a race car, flew the flag for Ford-of-Germany until the end of 1970. Although there were no outright victories, in the European Championship these cars took second overall at Monza and Budapest. This car, though, needed more power to win – so the arrival of the RS2600 made it instantly obsolete.

Specification

Capri 2300GT/RS (MkI)

ENGINE

Type:	Ford-of-Germany Cologne
Capacity:	2,294cc
Bore/stroke:	90 x 60.1mm
Compression ratio:	9.0:1
Max power:	125bhp at 5,600rpm
Max torque:	135lb ft at 3,500rpm
Cylinders:	six, in 60° vee, longitudinally mounted
Cylinder heads:	cast iron
Block:	cast iron
Valve gear:	two valves per cylinder, single camshaft, pushrods and rockers
Fuelling:	Solex downdraught dual-choke carburettor
Installation:	Front-mounted, longitudinal

TRANSMISSION

Type:	front-engine, rear-wheel-drive
Gearbox:	four-speed manual

SUSPENSION

Front:	independent by MacPherson struts, lower track control arms, coil springs, anti-roll bar and telescopic dampers
Rear:	live (beam) axle, half-elliptic leaf springs, anti-roll bar, radius arms and telescopic dampers

STEERING

Type:	rack-and-pinion
Lock-to-lock:	3.3 turns

BRAKES

Front:	9.63in (244.6mm) discs
Rear:	9.0 x 2.25in (57.15mm) drums
System:	hydraulic, with vacuum servo assistance

WHEELS & TYRES

Wheels:	sculpted steel discs, with four-stud fixing, 5.0J x 13in
Tyres:	185/70HR13in

BODY

Type:	two-door four-seater coupé monocoque
Weight:	2,293lb (1,040kg)

PERFORMANCE

Max speed:	118mph (190kph) (claimed)
Acceleration:	0–60mph in 9.8sec (claimed)

PRICE at LAUNCH

Not officially sold in the UK

Capri 2300GT/RS

1969–1970

In the early days Capris were built in two locations – at Halewood, and in Cologne, Germany. Although the two cars were visually similar, there were important differences to the choice of engines, and to the decoration of the coupé style.

This was the period in which all German-built Capris had V-formation engines – for all of them used one or other of the V4 or V6 Cologne engines which Ford-of-Germany had launched way back in 1962. Top of the range, at first, was a 108bhp/2.3-litre V6, but from September 1969 a 125bhp version of the same engine was made available. This powered the 2300GT/RS, a short-lived model which would soon be overshadowed by the more famous RS2600.

Although the 2,294cc German V6 was almost as powerful as the entirely different 3.0-litre British V6, it was not nearly as torquey, so it was by no means as easy to drive quickly in a 'lazy' manner. The original 2300GT had always been marketed with a 'power bulge' in the bonnet – that would not be added to UK cars until the start of the 1973 model year. It was already equipped with the gearbox which would later grace the Escort RS2000, and other related models in the 1970s.

The 2300GT/RS featured the 125bhp engine which had also been developed for use in the Taunus 20MRS saloon. Compared with original and smaller-engined German Capris, it had stiffer suspension, and wider-rims, and featured the best possible trim package which was then being used on these cars.

Here was a left-hand-drive car for which Ford-of-Germany claimed a top speed of 118mph (some Capri experts reckon that 110–115mph was more likely to be available), although such a car was never tested in British magazines.

The 2300GT/RS was never officially imported to the UK, not only because it was always destined to be a very short-lived model (assembly ran from September 1969 to September 1970), but because it would have sat rather uneasily in the middle of the British-Capri range, faster than the Essex V4 engined 2000GT, and not nearly as fast as the Essex V6-engined 3000GT.

Capri **RS2600**

1970–1974

When Ford launched the Capri RS2600 they meant business, for this would become an ultra-successful race car in the early 1970s.

In 1970, the first specialised Capri, the RS2600, went on sale and within two years it was winning European Touring Car Championship races. Ford-of-Europe, in fact, had planned this for some time as this once-confidential document tells us: 'Generally in European sales areas the Capri has not acquired the sporting, as opposed to merely sporty, image expected . . . it is believed that some competitions support is necessary. To this end Advanced Vehicle Operations have engineered and Ford Germany Manufacturing staff are producing a special 2.6-litre fuel-injected V6 derivative with obvious sporting appeal.'

Whoever wrote that submission was pushing against an open door, because Ford-of-Germany had settled on a policy for the 1970s – if Ford-of-Britain, at Boreham, intended to dominate rallies, Ford-of-Germany wanted to win motor races. Boreham, in other words, was well-provided for with the Escort Twin-Cam, and the up-and-coming Escort RS1600 – Cologne wanted to see the Capri evolve into a winning race car.

No single person designed, or developed, the RS2600. In Cologne competitions manager Jochen Neerpasch and his deputy Mike Kranefuss (with help from Weslake of Rye, in Sussex) had already started work on an enlarged version of the Cologne V6 engine. Most important of all, though, was that Walter Hayes gleefully accepted the RS2600 concept.

RS2600 and RS3100 – different Capris, different markets

I should emphasise that the RS2600 and the (later) RS3100 were related, but not very closely. Both cars were quite closely based on the original Capri MkI, and were intended to be competition cars. However, engine work on the RS2600 was carried out in Germany, but on the RS3100 it was done in the UK.

In summary, the RS2600 was a German-market car with a German engine, while the RS3100 was its successor but British, with a British V6. The RS2600 was never meant for sale in the UK, and was never built with right-hand steering. The RS3100 was a home-market car, and not built with left-hand steering.

When the RS2600 was new, it was never officially sold over here, although in recent years a small number have been imported. It appeared early in the life of the original Capri, but the RS3100 came at the end. In both cases the racing versions were as totally different from the road cars as possible – the 'works' RS2600s used special Weslake cylinder heads.

It is important to remember that in those days the Capri was manufactured in two different factories – Halewood on Merseyside, and Cologne in West Germany. In Britain, of course, the first Halewood-built Capris used the British range of four-cylinder and six-cylinder engines, while early Cologne-built cars used V4s and V6s which were made entirely in that country. It was not until the early 1970s that any kind of commonisation took place.

The Capri RS2600 was the first Ford to use fuel-injection – and was the fastest Capri of all through the 1970s.

Engineering development

All MkI Capris had two-door coupé body styles, with long noses, short tails with a rather small boot, and had very cramped rear seats. All had MacPherson strut front suspension, and their axles were suspended on leaf springs. Early RS2600s also had twin radius arms at the rear, but most of them, and all RS3100s, lacked those items, but were fitted with rear anti-roll bars instead.

Except for the special parts developed for RS models, it is quite amazing to note how many totally 'mainstream' Ford parts were used in Capri Is, which probably explains why the less-extreme models cost so little to service, and why the insurance ratings could be so reasonable. The RS Capris used many of the same parts as standard vee-6 engined Capris – which, I am sure, are still thoroughly familiar to every Ford dealer.

Well-equipped, and completely purposeful, the driving compartment of the Capri RS2600. All these cars were built with left-hand steering.

RS2600 – very rare in the UK

The 2.6-litre RS2600 was launched in March 1970, complete with the characteristic four-headlamp nose, although the cars which would really count as production models were very different from the originals, which were rushed through to go motor racing.

The first 50 cars, built specifically to Ford-of-Germany Competition Manager Jochen Neerpasch's specific requirements, were very light and very crude, with carburetted engines, magnesium Minilite wheels, glass-fibre doors, bonnets and boot lids,

no carpets or heaters, and with Perspex side windows. They weighed a mere 1,985lb and their general build quality was awful: racing drivers, though, don't complain about noise and vibration!

Proper production cars (or what we now call 'real' RS2600s) did not appear until the autumn of 1970, and were so much more civilised that they weighed a lot more than the normal 2300GT/2600GT series. They had glass all round, carpets, heaters and all such up-market fittings that the price demanded. The Cologne engine was a 2,637cc/150bhp unit with Kugelfischer fuel injection and was backed by the heavy-duty (Taunus 26M, at first) gearbox and back axle: the final drive ratio was 3.22:1.

To alter the suspension geometry, and to provide more front negative camber there was a special reinforced front cross member, along with stiffened coil springs, while there were special single-leaf rear springs, and gas-filled Bilstein dampers all round. Cast alloy wheels with 6J section rims, and 185/70HR13in tyres, were standard.

Inside the car there were special bucket seats, while outside the quadruple headlamps were joined by front quarter bumpers, Escort Twin-Cam and RS1600 style. There was no rear spoiler of any type.

From October 1971 the latest Granada/Capri 3-litre gearbox was standardised, along with a different style of FAVO four-spoke cast-alloy wheel and 9.75in ventilated front brake discs.

Visually, a true RS2600 had a contrasting (usually black) bonnet panel, and from late 1971, RS2600 stripes and identification were added. At the end of the run matt black bumpers were being fitted.

Every RS2600 had left-hand-steering, and about 4,000 such cars were built before the end of 1973. The only cars to be officially brought into the UK at the time were for the use of such Ford Motorsport personalities as Walter Hayes and Stuart Turner, but a few more may have been brought in since then.

The 'works' Capri RS2600s won the European Touring Car Championship in 1971 and again in 1972.

Specification	
Capri RS2600	
ENGINE	
Type:	Ford-of-Germany Cologne
Capacity:	2,637cc
Bore/stroke:	90.0 x 69.0mm
Compression ratio :	10.5:1
Max power:	150bhp at 5,800rpm
Max torque:	165lb ft at 3,500rpm
Cylinders:	six, in 60° vee, longitudinally mounted
Cylinder heads:	cast iron
Block:	cast iron
Valve gear:	two valves per cylinder, single camshaft, pushrods and rockers
Fuelling:	Kugelfischer fuel injection
Installation:	front-mounted, longitudinal
TRANSMISSION	
Type:	front-engine, rear-wheel-drive
Gearbox:	four-speed manual
SUSPENSION	
Front:	independent by MacPherson struts, lower track control arms, coil springs, anti-roll bar and telescopic dampers
Rear:	live (beam) axle, half-elliptic leaf springs, radius arms (anti-roll bar from late 1970), and telescopic dampers
STEERING	
Type:	rack-and-pinion
Lock-to-lock:	3.3 turns
BRAKES	
Front:	9.62in (244.3mm) solid discs [9.75in (247.6mm) ventilated discs from late 1973]
Rear:	9.0 x 2.25in (228.6 x 57.1mm) drums
System:	hydraulic, with vacuum servo assistance
WHEELS & TYRES	
Wheels:	cast alloy discs, with four-stud fixing, 6.0J x 13in
Tyres:	185/70HR13in
BODY	
Type:	two-door four-seater coupé, early cars with lightweight panels
Weight:	1,985lb (900kg) [early lightweights] to 2,381lb (1,080kg) [mainstream cars]
PERFORMANCE	
Max speed:	124mph (200kph)
Acceleration:	0–60mph in 8.0sec
PRICE at LAUNCH	
Not officially sold in the UK	

The RS3100 was a very limited-production Capri, made only at the end of 1973, and identified by the RS wheels and this huge rear spoiler.

Capri RS3100
1973–1974

Commercially it made no sense for Ford-UK to introduce the Capri RS3100 only months before the entire MkI range was to be dropped in favour of the bigger, heavier, hatchback MkII. For motor racing purposes, however, Ford needed to counter BMW's latest 'winged-monsters' – the 3.0CSLs – by something even more extreme.

The racing RS2600 had reached its limit, and needed a replacement. A careful reading of the rules suggested that the engine should be over 3-litres, but simple, and that a rear spoiler should be added.

The RS3100, was built in Britain, in right-hand-drive only, with the late-model RS2600 chassis, including the lowered suspension, Bilstein dampers, the single-leaf rear springs, and negative-camber front end.

Visually it was easy to 'pick' an RS3100 from an ordinary 3-litre, by the four-spoke FAVO cast alloys, the quarter bumpers, and the large, rubberised, duck-tail spoiler. Unhappily, the RS3100 was never fitted with special front seats, but retained those being used in Capri 3-litres at the time. That spoiler, incidentally, was never seen on any other Capri, British or European.

The Essex V6 engine was modified, but only slightly. The maximum piston overbore approved by the service engineers was chosen (pistons of 95.19mm were freely available), the result being a swept volume of 3,091cc. There was no change to the downdraught Weber carburation. The tappet covers were different – blue instead of black! The result was peak power of 148bhp at 5,000rpm, which gave the RS3100 a top speed of about 125mph.

Deliveries began in December 1973 and ended in February 1974 when the Capri II came along. Only about 200 of the planned 500 cars were ever built.

Although priced at £2,450, the RS3100 proved difficult to sell: a number had to be heavily discounted. The RS3100's reputation reached its low point in about 1981, when the new 2.8i Capri arrived to make all other old Capris look out of date – the result being that not many RS3100s have survived.

Capri 3-litre

1974–1978 (MkII) & 1978–1981 (MkIII)

New shape, new hatchback feature, but the same platform – this was the secret of the Capri II, announced in 1974.

Spare a thought for the most neglected of Capris – the MkII/III 3-litre types. These tend to be overshadowed, either by the earlier MkIs, or by the later 2.8 Injection model.

Ford changed the Capri's image considerably for 1974. Although billed as a 'reskin', the MkII was effectively a new style on the original body/chassis platform. Not only was the new style smoother than before, but there was a more roomy cabin (especially in the rear seats), and a new type of hatchback tail.

It was two inches wider and about an inch higher: most importantly, the hatchback layout offered three times the stowage accommodation, for the back seat cushion could now be folded down. You could, at a pinch, sleep in that space. It wasn't ideal, but it was possible – I know, because I've done it.

According to all the pundits, this was a much more versatile and better-developed Capri. Even so, sales were quite a lot lower. This seemed to be because times, and fashions, were changing, and not as many cars of this type were being sold in the motoring world. Between 1974 and 1978 318,758 Capri IIs were built. From mid-1976 UK assembly ended, after which all Capris were built by Ford-of-Germany in Cologne. For the 3000S model, first seen in 1975, there was up-rated suspension (including Bilstein dampers), cast-alloy wheels became standard while power-assisted steering also became available.

The MkIII of 1978 was really an improved MkII, with a reduced drag coefficient, new grille, new spoiler, and a nose with four circular headlamps. To make these cars easy to maintain, their drive lines were shared with contemporary Granadas.

This was the definitive Ghia specification fascia/instrument panel display of the Capri II, introduced in 1974.

Those were the days when much equipment was still optional. Power-assisted steering was standard on the MkIII, but an opening sun-roof, tinted glass, Recaro seats and headlamp washers were extra. On MkIIIs, inside the cars there was a hinged parcel shelf tied to the lift-up rear hatch – at least

The Capri II, and the III which followed it, both shared this hatchback feature. Automatic transmission was optional on the 3.0-litre models.

it covered up what the owners were carrying in the boot. Nice touches included mesh-type headrests on Recaro seats, the use of fashionable tartan trim for the seat coverings on S models, and that excellent, straight-legged, driving position.

In MkII and MkIII form, the 3-litre was on sale for seven years. Even before the much more expensive 2.8 Injection version came along in 1981 it had officially been retired, for the last 3000 Ghia was made in December 1980, and the last 3000S followed in April 1981.

Along the way, there was still time for a few development and equipment changes. From Autumn 1978 the cars' radio equipment was upgraded, and the S was fitted with rear fog lamps. Months later, in the spring of 1979, Ghia models inherited the S-type steering wheel, and headlamp washers, while S versions gained more of the Ghia's sound-deadening.

In a way the 3-litre Capris were almost too easy to drive. Just so long as the 3-litre engine was working at all, it delivered strong torque. Even though prices inevitably shot up during the inflationary 1970s, the 3-litre always offered remarkable value. Because of the rather nose-heavy weight distribution, and the limited rear suspension travel, the 3-litre was let down by its road-holding on poor surfaces. The ride was hard, and there was a lot of axle hop on rough surfaces.

Experienced drivers soon learned how to get the best out of the handling. It was best to cruise in to a corner, boot it as soon as you were sure there would be no inside-rear-wheel lift and wheelspin, but be ready to catch any power-oversteer with a quick flick of the power-assisted steering. Hooligan's car? You bet it was.

From 1978, the Capri became Capri III, complete with a four-headlamp nose. On 'S' models, too, there was unique colour decalling along the flanks.

Specification	
Capri 3-litre (MkII and MkIII)	
(Capri III differences in brackets.)	
ENGINE	
Type:	Ford-UK Essex
Capacity:	2,994cc
Bore/stroke:	93.7 x 72.4mm
Compression ratio:	9.0:1
Max power:	138bhp at 5,000rpm
Max torque:	174lb ft at 3,000rpm
Cylinders:	six, in 60° vee, longitudinally mounted
Cylinder heads:	cast iron
Block:	cast iron
Valve gear:	two valves per cylinder, single camshaft, pushrods and rockers
Fuelling:	Weber dual-choke 38/38 EGAS carburettor
Installation:	front-mounted, longitudinal
TRANSMISSION	
Type:	front-engine, rear-wheel-drive
Gearbox:	four-speed manual
(Optional three-speed Ford C3 automatic transmission)	
SUSPENSION	
Front:	independent by MacPherson struts, lower track control arms, coil springs, anti-roll bar and telescopic dampers
Rear:	live (beam) axle, half-elliptic leaf springs, anti-roll bar, and telescopic dampers
STEERING	
Type:	rack-and-pinion (power-assisted)
Lock-to-lock:	3.3 turns
BRAKES	
Front:	9.75in (247.6mm) ventilated discs
Rear:	9.0 x 2.25in (228.6 x 57.1mm) drums
System:	hydraulic, with vacuum servo assistance
WHEELS & TYRES	
Wheels:	cast-alloy discs, with four-stud fixing, 6.0J x 13in (some sub-variants 5.5J x 13in)
Tyres:	185/70HR13in
BODY	
Type:	two-door four-seater hatchback monocoque coupé
Weight:	2,577lb (1,171kg)
PERFORMANCE	
Max speed:	117mph (188kph)
Acceleration:	0–60mph in 8.6sec
PRICE at LAUNCH	
3000GT (MkII): £1,932 in March 1974	
3000S (MkIII): £4,327 in March 1978	

Capri 2.8 Injection & Special

1981–1986

The Capri 2.8 Injection model of 1981 was a brilliant rework of an ageing design. Faster, more purposeful, and with those unique wheels, it was a very successful Capri.

As far as the Capri was concerned, Ford kept the best until the last. The 2.8-litre Injection model, produced from 1981 to 1986, was the most satisfying Capri of all. It was the fastest of all the production-line models, it looked best, and for sure, it had the best roadholding. How do I know this? Because I owned a new one for two very happy years.

The miracle was that this model came to be made at all. By 1980 the Capri 3000 was looking old, for it had been in production for more than ten years, and there had been no significant style changes for six years. Technically, too, it was in trouble, for the Essex V6 had reached its limits, and would shortly not be able to meet the exhaust emission regulations which were expected to flood across Europe.

Fortunately, Rod Mansfield's Special Vehicle Engineering department (SVE) had just been set up at Ford-UK's engineering centre, and was encouraged to produce a special Capri to keep this charismatic car on the road. Even so, this was a real challenge, for they were given little more than a year to do the job, and they had to find almost every innovation by delving into Ford's capacious 'parts bin'.

Surrounded by so many restrictions, it would have been so easy to get it wrong. Yet the new car, called 2.8 Injection for what were obvious reasons, would be the best, the finest-balanced, and the most satisfying of all Capri types built. SVE approached their task with logical intent – compared with the old 3-litre, they wanted to produce a faster Capri which handled better and felt altogether more modern. From the day that it was announced, in March 1981, almost everyone seemed to love it.

The first, and probably the easiest, decision was to fit a fuel-injected Ford

51

For the Capri 2.8 Injection, Ford settled on this fascia layout, complete with chunky three-spoke steering wheel.

Cologne 2.8-litre V6 engine – one identical in almost every detail with that currently used in the Granada saloon. As a direct descendant of the RS2600 power unit, it slotted easily into the big engine bay, and it was easy to adapt it to fit the existing 3-litre's sturdy (if not very refined) four-speed gearbox. Unlike the 3-litre, though, there would be no automatic transmission option, for SVE intended this to be a real sports coupé, not a car which could waft around in overcrowded cities.

When this was a new model, the engine was rated at 160bhp, but over the years this figure was quietly down-graded to 150bhp (exactly the same, in other words, as the Granada from which it was derived). There had been no changes, and no loss in performance, but independent tests showed that most engines more nearly approximated to the lower figure. Ford was forever honest (they told us) so . . .

In detail the chassis was much improved. Not only were unique-style 7.0in rim cast-alloy wheels specified (with 205/60-section radials – the widest yet specified on any Capri), but spring and damper rates were all rerated, Bilstein gas-filled dampers were chosen, and the whole car was hunkered down by one inch. Power-assisted steering was standard, and even that was carefully and thoughtfully retuned to match the latest suspension settings.

The result was magical, for without altering anything significant (except the settings) SVE had produced the best-handling Capri which any of us had, or would ever drive. And it was all so reassuring, too, for ventilated front discs had also been standardised.

In the cabin, there was one significant improvement over the old 3-litre (which was immediately discontinued when the Injection model was announced) – which was that a pair of splendid figure-hugging Recaro seats were standardised. The fascia panel looked, and was, very familiar, for it was the same style which had been introduced as long ago as late 1972. The familiar tilt-and-slide sunroof of the outgoing 3000S was also retained.

Early cars went on sale in the UK at £7,995, although it was easy to push this up by specifying metallic paint, specially ordering a limited-slip differential, or dipping further into the options catalogue. Within weeks, it seemed, the 'old' Capri's reputation had perked up considerably, for independent tests showed that here was a car which could approach 130mph where such speeds were allowed, and that the ultra-wide wheel/tyre combination gave it the best balance which we Capri-owners had ever experienced.

From the winter of 1982/83, there was one significant mechanical change, when the clunky old four-speed gearbox was ditched in favour of the Type 9 five-speeder which had just been inaugurated in Sierra models (and was about to be standardised in the new Sierra XR4i hatchback).

Because fifth gear was an overdrive, and fourth gear was direct, this automatically made the 2.8 Injection into a higher-geared car, something which seemed to suit it very well indeed.

British sales of this German-built Capri then carried on at a rate of about 4,000 cars a year for another two years. This was the point at which the model name was changed – for henceforth it would be called 2.8 Injection Special. From that moment on, all Capris would have right-hand-drive, so exclusively for British customers the 'Special' meant that a different style of 7.0in wide alloy wheel rims were to be standard (they would have seven spokes instead of being 'pepperpots'), a Salisbury limited-slip differential would also be standard, while inside the cabin there was liberal use of leather on seat trims, steering wheel and door panel inserts.

No changes were, however, ever made to the smooth fuel-injected 2.8-litre engine, nor were they made at the very end of the run when the limited-edition 'Brooklands' type was also revealed. Only 1,038 such cars were ever produced, all of them in the same green hue, all priced at £11,999.

The last Capri of all was produced in Cologne in December 1986. But through a quirk of marketing the Brooklands limited-edition was not even announced until February 1987, when all cars had been built, and the line had been closed down!

It is a dreadful indictment on the morality of this country that the last of the Capris instantly became a target for theft. Many of the Brooklands models were stolen and, if recovered, had often been extensively vandalised. This, if nothing else, was a measure of how desirable the fuel-injected Capri had become.

Ford once wanted us to think that the Sierra XR4i was a worthy successor to the injected Capri, but we all knew better. Unhappily, the financial sums never added up far enough for a genuine replacement ever to be developed.

Specification	
Ford Capri 2.8 Injection and Special	
ENGINE	
Type:	Ford Cologne
Capacity:	2,792cc
Bore/stroke:	93 x 68.5mm
Compression ratio:	9.2:1
Max power:	150bhp at 5,700rpm (originally rated at 160bhp)
Max torque:	162lb ft at 4,300rpm
Cylinders:	six, in 60° vee, longitudinally mounted
Cylinder heads:	cast iron
Block:	cast iron
Valve gear:	two valves per cylinder, single camshaft, pushrods and rockers.
Fuelling:	Bosch K-Jetronic fuel injection
Installation:	front-mounted, longitudinal
TRANSMISSION	
Type:	front-engine, rear-wheel-drive
Gearbox:	four-speed manual (five-speed from January 1983)
SUSPENSION	
Front:	independent by MacPherson struts, lower track control arms, coil springs, anti-roll bar and telescopic dampers
Rear:	live (beam) axle, half-elliptic leaf springs, anti-roll bar, and telescopic dampers
STEERING	
Type:	rack-and-pinion (with power assistance)
Lock-to-lock:	3.3 turns
BRAKES	
Front:	10.3in (257mm) ventilated discs
Rear:	9.0 x 2.25in (228.6 x 57.1mm) drums
System:	Girling hydraulic, with Girling vacuum servo assistance. No ABS
WHEELS & TYRES	
Wheels:	cast-alloy discs (original with eight-hole pattern), with four-stud fixing, 7.0J x 13in
Tyres:	205/60VR13in
BODY	
Type:	two-door four-seater hatchback coupé
Weight:	2,620lb (1,190kg)
PERFORMANCE	
Max speed:	127mph (204kph)
Acceleration:	0–60mph in 7.9sec
PRICE at LAUNCH	
£7,995 in 1981	

The 280 Brooklands was the final Capri of all, mechanically the same as other late-model 2.8is, but with unique trim and colour scheme.

Capri 2.8 Turbo

1981–1982

Pictured at the Nürburgring is one of the rare Capri 2.8 Turbos, for which Zakspeed had some involvement.

Sold only in Germany, the Capri 2.8 Turbo was a conversion of the 2.8i – although with a carburetted turbo engine. Note the special big rear spoiler.

The turbocharged Capri is the least known of all derivatives. It was only in production for a short time, it was only ever built in left-hand-drive form, and it was officially never sold in the UK. Nor was it well known in its native Germany, for only 200 were ever built, all of them being sold on the Continent.

Deep down, the 2.8 Turbo was intended to benefit from the great publicity garnered by the flamboyant Zakspeed 'silhouette' race cars of the late 1970s. Although the aerodynamic add-ons in the Turbo gave an impression of these two cars being related, in fact they had nothing in common. Even so, the 'halo' effect of one must surely have helped the other.

The key to this development was Zakspeed, the much-respected German tuning house, based at Niederzissen, for all 200 cars were part fettled there, by modifying partly completed production Capri 2.8i body shells which had been transported up the road from Cologne. The GRP wheelarches, in fact, were glued rather than riveted into place – which sometimes caused some quality problems, especially on finished cars. They were then returned to Cologne for completion.

One of the visual features which made the Capri 2.8 Turbo special was the deep front spoiler.

Specification

Ford Capri 2.8 Turbo

ENGINE

Type:	Ford Cologne
Capacity:	2,792cc
Bore/stroke:	93 x 68.5mm
Compression ratio:	9.2:1
Max power:	188bhp at 5,500rpm
Max torque:	206lb ft at 4,500rpm
Cylinders:	six, in 60° vee, longitudinally mounted
Cylinder heads:	cast iron
Block:	cast iron
Valve gear:	two valves per cylinder, single camshaft, pushrods and rockers
Fuelling:	downdraught dual choke Weber carburettor and KKK turbocharger
Installation:	front-mounted, longitudinal

TRANSMISSION

Type:	front-engine, rear-wheel-drive
Gearbox:	four-speed manual

SUSPENSION

Front:	independent by MacPherson struts, lower track control arms, coil springs, anti-roll bar and telescopic dampers
Rear:	live (beam) axle, half-elliptic leaf springs, anti-roll bar, and telescopic dampers

STEERING

Type:	rack-and-pinion (power-assisted)
Lock-to-lock:	3.3 turns

BRAKES

Front:	10.3in (257mm) ventilated discs
Rear:	9.0 x 2.25in (228.6 x 57.1mm) drums
System:	Hydraulic, with vacuum servo assistance

WHEELS & TYRES

Wheels:	cast-alloy discs, with four-stud fixing, 6.5J x 13in
Tyres:	235/60VR13in

BODY

Type:	two-door four-seater hatchback coupé with Zakspeed-style flared wheelarches
Weight:	2,695lb (1,225kg)

PERFORMANCE

Max speed:	134mph (216kph)(claimed)
Acceleration:	0–60mph in 8.0sec (claimed)

PRICE at LAUNCH

Not officially sold in the UK

Its important to realise, however, that these were not turbocharged versions of the 2.8i – for the Turbo had a carburetted engine. Except on the very first cars (which were 3000S types), the base car, indeed, was a 2.8 Injection Capri, but the power output was actually taken from a carburetted version of the 2,792cc V6 engine, as normally fitted to the Granada at this time. Zakspeed completed the tune-up by fitting a KKK turbocharger. Even though maximum boost was only 0.4 Bar, this was enough to push peak power up from 135bhp (normally aspirated) to 188bhp (Zakspeed Turbo). This engine, in fact, was so lusty that 150bhp (Capri 2.8i peak levels) was already being developed at 4,000rpm, at which point the power curve was still thrusting confidently upwards.

No changes were made to the familiar, beefy, old four-speed gearbox (there never was a five-speed Capri Turbo), although a limited-slip differential was always optionally available in the (Atlas-type) rear axle.

Because this was a torquey, rather than a peak-output, turbocharging tune, the Turbo had easy-to-find, stump-pulling performance, for which Ford-of-Germany claimed a top speed of 134mph, and 0-62mph acceleration in 8.0sec. As far as I can see, there were no independent tests, but both these, surely, were conservative figures – for tests showed that the 150bhp 2.8 Injection was almost as fast.

Zakspeed went all out to make the Turbo obvious, so it attached a deep front spoiler under the front bumper, and an even more flamboyant plastic rear spoiler on the hatchback. Flared glass-fibre wheelarches were also added. The visual effect was completed by the chunky, 6.5in (some cars even had 7.5in. Ford Motorsport-style four-spokers) alloy wheels and the 235/60-section tyres.

Except for the use of Ford RS-branded velour seating, and an Escort RS1600i type of four-spoke steering wheel, that was the extent of the conversion which, crucially, left the braking and suspension unmodified. The result was a melange, by no means as elegantly done as the Ford-UK 2.8 Injection car, and although it did its job (and all 200 cars were sold in the year in which they were marketed), it never became an icon in the way that the British model most certainly did. Except for the Capri Tickford this was the fastest of all factory-approved Capris – yet there was no obvious category in which it could go motor racing, and I have not traced any successes in that field.

Capri Tickford

1983–1987

The Capri Tickford not only had a turbocharged Essex engine, but a much-restyled body shell.

The Capri Tickford featured a turbocharged V6 engine – the turbo being mounted up front, ahead of the engine block itself.

The Tickford Capri had rather complex origins. First came ex-F1 driver John Miles, then Aston Martin Tickford, finally Ford, who were persuaded to back its development. However, by 1983, much Ford support had been lost. Tickford Capris started life as conventional Capri 2.8is before being stripped at the Bedworth factory (which later produced Sierra RS500 Cosworths, and reprepared most of the RS200s), and completely re-engineered and re-equipped.

Because they were costly, and there were many options, these cars were never built for stock. Each and every one was produced in response to an order, and no two cars seemed to be exactly alike.

Think of the best handling of all fuel-injected Capris, faster with a turbocharged engine, improved handling, all kept in check with a conversion to four-wheel disc brakes. Then make it look sensational, built in lots of value-adding extras – and it made every other Capri owner jealous. The problem was the price. In October 1983, when the 2.8i retailed at £8,653, a 'basic' Tickford was listed at £14,985, but by the time you had added leather interior, Wilton carpets and more to the interior, the invoice price had probably risen to £18,000, and more.

There were major changes to the engine, the rear suspension, the brakes, the bodywork and the interior. The 2.8-litre Ford Cologne V6 was turbocharged and produced 205bhp. The turbo was ahead of the engine, the Bosch fuel injection gizmos were moved and an intercooler was fitted. Surprisingly, there were no gearbox or axle changes.

The rear suspension was considerably improved, with an 'A frame', this actually comprising two diagonal radius arms which linked the axle centre piece to the leaf spring-mountings. At the rear, solid rear discs replaced drums.

Style changes

Tickford also provided fresh looks to match the performance, and also made it handle better and feel more stable at high speeds. Although the Tickford was no lower, extra-sized front and rear bumpers made it look like that. A glass-fibre body kit included integrated front and rear 'bumpers', sill kits along the flanks, a complete blanking panel for the front grille, and a large but effective rear spoiler.

Blanking off the original grille did not cause overheating problems: for most of the cooling air (and air for the intercooler) entered through a large bumper slot.

We now know, that the kit reduced the drag coefficient to Cd = 0.37, with reduced front and rear lift compared with the standard 2.8i. Two different types of road wheel were used – first the standard 2.8i 'pepperpot' style, and later the seven-spoke variety from the 280 Special.

The interior was rejigged, with a new and more impressive plastic (but leather-covered) instrument panel surround, and with a wooden fascia insert. Early cars used walnut veneer, later cars had satin black veneer instead. The standard instruments were all retained.

Colour and trim? Surprisingly, not as many as you might think are white with black leather interiors, though such cars seem to have hogged the limelight over the years. Basically, there were three colours: Cardinal Red, Diamond White and black – and leather was always an expensive option (£1,885 in 1983, more costly as the years passed). White is the most common paint colour, and one or two oddball colours were also provided by Tickford, which was always able to provide such a hand-tailoring service.

Incidentally, beware imitations. Tickford stylist Simon Saunders later moved on from the company and set up his own company – KAT – to make and sell body kits for Capris. At first Tickford thought these were too close to their own trademarked layout and threatened legal action, after which those styles were modified enough to keep all parties happy.

Because it was possible to jack up the invoice of a new Tickford to nearly £20,000, sales were slow. Only one hundred Tickfords were built before 1987. Nowadays, there are less than 50 roadworthy survivors in this country.

Specification	
Capri Tickford	
ENGINE	
Type:	Ford-of-Germany Cologne
Capacity:	2,792cc
Bore/stroke:	93.0 x 68.5mm
Compression ratio:	9.2:1
Max power:	205bhp at 5,000rpm
Max torque:	260lb ft at 3,000rpm
Cylinders:	six, in 60° vee, longitudinally mounted
Cylinder heads:	cast iron
Block:	cast iron
Valve gear:	two valves per cylinder, single camshaft, pushrods and rockers
Fuel and ignition:	Bosch K-Jetronic fuel injection, with IHI RHB6 turbocharger
Installation:	front-mounted, longitudinal
TRANSMISSION	
Type:	front-engine, rear-wheel-drive
Gearbox:	five-speed manual
SUSPENSION	
Front:	independent by MacPherson struts, lower track control arms, coil springs, anti-roll bar and telescopic dampers
Rear:	live (beam) axle, half-elliptic leaf springs, anti-roll bar, A-bar axle-location, telescopic dampers
STEERING	
Type:	rack-and-pinion (power-assisted)
Lock-to-lock:	3.3 turns
BRAKES	
Front:	10.3in (262mm) ventilated discs
Rear:	10.43in (265mm) solid discs
System:	Girling hydraulic, with Girling vacuum servo assistance
WHEELS & TYRES	
Wheels:	cast-alloy discs, with four-stud fixing, various styles
Tyres:	205/60VR13in
BODY	
Type:	two-door four-seater coupé, large transverse rear spoiler
Weight:	from 2,650lb (1,202kg)
PERFORMANCE	
Max speed:	135mph (217kph)
Acceleration:	0–60mph in 6.5sec
PRICE at LAUNCH	
£14,985 in 1983	

The Capri Tickford not only had more performance, but an extrovert body style which included a vast rear spoiler.

Escort RS2000 MkII

1976–1980

The beaky-nosed Escort RS2000 of 1976–1980 became the best-selling rear-drive Escort RS model of all.

Between 1976 and 1980 the beaky-nosed Escort RS2000 MkII became the most successful, best-selling, rear-drive RS model of all. Even twenty years later, when other RS models have come and gone, it is still well-regarded. In the long list of RS models which reached its 30th anniversary in 2000, only the front-wheel-drive Escort RS Turbo attracted more customers.

When the time came to start work on a second generation of Escort RS models in 1973, the market place was booming. Ford planned to develop cars to replace all their existing RS types – Mexico, RS1600 and RS2000 – and thought that they could continue to assemble them at Aveley.

Although the Suez War/Energy Crisis of 1973/74 then changed everything – because Ford sales were badly hit, it meant that the Aveley plant would have to be closed down – the product plan survived. For the new MkII models, the major difference was that they would be assembled in the dedicated Escort plant at Saarlouis, in West Germany, close to the French border.

There would be three new MkII RSs – an RS1800 for competition, an RS Mexico at 'entry level', and an RS2000 to take up the profitable, prestigious, middle ground. Although the original RS2000 would only be on sale for a year and a half, it was an obvious success, so the new-style car would build on that.

Although all three Escort RS MkIIs shared the same basic body shell and chassis/running gear architecture, the RS2000 MkII was the only version which AVO was allowed to restyle. To make it stand out, and to make it unique in marketing terms, it was given a smart new nose, where a special wedge-shaped style, in polyurethane, not only jutted out more, but had an integral low spoiler, seemed to be more aerodynamically efficient, and enclosed four circular headlamps. The polyurethane was flexible (which

Derivatives

In Australia and in South Africa, flat-nosed (i.e. RS Mexico-shaped) versions of this car were built – but not always given the 'RS' badge. The flat-nose version became the rally car weapon of choice in the UK until it ran out of eligibility in the mid-1980s. A quantity of four-door RS2000s, complete with beak-noses, were assembled in Australia, and sold on the market, but this version was never offered elsewhere.

X-pack versions, featuring flamboyantly flared front and rear wheelarches by Zakspeed, were made available, and were completed as after-market RS dealer conversions. Hundreds of these kits were sold, and surviving cars are among the elite at Ford club gatherings.

Thanks to some clever homologation, and a lavish list of off-the-shelf performance-enhancing extra equipment, the RS2000 MkII became a very successful Group 1 model, especially in rallies, and sometimes in racing too. Ari Vatanen won the Tour of Britain in 1976, other cars won the Group 1 category of the RAC Rally in 1979 and 1980, and flat-nosed derivatives were used in British road rallies for a good many years.

meant that it was not as vulnerable to minor damage as was once feared), and changes were made to the bonnet panel (which was lengthened) and the steel front wing pressings (which were shortened) to accommodate it. Inner pressings, however, were not changed.

At the rear, a rubberised spoiler was now mounted, transversely, on the rear edge of the boot lid. Ford insisted that the combination of new aerodynamic features meant a 16 per cent lower drag coefficient, 25 per cent less front end lift and no less than 60 per cent lower rear end lift.

The running gear was all a sensible update of that which had been used in the first type of RS2000. Once again, power was provided by the single-overhead-camshaft Pinto engine (rally enthusiasts had already seen that there was a lot of potential locked away inside it!). Changes included a better, more through-flow, exhaust system, which saw the peak raised to 110bhp at 5,500rpm.

Behind the engine, the German 'E' gearbox was as before, as was the 3.54:1 rear axle ratio, although the rear drum brakes had been enlarged to 9 x 1.75in. MacPherson strut front suspension and radius-arm location for the rear axle was also as before, the entire suspension installation being shared (except in tiny detail) with the RS Mexico and the very rare RS1800 road car.

It was inside the car that the MkII was such an advance on the MkI, for Ford. Along with the RS1800 and the RS Mexico, the new car shared a much more modern-looking, and nicely equipped, fascia/instrument panel, with a smart three-spoke RS steering wheel. Rally-type front seats were the best possible fittings for a car where the driver needed to have a reassuring 'seat-of-the-pants' feel, there was a sensible clock alongside the glove box, and the simple console was another advance.

Ford's big decision was that this 'executive' machine would only ever be sold as a two-door saloon, which took the edge off some potential sales, I am sure. For very good family reasons I would have needed four doors on my RS2000 – and although I pulled every possible string with my contacts at the factory, such a request was always refused: interestingly, there was a four-door eventually – but only built and sold in Australia!

Much more expensive than the last of the MkI cars – £2,857 in January 1976 compared with £2,076 for a 1975-model MkI – it nevertheless looked like selling well, and always did. And why? Here, more than on many

When Ford launched the X-Pack range in the late 1970s, the RS2000 took pride of place. Scores of cars, complete with those Zakspeed-style wheelarch extensions, were sold.

occasions, I think we can say that the entire package – not just the style, not just the performance, not just the image – was right. If it could be distilled and bottled, Ford's product planners would certainly have done so, for it sold better than they had dared hope, it received more favourable press attention than expected and – very important, this – it was profitable too.

Management already knew that the handling would appeal to RS as well as less-committed enthusiasts – they had already driven prototypes, whose balance had been influenced by no less a character than Tom Walkinshaw – but they must have been quite delighted with the out-and-out performance. Although this was a car which was nominally less powerful than the RS1800 (it had 110bhp, compared with 115bhp), all the independent tests showed that it accelerated just as fast, and had a top speed which was broadly similar. More than this, it was blessed with the same simple-to-maintain power train as 'ordinary' Fords such as a 2-litre Capri or even a 2-litre Cortina.

Yet there was something else, too. The RS2000 MkII looked flamboyant without being vulgar (there was an array of exciting colours in the line-up), it was fast without being noisy, and it could not only be used for commuting in busy traffic, but tuned-up for motorsport with every chance of class success. Even in those inflationary days, when the price had to be increased twice or more times every year, it never ran out of customers.

It was versatile too, as from the autumn of 1978, Ford discontinued the RS Mexico, and rejigged the RS2000 MkII line to compensate. From this point, there would be two different RS2000s – both still looking the same, and both sharing the same, unchanged, running gear, but with different levels of equipment. There was now a 'base' RS2000 model (£3,902) which had 1600 Sport-style low-back reclining front seats, and 5.5in rim steel road wheels, while there was also to be a 'Custom' RS2000 (£4,416) with high-back Recaro reclining front seats, 6.0in rim cast alloy wheels, and bronze-tinted glass all round the cabin.

Although the 'base' RS2000 was really intended to provide an alternative to the obsolete RS Mexico, it never sold well – dealers reckon that four out of every five sales were of the 'Custom' variety. Between them, though, these cars sold well until the last rear-drive Escort of all was built in the summer of 1980. In the UK the last few, I understand, were registered in 1981.

The Escort RS2000 MkII was more of a 'life-style' car than a competition vehicle. Gliding for a hobby, anyone?

Specification	
Escort RS2000 MkII	
ENGINE	
Type:	Ford Pinto
Capacity:	1,993cc
Bore/stroke:	90.82 x 76.95mm
Compression ratio (nominal):	9.2:1
Max power:	110bhp at 5,500rpm
Max torque:	119lb ft at 4,000rpm
Cylinders:	four, in-line, longitudinally mounted
Cylinder head:	cast iron
Block:	cast iron
Valve gear:	two valves per cylinder, belt-driven single overhead camshaft, fingers and rockers
Fuelling:	Weber 32/36 downdraught carburettor
Installation:	front-mounted, longitudinal
TRANSMISSION	
Type:	front-engine, rear-wheel-drive
Gearbox:	four-speed manual
SUSPENSION	
Front:	independent by coil springs, MacPherson struts, anti-roll bar, telescopic dampers
Rear:	live (beam) axle, with half-elliptic leaf springs, radius arms, telescopic dampers
STEERING	
Type:	rack-and-pinion
Lock-to-lock:	3.5 turns
BRAKES	
Front:	9.62in (244mm) discs
Rear:	9.0 x 1.75in (228.6 x 44.45mm) drums
System:	hydraulic with vacuum servo assistance
WHEELS & TYRES	
Wheels:	cast-alloy disc (steel from 1978 on 'base' models), 6.0J x 13in (5.5J x 13in)
Tyres:	175/70HR13in radial-ply
BODY/CHASSIS	
Type:	pressed-steel monocoque, in two-door saloon style
Weight:	2,075lb (941kg)
PERFORMANCE	
Max speed:	109mph (175kph) approx
Acceleration:	0–60mph in 8.6sec
PRICE at LAUNCH	
£2,857 in January 1976	

Escort RS1800

1975–1977

This is why the RS1800 was truly famous – it was an astonishingly successful rally car. This was Ari Vatanen, on the way to winning the Cyprus Rally of 1979.

Motorsport

The RS1800, quite simply, became the most successful of all Ford rally cars, and hundreds are still in use at club level today. Except to note that Ford won the World Rally Championship for Makes in 1979, and that Bjorn Waldegard (1979) and Ari Vatanen (1981) used RS1800s to win the World Drivers' Championship, little further detailing is needed. RS1800s won the world's toughest events – including the Safari, the RAC, the Acropolis and the Finnish 1000 Lakes – and after much development also become winners on tarmac events all round the world.

It was only the arrival of four-wheel-drive cars which brought their reign to an end.

Here are two different cars for you to consider, and two different characters to assess. How are you going to choose between the Escort RS1800 and the Escort RS 2000 MkII? RS1800s were price-listed from mid-1975 to late 1977, RS2000 MkIIs from January 1976 to late 1980.

The fact is that it is the RS1800 which usually causes most interest at an enthusiasts' meeting, for it is relatively rare, and not often seen in standard and carefully preserved form. Very few were built – indeed, they were homologated suspiciously quickly. Early cars were hand-built at Halewood, and later ones part-assembled at Saarlouis in West Germany, where RS1800s were actually programmed as RS Mexicos to start with! It seems that only 109 RS1800s were delivered in the UK compared with 10,039 UK-market RS2000 MkIIs, so you will see why this is a rarity . . .

Noting that only 155 built-up RS1600s had actually been sold in Britain from 1973 to 1975, with hundreds more created in private workshops for motorsport, Ford decided only to make RS1800s if asked – doing it by using partly built RS Mexicos as the basis for a 'conversion' job.

Both RS1800 and RS Mexico MkIIs shared the new platform, and rather angular two-door body styles, along with front 'chin' spoilers, and with a transverse spoiler across the boot lid. The new RS body shell was much less specialised and almost entirely common with the mainstream cars except for local strengthening of front strut top mounts and provision for radius arm rear suspension locations. Inside the cabin, the cars used a new 1300 Sport or 1600 Sport type of fascia/instrument layout.

RS1800 'production cars' started life at Saarlouis as RS Mexicos, were painted, trimmed and completed as far as possible, but were then shipped to a small workshop at Aveley in Essex, where engines and transmissions were fitted. They were then completed as RS1800s.

The engine measured 1,835cc (it was an over-bored BDA), and was normally fitted with a single, downdraught, dual-choke Weber 32/36 DGAV carburettor. Ford had reckoned that motorsport users would have the engine super-tuned. Behind the latest engine was yet another derivative of the Type E 'German' gearbox, with a close ratio gear set. The new ratios, when allied to a modified gear casing and an extra fifth, overdrive gear, would later be found on cars like the Sierra XR4i and the Capri 2.8i of the early 1980s.

The different types of road wheels seen on these cars – sculptured steel or cast alloys – were the same as those used on Escort RS2000 MkIIs or RS1800s. RS1800s had '1.8' badges on the front wings, a single, broad, two-tone blue strip on the flanks at wheelarch-top level, and 'RS1800' decals on the rear quarters, and on the boot lid, along with a black-painted panel across the tail. There were two types of RS1800. The RS1800 'base' was fitted out rather like the Escort 1600 Sport of the day, whereas the more expensive RS1800 'Custom' had superb contoured/reclinable front seats, a centre console with provision for a radio mounting, a fascia-mounted clock, and the extra fascia/instrument equipment normally found in RS2000 MkIIs of the day. There was little demand for the 'Custom' pack, so this was dropped at the end of 1976.

As road cars the standard RS1800 was rather overshadowed by the all-round excellence of the RS2000 MkII, but in later years its own distinctive character came to be recognised. Today's values, I believe, reflect their worth – for the RS1800 in particular is a rare and ultra-desirable beast.

Specification	
Escort RS1800	
ENGINE	
Type:	Cosworth-Ford BDA
Capacity:	1,835cc
Bore/stroke:	86.75 x 77.62mm
Compression ratio:	10.0:1
Max power:	115bhp at 6,000rpm
Max torque:	120lb ft at 4,000rpm
Cylinders:	four, in-line, longitudinally mounted
Cylinder head:	cast aluminium
Block:	cast aluminium
Valve gear:	four valves per cylinder, twin belt-driven overhead camshafts, bucket tappets
Fuelling:	single downdraught dual-choke Weber Type 32/36 DGAV carburettor
Installation:	front-mounted, longitudinal
TRANSMISSION	
Type:	front-engine, rear-wheel-drive
Gearbox:	four-speed manual
SUSPENSION	
Front:	independent by coil springs, MacPherson struts, anti-roll bar and telescopic dampers
Rear:	live (beam) axle, with half-elliptic leaf springs, radius-arms and telescopic dampers
STEERING	
Type:	rack-and-pinion
Lock-to-lock:	3.0 turns
BRAKES	
Front:	9.62in (244mm) discs
Rear:	9.0 x 1.75in (229 x 44.5mm) drums
System:	hydraulic, with vacuum servo assistance
WHEELS & TYRES	
Wheels:	steel disc, 5.5J x 13in
Tyres:	175/70HR13in radial-ply
BODY/CHASSIS	
Type:	pressed-steel monocoque, in two-door saloon style
Weight:	2,015lb (915kg)
PERFORMANCE	
Max speed:	111mph (179kph) approx
Acceleration:	0–60mph in 9.0sec
PRICE at LAUNCH	
£2,416 in 'base', or £2,527 in 'Custom' trim, in 1975	

Although the Escort RS1800 road car was rare, it was a genuine production car – it was just that demand was limited! This car has motorsport wheelarches and driving lamps fitted.

The Escort RS Mexico MkII was almost the 'unknown RS' model. It was only on sale from 1976 to 1978.

Escort RS Mexico
MkII 1976–1978

Specification	
Escort RS Mexico (MkII)	
ENGINE	
Type:	Ford Pinto
Capacity:	1,593cc
Bore/stroke:	87.65 x 66mm
Compression ratio:	9.2:1
Max power:	95bhp at 5,750rpm
Max torque:	92lb ft at 4,000rpm
Cylinders:	four, in-line, longitudinally mounted
Cylinder head:	cast iron
Block:	cast iron
Valve gear:	two valves per cylinder, single belt-driven overhead camshaft and fingers
Fuelling:	single downdraught dual-choke Weber Type 32/36 DGAV carburettor
TRANSMISSION	
Type:	front-engine, rear-wheel-drive
Gearbox:	four-speed manual
SUSPENSION	
Front:	independent by coil springs, MacPherson struts, anti-roll bar and telescopic dampers
Rear:	live (beam) axle, with half-elliptic leaf springs, radius-arms and telescopic dampers
STEERING	
Type:	rack-and-pinion
Lock-to-lock:	3.0 turns
BRAKES	
Front:	9.62in (244mm) discs
Rear:	9.0 x 1.75in (229 x 44.5mm) drums
System:	hydraulic, with vacuum servo assistance
WHEELS & TYRES	
Wheels:	cast-alloy disc, 6.0J x 13in
Tyres:	175/70HR13in radial-ply
BODY/CHASSIS	
Type:	pressed-steel monocoque, in two-door saloon style
Weight:	1,990lb (902kg)
PERFORMANCE	
Max speed:	106mph (170kph) approx
Acceleration:	0–60mph in 11.1sec
PRICE at LAUNCH	
£2,443 in January 1976	

After a year off the market, the Escort Mexico name reappeared in January 1976, as the 'entry level' to the new range of MkII RS models. Closely related to the RS1800 in many ways, it was manufactured until the summer of 1978. To differentiate it from the earlier type, it was always known as the RS Mexico – the 'RS' acronym never having been attached to the original car.

Like the RS2000 MkII, it was always built at Saarlouis in West Germany, and a total of 2,290 such RS Mexicos were delivered to British customers.

As on all mainstream MkIIs, the battery tray/battery were now under the bonnet. All cars used a new 1300/1600 Sport-type of fascia/instrument layout, but the RS Mexico's was simpler than the RS1800/RS2000 types.

The RS Mexico was the first, and only, RS model to use the 1.6-litre overhead-cam Pinto engine, the same basic 1,593cc unit as used in Capris and Cortinas of that period, but in a higher state of tune. It was rated at 95bhp (DIN) at 5,700rpm which guaranteed a top speed of around 105mph. This, of course, was a smaller-capacity relative of the Pinto engine fitted to RS2000s of both types, and in bhp/litre terms was more highly rated than either of them. Visually, in fact, there was little to distinguish one type from the other.

Externally, the RS Mexico looked very much like the 1600 Sport except that it used a moulded front spoiler under the front bumper. Naturally it had front 'quarter' bumpers instead of the full-width variety, and there were '1.6' badges behind the front wheelarches, together with the same pin-striping along the flanks, although the 'Mexico' decal appeared on the rear quarters instead of the 1600 Sport's own badges. The road wheels seen on this model – sculpted steel or (optionally extra) cast alloys – were the same as those used on Escort RS2000 MkIIs or RS1800s. There was only one RS Mexico trim specification (which was virtually identical with the 'basic' RS1800 trim) – for the 'Custom' pack never featured on this model.

As road cars, at the time, there is no question that the Mexico MkII was always overshadowed by the all-round excellence of the RS2000 MkII. Even so, for those who did not want to spend extra money on the RS2000 MkII, the RS Mexico found its own particular niche. It was a fast and compact car (considerably faster, need I add, than the original-style Mexico) which handled equally as well as the other MkII RS models, yet it did not suffer from any of the parts supply problems (or parts cost problems) of the other types.

Escort XR3

1980–1982

The first front-wheel-drive Escorts were built in 1980. In the early years, the 96bhp XR3 was the most powerful type on offer.

The Escort XR3 was a new type of Ford, but it could not have arrived at a more awkward time. Even before they understood the new car, almost every Ford enthusiast was ready to hate it. Not for what it was, maybe, but for what it elbowed aside.

The XR3 signalled the end of an era, not the beginning of another. The end of the traditionalists' world had seemed to come fairly regularly in the 1970s. First there was that awful week when the AVO plant was closed down, and then the RS range went off the market for a full year. Next it was when Escort RS2000 MkII assembly ran down. Most shattering of all, was in 1980, when rear-wheel-drive Escort production came to an end. Could there ever be any enjoyable Fords, ever again?

The original XR3 was not a bad car, it just wasn't an RS. In fact, the XR3 was a faster car than the well-loved RS2000 MkII – faster in a straight line, a better traffic-light sprinter, lighter and more economical into the bargain. So, what was the problem? If you asked enthusiasts why they didn't fancy an XR3, there would be a lot of foot shuffling, averted eyes, staring into the depths of a pint glass, and some muttering about 'character': 'Well, it just isn't an RS, is it? What's an XR? Who cares, anyway?'

Yet the XR3 was always a success. Within a year there were so many XR3s on the road that the RS2000 had already been outnumbered. It did so many things so relatively well that the RS2000 looked old-fashioned. It handled well, it had more grip, a more spacious cabin, and all-independent suspension. It even had a hatchback body.

Walter Hayes once said why Ford decided to change the RS label in favour of XR. Ford, he said, realised that 'RS' appealed only to a tiny minority, and the cars were too specialised. What was wanted was a new type of car with as much performance, but with more equipment, more refinement, and a less extrovert nature.

To quote an anonymous Ford marketing man: 'The relationship (between XR and RS . . .) is exactly as for soft and hard porn! One is just a little further up the totem pole than the other . . .'

Sales figures prove that Ford was right. Although just over 10,000 RS2000 MkIIs were sold in the UK, that figure was overshadowed by 25,550 XR3s – more XR3s were sold in 1981 alone, and again in 1982, than the total number of RS2000s.

MkIII – the new layout

Original Escorts had been rear-drive cars, but for its third generation, Ford decided on change. New cars would have front-wheel-drive, with transverse engines, and every major component – body shell, engine, transmissions and suspensions, would be newly developed.

All MkIIIs were based around the same hatchback shell, with a 94.4in wheelbase, MacPherson strut front suspension, and a unique type of coil spring/transverse arm independent rear end. There would be three-door, five-door and estate car types, and engines from 1.1-litre/55bhp to 1.6-litres/96bhp.

Central to the entire project was the CVH engine (compound valve angle, hemispherical combustion chamber), to be built at Bridgend in South Wales – and which had a single belt-driven overhead camshaft. The aluminium cylinder head had two valves per cylinder, those being opposed at 45°, with a 7° skew angle across the combustion chamber – and hydraulic tappets. There was a four-speed, all-synchromesh gearbox, which was really an up-rated development of that which was used in the Fiesta.

The XR3 had a totally new layout of fascia/instrument panel arrangement, and those stripey seats were very fashionable at the time.

XR3 – the high-performance version

XR3? Why XR? This was the first European use of the title. Ford never defined what XR meant, so let's settle for XtRa performance, and have done with it!

Visually, the XR3 differed from normal 1.6-litre Escorts in many detail ways. Not only was there a noticeable, and entirely functional front spoiler under the bumper, but there was a wide and equally functional flexible spoiler around the tail. When the special four-hole 14in alloy wheels (inspired, they say, by those fitted to Porsche 928s), low-profile (60-section) radial-ply tyres, the plastic shrouding ahead of the rear wheelarches, and the XR3 badging were all taken into account, there was never any excuse for ignoring the new car on the road.

Like all Escorts of the period, the

The Escort XR3 had a large, moulded, rubberised spoiler across the tail of the hatchback.

For the original Escort XR3, Ford provided a vee-style, two-spoke steering wheel, and there was space for cassette tapes in the centre console.

chassis of the new XR3 was set up with a slightly tail-down attitude. This meant that there was positive camber on the front wheels, and negative camber on the rears – all, it seemed, chosen to get the handling balance right, although it did little for the car's looks, especially when it was heavily laden in the tail.

Compared with other Escorts, the suspension was firmed up quite a lot, the rear springs being progressive-rate types, with an 0.87in diameter front anti-roll bar, and the use of Bilstein shock absorbers. Unhappily, although this produced a marvellous handling package, especially on smooth tarmac, initially the ride was harsh – the XR3i, which took over, would be softened off considerably.

In the beginning, the normal range of MkIII Escorts was topped out by the 79bhp/1.6-litre version of the CVH engine, so the XR3 went one better and was equipped with a 96bhp version of that size, where the extra power was provided by a different camshaft grind, a four-branch exhaust manifold, and the use of a Weber downdraught twin-choke carburettor.

When I ran an XR3 for two years in the mid-1980s I used to think that this was an eager, high-revving engine, which peaked at 6,000rpm, while the hydraulic lifters began to float (and froth!) at 6,300rpm. Nowadays it is fashionable to call a CVH engine arthritic, so who is right? Was it always arthritic, or was the engine to be progressively strangled by exhaust emission regulations throughout its life?

The gearbox, although still a four-speeder like the Fiesta, had been considerably beefed up, by providing it with a more massive transaxle casing, wider gear wheels and stronger bearings. To take account of the XR3's high-revving engine and the 14in wheels, the XR3 was given a unique, 3.84:1 final drive ratio. Once again, times and standards, seem to have changed, for in the early 1980s we always thought this transmission had a high-quality change, but now we tend to dismiss it as 'sticky', 'lumpy' or at least not as precise as that of the modern MTX75 transmission.

Inside the cabin there was a special seat pattern, a two-spoke steering wheel with droopy spokes pointing considerably downwards when the car was being driven straight ahead, and with a rev counter encouragingly red-lined at 6,500rpm, if you could persuade the CVH power unit to spin so far up the range.

XR3 on the market

Ford's first European XR was only in production for two years – two very successful years – before it was replaced by the more powerful, fuel-injected, XR3i derivative. During that time, too, the RS1600i was developed from the XR3, as a limited-life homologation special version.

The Escort MkIII range was introduced in September 1980, with XR3 deliveries beginning almost at once, and very few changes were made to its design before the spring of 1982.

Specification	
Escort XR3	
ENGINE	
Type:	Ford-UK CVH
Capacity:	1,596cc
Bore/stroke:	80.00 x 79.52mm
Compression ratio:	9.5:1
Max power:	96bhp at 6,000rpm
Max torque:	98lb ft at 4,000rpm
Cylinders:	four, in line, transversely mounted
Cylinder head:	cast aluminium
Block:	cast iron
Valve gear:	two valves per cylinder, single overhead camshaft, rockers, and hydraulic tappets
Fuelling:	single downdraught dual-choke Weber DFT carburettor
Installation:	front-mounted, transverse, driving front wheels
TRANSMISSION	
Type:	front-engine, front-wheel-drive
Gearbox:	four-speed manual, later five-speed manual
SUSPENSION	
Front:	independent by coil springs, MacPherson struts, anti-roll bar and telescopic dampers
Rear:	independent, by coil springs, lower wishbones, radius arms, and telescopic dampers
STEERING	
Type:	rack-and-pinion
Lock-to-lock:	3.7 turns
BRAKES	
Front:	9.4in (239.5mm) ventilated discs
Rear:	7.0 x 1.5in (178 x 38mm) drums
System:	hydraulic, with vacuum servo assistance
WHEELS & TYRES	
Wheels:	four-perforation cast alloys, 5.5J x 13in
Tyres:	185/60HR13
BODY/CHASSIS	
Type:	pressed-steel monocoque, based on conventional Escort, in three-door hatchback style
Weight:	1,969lb (895kg)
PERFORMANCE	
Max speed:	113mph (182kph) approx
Acceleration:	0–60mph in 9.2sec
PRICE at LAUNCH	
£5,123 in 1980	

Throughout the period a number of desirable (but costly!) fittings were optional extras, including central locking, the tilt-and-slide glass sunroof which became so popular, electric window lifts, and higher-specification radio/cassette installations.

This means that although XR3 prices theoretically started at £5,123, it was easily possibly to add £600–£800 or more to that sticker price, and if items like metallic paint, headlamp washers, long range driving lamps, and more were all specified from the 46-item list of MkIII options, in excess of £1,000 could be added.

Then, in response to a general trend among all European car-makers, Ford suddenly changed the transmission, making an all-direct five-speeder standard on the XR3. To over-simplify a little, the new transmission was merely the old one with an overdrive fifth gear added, which lifted the overall gearing considerably (from 17.9mph/1,000rpm in the old fourth to 22.4mph/1,000rpm in the new fifth), making the XR3 considerably more relaxing on high-speed motorway journeys.

The XR3 finally went out of production in the autumn of 1982, being replaced immediately by the fuel-injected, 105bhp, XR3i.

To celebrate the opening of the Bridgend factory, where CVH engines were assembled, and to emphasise the launch of the XR3, Ford set up this startling display of new cars in the autumn of 1980.

Escort XR3i

1982–1990

Early XR3is looked exactly like the XR3, but from 1986 all Escorts were treated to this new nose, and different-style alloy wheels.

Never forget that there was also a cabriolet version of the XR3i, which sold in tens of thousands.

More than any other Performance Ford of that period, the 1980s-style XR3i was the model which confirmed the company's decision to embrace 'XR-ism'. In production for eight years, and selling faster either than the XR3, or than any previous RS-badged rear-drive Escort, it made a lot of friends, and a lot of money for the company. In its first full year, 1983, no fewer than 25,058 XR3is were sold in the UK alone. So many of the trendy pundits queued up to mock it, in spite of its obvious commercial success, that it must have been a good car.

Although the XR3i was a direct development of the Escort XR3, it came about in a rather different manner. The XR3 had been developed by Ford's mainstream engineers, while the XR3i was produced by Special Vehicle Engineering (SVE), which had already completed work on the Fiesta XR2

and the Capri 2.8 Injection. SVE, as usual, was given little time to do the job, but was expected to improve on the XR3 in almost every way.

Simply, their job could be summed up like this – make it faster, make it handle better, but retain the fuel efficiency, and keep down the costs. Starting from scratch in October 1981, it had to be ready for sales to begin within a year. Saarlouis production began in October 1982, with Halewood assembly commencing in January 1983. The one concession granted was that this could become the very first mainstream Escort model to be sold with a fuel-injected engine.

Fuel injection, as far as Ford was concerned, was not new, for models such as the Capri RS2600, plus the 2.8-litre V6 engined Granadas and Capris had already gone on sale and the limited-production Escort RS1600i was about to join in. Although experimental work had been going ahead for some time, in association with Bosch, it had not, however, been blooded on smaller Fords – and neither, for that matter, had it appeared on any rival makes. It was to be the big advance, and one that had to be made.

In the end, there were three phases of XR3i assembly. The first cars had a modified type of XR3 suspension, the 1983–1986 type which followed had improved geometry and handling, and the 1986–1990 cars had what became the 'MkIV' type of rounder nose, modified interior fittings and rejigged suspension.

Mechanically sensed fuel injection, engineered by Bosch, was central to the original specification, and I should emphasise that it differed in almost every important detail from the Escort RS1600i (which had been engineered by Ford Motorsport in Germany). As originally specified, the 1.6-litre CVH engine gave 105bhp at 6,000rpm, compared with the 96bhp peak figure quoted for the carburetted XR3. Note that although this was less than that quoted for the Escort RS1600i, it never felt less, and in any case, the RS1600 was graced with solid instead of hydraulic tappets, and different manifolding.

As with the late-model XR3s, it was linked to a five-speed transmission, although the final drive was changed from 3.84:1 (XR3) to 4.29:1 (XR3i). This meant that the new car was a more relaxed car than the original four-speed XR3, but it was by no means over-geared.

For the all-independent suspension, SVE's objective was always to realign the wheels, getting rid of the positive camber of the XR3 at the front, and by making the rear wheels more upright. At first they achieved this by modifying the suspension members themselves and moving a rear suspension mount. From May 1983, however, company-wide modifications which applied to all Escorts saw the same thing achieved by moving front and rear bodyshell mounting positions. For the XR3i, too, the whole car was lowered and the spring and damper settings rerated.

This was an excellent package which clearly did a great job. Just as soon as customers realised that the XR3 had been replaced by a faster (114mph) car, which handled better, rode better, and both looked and felt more like a sports saloon, sales rocketed. The only tiny controversy was over the choice of wheels, for although a 6.0in rim steel wheel (with fake 'pepperpot' plastic covers) was standard, the XR3 type of 5.5in rim alloy (the one with four spokes and four large holes) proved to be much more popular.

So, why did the XR3i sell so well, right from the start? It always looked right, without being flamboyant (the only visual change was that it looked slightly lower, and there was a different badge on the hatchback). It now had the five-speed transmission which made it so much less frantic in motorway driving, and the Bosch-injected engine gave it seamless power all the way up the range.

Another derivative, which was introduced without fuss, appeared in 1984, this being the Cabriolet, which was built for Ford by Karmann at

The XR3i featured genuine hip-hugging Recaro seats, and a centre console with space for tape storage. Customers loved all that.

The XR3i's fascia layout was an evolution of that of the original XR3, now coming complete with a three-spoke steering wheel.

Specification	
Escort XR3i	
ENGINE	
Type:	Ford-UK CVH
Capacity:	1,596cc
Bore/stroke:	80.00 x 79.52mm
Compression ratio:	9.5:1 (9.75:1 from mid-1989)
Max power:	105bhp at 6,000rpm (108bhp from mid-1989)
Max torque:	102lb ft at 4,800rpm
Cylinders:	four, in line, transversely mounted
Cylinder head:	cast aluminium
Block:	cast iron
Valve gear:	two valves per cylinder, single overhead camshaft, rockers, and hydraulic tappets
Fuelling:	Bosch K-Jetronic fuel injection (Ford EEC IV engine management/injection from 1989)
Installation:	front-mounted, transverse, driving front wheels
TRANSMISSION	
Type:	front-engine, front-wheel-drive
Gearbox:	five-speed manual
SUSPENSION	
Front:	independent by coil springs, MacPherson struts, anti-roll bar, and telescopic dampers
Rear:	independent, by coil springs, lower wishbones, radius arms, and telescopic dampers
STEERING	
Type:	rack-and-pinion
Lock-to-lock:	3.7 turns
BRAKES	
Front:	9.4in (239.5mm) ventilated discs
Rear:	8.0 x 1.5in (203 x 38mm) drums
System:	hydraulic, with vacuum servo assistance
WHEELS & TYRES	
Wheels:	cast-alloys, 5,5J x 13in (steel disc, 6.0J x 14in, optional), 6.0J x 14in from 1986
Tyres:	185/60-13 or 185/60-14
BODY/CHASSIS	
Type:	pressed-steel monocoque, in three-door hatchback style (and Cabriolet option from 1984)
Weight:	2,024lb (920kg)
PERFORMANCE	
Max speed:	114mph (183kph) approx
Acceleration:	0–60mph in 9.0sec
PRICE at LAUNCH	
£6,155 in 1982 (Hatchback)	
£10,189 in 1986 (Cabriolet)	

The message on the tail of the XR3i was loud and clear: i = injection, which was worth nine more horsepower.

Osnabruck in West Germany. Fitted with two passenger doors and (because of the way the soft-top folded back and stowed) with a small boot lid instead of the hatchback, the Cabriolet would be built in several versions in the next few years. Although the XR3i version was just like the famous hatchback under the skin, somehow it was a more restrained car, and would not officially be badged as an XR3i until facelift-time in 1986.

Even after the much faster and much more expensive Escort RS Turbo arrived (in the spring buying season of 1985 the Turbo cost £9,951, the XR3i £7,274) demand for the XR3i was still as high as ever. Sales held up well until the spring of 1986, when the 'facelift' or (unofficially titled 'MkIV') Escorts arrived.

Each and every Escort – from the Turbo down to the light vans, received the same soft-lined changes to front-end panels. Hatchbacks had a reshaped pressing (and a different, colour co-ordinated spoiler on the XR3i), there was a different type of aluminium wheel style, and there were important changes and improvements to the fascia/instrument panel display. The ride height was lifted, and spring rates altered yet again. This time SVE had not been involved, but as this was purely an evolutionary change, nothing was lost. The 'MkIV', however, was a little slower than the MkIII variety, because it was about 100lb heavier than before, this increase being caused by extra safety features in the structure.

Mechanically the big advance was the offering of Lucas-Girling SCS anti-lock braking, which became optional (for £315) on the XR3i (and standard on the RS Turbo). Although not as sophisticated as Bosch or Teves ABS, this was an effective system ('cheap and cheerful' is what some people called it), which could be felt pulsing strongly back through the brake pedal if the friction limits were exceeded. Even so, it was not a popular option (only 3 per cent of customers specified it), and it would not be used on later Fords in the 1990s.

The final change to this long-running model came in 1989, when a different type of fuel injection and engine management (by Ford/EEC IV, rather than by Bosch) was fitted. Under the bonnet, such engines could easily be recognised by the 'EFI' lettering on the top of the inlet manifold. Although the peak power rating was nominally increased – from 105bhp to 108bhp – this made no obvious difference to the performance: the principal gain was in fuel efficiency, and the ability to run on unleaded fuel.

Except that yet another alloy wheel style was optionally available on 1990 model year cars, and there were further changes to the shape of the tailgate spoiler, this was really the end of the XR3i's 1980s evolution, as this complete range of Escorts went out of production in the summer of 1990. Although there would eventually be a replacement XR3i, complete with a new type of Zetec 16-valve twin-cam engine, this would not be launched until 1992.

From 1982 to 1990, however, more than 200,000 of these versatile and popular models had already been made, which assured their reputation for all time.

Escort RS1600i

1981–1983

Carefully developed to be a useful 'class' car in motor racing, the Escort RS1600i was an improved version of the XR3, complete with fuel injected engine, and special suspension.

Many RS1600is were white, but the red cars, with contrasting black decoration, looked quite startling. The four extra driving lamps were standard on UK-market examples.

In the early 1980s the Escort RS1600i cost more than the XR3i, was no faster, and didn't sell as well. Fewer than 9,000 RS1600is were sold in two years – but now they are highly prized. So, what's in a name? RS, that's what. The RS1600i of the early 1980s proves the point.

An RS1600i had 10bhp more than an XR3i, but it didn't seem to have any more performance. In spite of its fancy front suspension, it didn't appear to handle any better. It cost £6,700, but you needed only £6,030 to buy an XR3i. Very odd, for the RS1600 was based on the design of the obsolete XR3 . . .

In 1980, Ford Motorsport of Germany convinced President Bob Lutz that a new Escort-based model (for motor racing, rather than rallying) was needed for use in the new-fangled Group A category, and a production run of at least 5,000 cars was required. In improving the XR3, their options were limited, for they were obliged to keep the same basic body structure, engine/transmission unit, and suspension.

For the engine, there was Bosch K-Jetronic injection, a new camshaft profile, different exhaust manifolding and solid (instead of hydraulic) valve lifters. Even with an electronic rev-limiter, the engine felt more sporting than that of the XR3. Even so, these power figures tell their own story:

XR3	96bhp (DIN) at 6,000rpm	
RS1600i	115bhp (DIN) at 6,000rpm	
XR3i	105bhp (DIN) at 6,000rpm	

As we soon realised, tuned versions for use in Group A motorsport could produce at least 150bhp at 7,000rpm. Like late-model XR3s, the RS1600i featured a five-speed transmission, but it had a closer-ratio fifth gear.

Although the basic suspension layout was unchanged, at the front there were separate drag links to locate the front struts more accurately, while anti-roll bars were fitted at front and rear. Seven-spoke 15in wheels with 6in rims, and 50-section tyres were chosen, while the front ride height was cut down, and harder-rate Koni dampers were used.

Visually there were new types of front and rear spoiler, a new striping and paint job, better front seats, and (for the UK market) a four-spoke RS steering wheel, with a useful but drag-enhancing set of four extra auxiliary lamps.

The result, subjectively, was that the RS1600i felt (and looked!) harder, twitchier and altogether more 'race-track' bred than the XR3. If the XR3i had not arrived so soon afterwards, it would probably have been hailed as the best-handling MkIII of all. As it was, in a test of a UK-market car published in February 1983, *Autocar* described the handling as: 'distinctly twitchy', and commented that 'the RS1600i is a more nervous, throttle-sensitive car below the limit than the XR3i . . . There are two main areas of complaint – straight-line stability and braking . . . despite the low-profile tyres and increased roll stiffness, the RS1600i has a very good primary ride. The ride, it could be said, is very good and entirely in keeping with the nature of the car.'

Previewed in September 1981, deliveries from Saarlouis began properly in 1982. In the meantime, it was re-engineered for right-hand-drive production, with UK launch at the Birmingham Motor Show in October 1982.

British enthusiasts loved it, especially in 'MkII' form from May 1983, when the XR3i chassis changes (including a new front cross-member and revised suspension geometry) were adopted. For the extra cost, it was special, it looked special, and it handled in a special way too.

Although Ford planned to make only 5,000 RS1600is, that run was extended. No fewer than 8,659 RS1600is were eventually manufactured: 2,608 were sold in the UK, almost all of them in 1983. Then, in 1984, the RS1600i was displaced by the first-generation Escort RS Turbo, which shared some of its chassis technology, but more power, more potential, and a viscous-coupling limited-slip differential. Within five years an RS1600i 'classic' cult had grown, there was a big demand for surviving cars, and values began to rise. It has remained desirable to this day.

Specification

Escort RS1600i

ENGINE

Type:	Ford-UK CVH
Capacity:	1596cc
Bore/stroke:	80 x 79.5mm
Compression ratio:	9.9:1
Max power:	115bhp at 6,000rpm
Max torque:	109lb ft at 5,250rpm
Cylinders:	four, in-line, transversely mounted
Cylinder head:	cast aluminium
Block:	cast iron
Valve gear:	two valves per cylinder, single belt-driven camshaft, tappets and rockers
Fuelling:	Bosch K-Jetronic fuel injection
Installation:	front-mounted, transverse

TRANSMISSION

Type:	front-engine, front-wheel-drive
Gearbox:	Ford five-speed manual

SUSPENSION

Front:	independent by MacPherson struts, lower track control arms, coil springs, anti-roll bar and telescopic dampers
Rear:	independent, coil springs, lower wishbones, radius arms, anti-roll bar and telescopic dampers

STEERING

Type:	rack-and-pinion
Lock-to-lock:	3.69 turns

BRAKES

Front:	9.4in (239mm) ventilated discs
Rear:	7.1 x 12.25in (180 x 32mm) drums
System:	Girling hydraulic, with Girling vacuum servo assistance

WHEELS & TYRES

Wheels:	cast-alloy seven-spoke discs, with four-stud fixing, 6.0J x 15in
Tyres:	195/50VR15in

BODY

Type:	three-door four-seater hatchback
Weight:	2,027lb (919kg)

PERFORMANCE

Max speed:	118mph (190kph)
Acceleration:	0–60mph in 8.7sec
Standing start ¼-mile:	16.7sec

PRICE at LAUNCH

£6,700 in November 1982

Escort RS1600is had 115bhp, compared with 105bhp in the XR3i, and only 96bhp in the XR3 – plus, of course, the seven-spoke Motorsport wheels, and special spoiler.

Escort RS Turbo

1984–1990

'White Lightning', the original Escort RS Turbo, featured massive wheelarch flares and an Orion-type front grille, with 132bhp under the bonnet.

From the rear, the original Escort RS Turbo was easily recognised by those wheelarch extensions, the fat tyres and by the badging.

Go on, admit it. Once you had seen the first of the front-wheel-drive Escort MkIIIs, you were feeling depressed, right? You feared that the RS badge was dead. We all thought we could see the trends – and we were all wrong. Then came the rebirth, with the launch of the Escort RS Turbo – a great occasion.

To use horse-racing terms, the original RS Turbo was by SVE and Boreham, out of RS1600i, but a lot of people had an input. Officially, the project was born in April 1983 and put on sale before the end of 1984, but the need was identified way before that. Soon after Stuart Turner had returned to Motorsport, he set out his demands for three new motorsport-orientated models – the Escort RS Turbo to be a Group A rally car, for which at least 5,000 cars had to built, at Saarlouis.

When 'White Lightning' (as it was nicknamed) came on the scene in October 1984, its chassis was almost pure RS1600i, complete with the tie-bar front suspension layout plus front and rear anti-roll bars, while the turbo engine had Bosch fuel-injection.

The Ferguson limited-slip differential made its road-car debut while 15in road wheels, a deep spoiler, all-white paintwork and a blue decal along the sides, were joined by shapely wheelarch extensions, and an Orion-type grille allowed more air into the engine bay.

The Escort RS Turbo was a nicely integrated improvement on the RS1600i concept, complete with turbocharged engine, and more functional styling.

Motorsport

Although it was a failure in rallying – torque steer and a fragile transmission handicapped it badly – in 1985 and 1986 the Escort RS Turbo was a formidable circuit racer. Richard Longman's 'Datapost' car raced with 270bhp, and was invariably a walkaway winner in its capacity class. Traction was always a limiting factor – especially in wet conditions – but it had a phenomenal straight-line speed and nimble handling.

The facelifted Escort RS Turbo appeared from mid-1986. In some ways it was a 'softer' car than the original, with a more rounded nose style, and with different wheels, spoiler and other decoration.

The Turbo did so many things well, competently, and without temperament. With the revs above 2,500rpm, the turbo produced full boost on call, and kept on pushing. As for the grip and the handling – think only of a well-sorted RS1600i, with even more grip, and that magic VC to keep everything in check.

It was an impressive little projectile, and RS fans loved it. If, that is, they could afford it. Priced at £9,250 in 1984 (with a £470 Custom Pack available, as well as a raft of options) – other Escort prices started at £4,363, and the ever-popular XR3i sold for £7,035.

The RS Turbo did a great job for Ford, not only on the track, but in the showrooms as well. When the time came for the entire Escort range to be facelifted – new nose, new fascia, new style details, and related engine changes – the RS Turbo was facelifted too. Acting more like a super-fast road car than a suppressed homologation special, and now available in a full range of colours, the revised car sold strongly for four more years.

The 'MkIV' RS Turbo was just as powerful as before, but was now a softer and more sophisticated machine. SVE's enthusiasts had reworked the chassis, making it subtly and successfully more of a road car than a detuned competition car. There were new features in the suspension, the transmission and the brakes, while there was a new look (including a new style of cast-aluminium road wheel) which made the changes obvious.

To make this a more relaxed road car, the overall gearing was raised (the final drive ratio had been changed from 4.27:1 to 3.82:1). For example, when using 4,000rpm in fifth gear the latest car cruised at 90mph, whereas the old car would have been doing a mere 81mph. For high-mileage users, that was the good news. For the traffic-light cowboys, and the club night boasters though, the bad news was that the new car didn't accelerate quite as rapidly as the old one had done. Even so, it was still good enough to see off most of the imported competition.

To get the best out of this car, you had to understand its engine, and the shape of the torque curve. If you pottered around town in fifth gear, then floored the pedal at the end of the 30mph limit, it took time to light up, and get going. You had to wait, but soon all would be well. Lots of torque soon came rushing over the horizon, and the VC took care of the rest.

If, on the other hand, you changed down one or more gears every time the rpm needle dropped below 3,000rpm, the turbocharger was always spinning rapidly, and response was immediate. The RS Turbo, in fact, was really two cars in one – there was the hard-and-fast turbo hatchback, but there was also the smooth, I-don't-want-to-make-a-fuss-about-anything, suburban cruiser. Some examples were used in both modes – mine certainly was.

Then there was the suspension, changed amid some controversy for the 1986 model. Mine felt fine, for the traction and poise were still there, in full measure, but compared with the original type this version had definitely been softened off a little. The braking, on the other hand, was even better than before, because there were larger front and rear brakes, plus the option (for about £300) of the new-fangled Lucas-Girling Stop Control System, which was a mechanically sensed type of anti-lock facility, not nearly as advanced as the usual Teves or Bosch ABS layout. On my car, this rarely kicked into operation, when I could certainly feel the mechanism pulsing back through the brake pedal.

Style changes included the addition of sill extensions linking the front and rear wheelarch bulges, a new nose (common to all other Escorts), cooling louvres in the bonnet panel, and a different (less effective, surely?) type of rear spoiler. Cars fitted with the Custom Pack (most were) also enjoyed electric window lifts, a sunroof and central locking. All cars, naturally, were fitted with Recaro seats, the best in the business.

Even though RS Turbo prices started at £10,028 (the Custom Pack an extra £572) in mid-1986, customers continued to flock, drooling, to Uncle Henry's showrooms, and the records show that more than four times as many were sold, compared with the original 'White Lightning' type. Perversely, this means that the original type is worth more as a Heritage Ford today . . .

By 1988, the Custom Pack had been incorporated in the standard specification, and when you consider that this also included a high-spec radio/stereo cassette, tinted glass, rear seat belts, full instrumentation and Recaro seats it is easy to see why RS Turbo prices crept up to £13,985 by mid-Summer 1990, when the last cars were made.

When the Escort range was replaced by the 'MkV' models, there was no turbocharged car in the range, and it was a mark of progress that the front-drive RS2000 which took over was normally aspirated, had 150bhp, and was a good deal more torquey than the CVH-Turbo ever was.

The end of the Escort RS Turbo, however, was not the end for the CVH-Turbo, which found a home, modified in many ways, in the short-lived Fiesta RS Turbo. In that car the turbocharger was smaller and the electronics more advanced, but the effect was just the same – paralysing performance and great character.

Escort RS Turbo – the important dates

1981: Development of the original turbocharged CVH engine, with carburettor.

1983: Kits sold for competitors to use in the one-make Escort Turbo Rally Championship.

October 1984: Launch of Escort RS Turbo production model.

June 1985: Homologation into Group A (5,000 cars completed by this date)

December 1985: Last original-style RS Turbo built. Total production 8,604, of which 5,576 sold in the UK.

July 1986: Introduction of facelifted RS Turbo, using the 'MkIV' Escort nose style.

Summer 1990: Last Escort RS Turbo built.

Specification	
Escort RS Turbo (Where different, details for MkII – 1986–1990 models, in brackets.)	
ENGINE	
Type:	Ford-UK CVH
Capacity:	1,596cc
Bore/stroke:	80 x 79.5mm
Compression ratio:	8.2:1 (nominal), plus turbo-charging to 7.2psi/0.5 Bar
Max power:	132bhp at 6,000rpm
Max torque:	133lb ft at 4,000rpm
Cylinders:	four, in line, transversely mounted
Cylinder head:	cast aluminium
Block:	cast iron
Valve gear:	two valves per cylinder, single overhead camshaft, rockers, and hydraulic tappets
Fuelling:	Bosch KE-Jetronic fuel injection, with Garrett T3 turbocharger and intercooling
Installation:	front-mounted, transverse, driving front wheels
TRANSMISSION	
Type:	front-engine, front-wheel-drive
Gearbox:	Ford Type B5, five-speed manual
SUSPENSION	
Front:	independent by coil springs, MacPherson struts, anti-roll bar and telescopic dampers
Rear:	independent, by transverse links, coil springs, anti-roll bar and telescopic dampers
STEERING	
Type:	rack-and-pinion
Lock-to-lock:	3.5 turns
BRAKES	
Front:	9.4in (239mm) ventilated discs [10.2in (260mm) ventilated discs]
Rear:	8.0 x 1.5in (203 x 38mm) drums [9.0in x 1.75in (228.6mm x 44mm) drums]
System:	hydraulic, with vacuum servo assistance (ABS on MkII)
WHEELS & TYRES	
Wheels:	seven-spoke cast-aluminium, 6.0J x 15in [Six-spoke, new pattern]
Tyres:	195/50VR15
BODY/CHASSIS	
Type:	pressed-steel monocoque, based on conventional Escort, in three-door hatchback style
Weight:	2,150lb (977kg) [2,247lb (1,017kg) – with Custom Pack]
PERFORMANCE	
Max speed:	125mph (200kph) approx
Acceleration:	0–60mph in 8.1sec [8.3sec]
Standing start ¼-mile:	16.2sec
PRICE at LAUNCH	
£9,250 in 1984/85 (£10,028 in mid-1986)	

Fiesta XR2

1981–1983

The style of the original Fiesta XR2 combined some elements of the US-spec model (circular headlamps), and the limited-edition Supersport. Amazingly, the wing/door/side transfers were still being manufactured, more than twenty years later.

In road-car terms, Ford's sporting image was revived considerably by Special Vehicle Engineering in the 1980s, when they had a hand in the design of many XR and RS models. An early example was the Fiesta XR2.

Like every such SVE project, the XR2 had to be developed quickly, and with the very minimum of expense. There was never any question of new engines, new transmissions or new suspensions being available. In this case all the elements of an agile little car were present, in other Ford departments.

In the late 1970s, no-one gave much thought to producing high-performance Fiestas. Then came the launch of the US-market model. For that country Ford installed a larger engine – 66bhp version of the 1,598cc Kent. In 1978 and 1979, too, Ford Motorsport had dabbled with the Fiesta as a front-wheel-drive rally car: in the 1979 Monte Carlo Rally Ari Vatanen took an excellent 10th place.

To improve the performance of the Fiesta, SVE dipped into Ford's parts

Every Fiesta XR2 had this rubberised rear spoiler, and the rather obvious large exhaust silencer. All types were three-door hatchbacks.

bin, and chose whatever would give them the best performance improvements. The engineers decided to follow the same philosophy as with the Capri 2.8i – to use the largest possible engine, to improve the handling, and to join forces with the stylists to jazz up the looks of the little hatchback without reshaping any of the body panels.

If you say it quickly, the spec of

the XR2 doesn't sound all that exciting (indeed, later XR2s were more sophisticated than the original), for the engine was merely the usual European-tune version of the 1.6-litre Kent, with a downdraught dual-choke Weber DFT carburettor and 84bhp, the gearbox was from an Escort XR3, but with a different final drive ratio, the suspension was really a stiffened-up version of any other Fiesta, and the interior was still much like that of other Fiestas – but there was more. The perforated cast-alloy wheels,which had a distinct family resemblance to those used on the SVE-developed Capri 2.8i, made the car look special.

In spite of the rush, there was time for a lot of detail thought to go into styling revisions, including a new nose with circular instead of rectangular headlamps (US-spec Fiestas were like this), allied to a new front spoiler, while there were carefully shaded decal stripes on the sides, and a rear hatchback spoiler too.

The result was a car which I drove often, a car which some described as 'a demented rollerskate', and which provided more fun per cc than most cars any Ford enthusiast had ever driven. Here was the fastest-yet Fiesta, with an urgent character. In a way, though, the XR2 looked so good, and handled so well, that it wouldn't even have mattered if there was no more performance other than the 1300S. Priced at £5,500 in 1981, the XR2 was a performance bargain, for the larger XR3 cost £6,245. The interior looked very inviting – for the trim was at Fiesta Ghia level, and XR3 type Recaro seats were fitted.

Everyone who drove the car discovered its urgent and extrovert little character – and its splendid handling. SVE had not only redeveloped the spring/damper/anti-roll bar settings, but the entire car sat one inch lower than standard, and the engine/transmission assembly had also been lowered in the body shell to idealise the drive shaft alignment. That package of changes, on its own, would have been an obvious improvement, but SVE added to the grip by specifying wheels with 6.0in x 14in rims (at the time the 1300S used 4.5in x 13in), and high-specification 185/60HR14in low-profile tyres, usually Pirelli P6 types.

Here was a breed of car which was quite new to Ford. *Autocar* set the testers' tone by describing the XR2 as a: 'fun-packed Fiesta', and reporting that it had: '. . . zesty performance, grip and sheer chuckability . . . It does most things delightfully, and is tremendous fun to drive.'

Only 253 UK-market XR2s were delivered in 1981, 8,174 in 1982, and no fewer than 11,445 in 1983. This, though, was facelift-time for the entire Fiesta range, so the XR2 was refreshed in 1984.

Specification	
Fiesta XR2 (MkI)	
ENGINE	
Type:	Ford-UK Kent
Capacity:	1,598cc
Bore/stroke:	80.98 x 77.62mm
Compression ratio:	9.0:1
Max power:	84bhp at 5,500rpm
Max torque:	91lb ft at 2,800rpm
Cylinders:	four, in line, transversely mounted
Cylinder head:	cast iron
Block:	cast iron
Valve gear:	two valves per cylinder, single camshaft, pushrods and rockers
Fuelling:	single downdraught dual-choke Weber DFT carburettor
Installation:	front-mounted, transverse, driving front wheels
TRANSMISSION	
Type:	front-engine, front-wheel-drive
Gearbox:	Ford Type A2, four-speed manual
SUSPENSION	
Front:	independent by coil springs, MacPherson struts, and telescopic dampers
Rear:	'dead' beam axle, coil springs, radius arms, Panhard rod and telescopic dampers
STEERING	
Type:	rack-and-pinion
Lock-to-lock:	3.0 turns
BRAKES	
Front:	9.4in (239.5mm) ventilated discs
Rear:	7.0 x 1.5in (178 x 38mm) drums
System:	hydraulic, with vacuum servo assistance
WHEELS & TYRES	
Wheels:	four-perforation cast-alloys, 6.0J x 13in
Tyres:	185/60HR13in
BODY/CHASSIS	
Type:	pressed-steel monocoque, based on conventional Fiesta, in three-door hatchback style
Weight:	1,848lb (839kg)
PERFORMANCE	
Max speed:	104mph (167kph) approx
Acceleration:	0–60mph in 9.4sec
PRICE at LAUNCH	
£5,500	

By 1983, the XR2 had become well-known. Many were sold in this distinctive colour scheme – and note the black-painted under-bumper front spoiler. Extra driving lamps were standard equipment.

Fiesta XR2 (Facelift)

1984–1989

From 1984, the XR2 gained the more-rounded nose of the facelifted family, with these smart wheels and wheelarch extensions.

The interior of the facelifted XR2 of 1984–1989 featured these smart front seats – not Recaros, but a good imitation.

The specification of the 'facelift' Fiesta XR2 might have been written by MkI owners themselves. If Ford had asked the questions, they would have got predictable answers: we wanted more power, higher gearing and better equipment please, all in the same package. No weight increases, though – and can you reduce the price?

Compared with the original XR2, therefore, the facelift car had 96bhp instead of 84bhp, five-speeds instead of four-speeds and . . . well, there was also a lot more, in detail. Previewed in August 1983, the first deliveries were made in June 1984.

Facelift cars retained the same floorpan, wheelbase, cabin and basic layout as before, with a more-rounded nose and a revised fascia layout, plus XR3i-style seats. There was a five-speed transmission and 13in wheels instead of 12-inchers. Most importantly, the overhead-cam CVH engine was used.

As you might expect, extra driving lamps at the front were standard, the bumper mouldings included a front spoiler, and a matching ridge at the rear. Naturally, there were wheelarch mouldings to cover the wide wheels, with plastic sills connecting them, front to rear. For the latest XR2, too, there was also a unique black plastic tailgate spoiler, by no means extrovert, which surrounded the top and sides of the glass. Did it do anything for the aerodynamics? Probably not, but at least it was discreet, and quite a talking point – and unlike the big whaletail on later Performance Fords, you didn't have to explain it away to your critics!

To make the latest XR2 faster and better-equipped than before, SVE raided the Escort 'parts bin'. Ditching the old 84bhp overhead-valve Kent engine, the team chose the 1.6-litre CVH engine, in Weber-carburetted 96bhp form, exactly as used on the original XR3, which had been made obsolete by the XR3i. This engine, naturally, had hydraulic tappets, and although it didn't seem to be as free-revving as the old Kent, it was a lot more powerful, and more torquey.

To match it, there was also an 'overdrive' five-speed gearbox, linked to a higher, 3.58:1, final drive ratio. Not only did this mean that the XR2 MkII cruised at 92mph when the rev counter pointed to 4,000rpm, but it also allowed Ford to claim a top speed of 112mph – which was a lot higher than before.

The rest of the chassis was much as before, although pressed steel wheels became standard (you now had to pay £158 more for the perforated alloys which had been standard on original XR2s), the suspension was subtly softer than before (but still a lot firmer than other Fiestas), and there was a larger fuel tank squeezed in under the rear seat pan.

This was not a noisy, urgent, 'boy-racer' machine. Inside, the Mk II's cabin and equipment was a combination of Fiesta Ghia and XR3. The seats, in particular, were a great improvement, these being faced by a new instrument panel cluster with finger-tip switch-gear, and a new steering wheel which featured two rather odd portholes: many an XR2 enthusiast made haste to change that at once!

The new car was a lot quieter than the first type of XR2 – higher gearing was partly responsible, but extra Ghia-standard sound deadening also helped – and other features included an electric release for the hatchback, remote control door mirror adjustment, and a 60–40 per cent split folding action for the rear seats.

Ford, being Ford, then listed a large number of extras including black paint, a glass sunroof, tinted glass and cast alloy wheels, plus metallic paint, upmarket radio/cassette installations, and rear seat belts . . .

At 1984 price levels, although an XR2 was listed at less than £6,000, one could easily boost that by £500.

No-one was arguing with the latest car's more relaxed character, for there was no doubt that the original Kent-engined XR2 had been noisy at continuous high speeds. Enthusiasts all over Europe clearly liked this car, which explains why so many were sold in five years.

The facelifted Fiesta XR2 had a much larger and more completely equipped fascia/instrument display than the original's. Many people did not like the new-style steering wheel, and made haste to fit an after-market item!

Specification	
Fiesta XR2 (Facelift model)	
ENGINE	
Type:	Ford-UK CVH
Capacity:	1,596cc
Bore/stroke:	79.96 x 79.52mm
Compression ratio:	9.5:1
Max power:	96bhp at 6,000rpm
Max torque:	98lb ft at 4,000rpm
Cylinders:	four, in line, transversely mounted
Cylinder head:	cast aluminium
Block:	cast iron
Valve gear:	two valves per cylinder, belt-driven single overhead camshaft, rockers, and hydraulic tappets
Fuelling:	single downdraught dual-choke Weber DFT carburettor
Installation:	front-mounted, transverse, driving front wheels
TRANSMISSION	
Type:	front-engine, front-wheel-drive
Gearbox:	Ford five-speed manual
SUSPENSION	
Front:	independent by coil springs, MacPherson struts, and telescopic dampers
Rear:	'dead' beam axle, coil springs, radius arms, Panhard rod and telescopic dampers
STEERING	
Type:	rack-and-pinion
Lock-to-lock:	3.0 turns
BRAKES	
Front:	9.4in (239.5mm) ventilated discs
Rear:	7.0 x 1.5in (178 x 38mm) drums
System:	hydraulic, with vacuum servo assistance
WHEELS & TYRES	
Wheels:	steel disc (optional cast alloys), 6.0J x 13in
Tyres:	185/60HR13in
BODY/CHASSIS	
Type:	pressed-steel monocoque, based on conventional Fiesta, in three-door hatchback style
Weight:	1,848lb (840kg)
PERFORMANCE	
Max speed:	112mph (180kph) approx
Acceleration:	0–60mph in 9.3sec
Standing start ¼-mile:	17.1sec
PRICE at LAUNCH	
£5,731 in 1984	

Sierra XR4i

1983–1985

The first high-performance Sierra was the XR4i of 1983–1985, which had a fuel-injected 2.8-litre V6 engine. The strange three-side-window style, and the red flashes made it instantly recognisable.

The Sierra XR4i featured this new-style fascia/instrument panel, which was picked out in red feature lines, and had its horn pushes on the steering wheel spokes. No Recaro seats, though!

The policeman on the Ilchester by-pass was most impressed. It was a sunny morning, my Sierra XR4i was going particularly well, but . . . maybe I would have got away with it if the XR4i hadn't looked so obvious. The policeman smiled politely as he handed me the ticket, commented that so far that morning I had clocked 'Fastest time of the day', and that 'these new Sierras go a bit, don't they?'

This is just one reminiscence of a long-time Sierra owner. In the Sierra decade, I ran an XR4i, an XR4x4 and two Sierra Cosworth 4x4s. I also drove a Merkur XR4Ti in its native habitat – the USA. The XR4i, which I kept for nearly two years and 40,000 miles, was my introduction to the Sierra style.

Any XR4i discussion starts with comment about the styling – you either loved it, or loathed it. I'll be honest – the XR4i was really far too visible for my tastes. In fact I seemed to spend more time defending the looks of the XR4i than in answering questions about its performance.

Yet the XR4i was much the fastest Sierra of the day. On the evidence of a day's testing in 1983, interrupted by a good lunch, some pundits suggested that the handling wasn't up to much, but after two years' ownership I can tell you, quite categorically, that they were wrong.

The XR4i was the flagship of the original Sierra range, using the same engine/gearbox as the much-loved Capri 2.8i. It had the same top speed as the Capri, the same acceleration, and it used no more fuel. Ford's original XR4i adverts carried the punch-line: 'Man and high-performance machine in perfect harmony.' Were they right?

One was that it didn't look as sleek as the Capri. But it was a full four-seater which, in my case, often accommodated myself, my wife, two teenage boys and two bulldogs of extrovert character on long journeys. I wasn't complaining.

Bob Lutz (then chairman of Ford-of-Europe), inspired the birth of the XR4 (the 'i' came later), demanding a flagship with more performance than any other Sierra, and a special style. Without Lutz I don't think the money would have been found to produce a unique style. His team evolved a special hatchback shell, which had the same doors and hatchback as a three-door Sierra, but which had a 'four-pillar' shell, with two windows on the flanks behind the doors, separated by a wide sheet steel pillar.

The new XR4 was always meant to share its front style with the new Sierra Ghias, but its plastic side-cladding was part of the special XR approach.

From the beginning, this was a Sierra derivative developed by PDG (the Product Development Group) in Cologne, with high-speed autobahn motoring in mind. There was no input from Special Vehicle Engineering at Dunton (which had only just been founded), no question of the new car carrying an RS badge, and no question of it ever being used in motorsport.

The first prototoype cars were actually fitted with 2.3-litre V6 engines (in this way it was intended to 'distance' the car from the Capri and Granada 2.8-litre models), but once testing began those particular cars were seen to be too slow. To quote Hans Gaffke, the engineering chief with much influence on the programme: 'We could have 130bhp from a fuel injection version of the 2.3, but when it was hitched up to the five-speed gearbox and in the car, we could see there was a real problem – just no torque!'

Bob Lutz himself was keen to retain the 2.3-litre engine, but once performance tests proved that prototypes could not reach 124mph, he was convinced. In the summer of 1982, only five months before the Sierra range was unveiled, the decision was made to fit the 2.8-litre engine instead.

Those of us who owned XR4is found them quite fast enough, found that the handling was just fine, and that they were thoroughly versatile four-seaters. Even so, we still had to live with that style, which always seemed to be a handicap to sales. Not even after power-assisted steering became optional in 1984 was that talking point finally quashed. In 1985, when the first of the four-wheel-drive Sierras appeared, the XR4i's career came to a premature end.

Ford admitted that the biplane rear spoiler was more for decoration than for aerodynamic effect – but it was certainly a talking point. The same body shell and spoiler would feature on the US-market Merkur XR4Ti.

Specification

Sierra XR4i

ENGINE

Type:	Ford Cologne V6
Capacity:	2,792cc
Bore/stroke:	93 x 68.5mm
Compression ratio:	9.2:1
Max power:	150bhp at 5,700rpm
Max torque:	161lb ft at 3,800rpm
Cylinders:	six, in 60° vee
Cylinder heads:	cast iron
Block:	cast iron
Valve gear:	two valves per cylinder, single camshaft, pushrods and rockers
Fuelling:	Bosch K-Jetronic fuel injection
Installation:	front-mounted, longitudinal

TRANSMISSION

Type:	front-engine, rear-wheel-drive
Gearbox:	Ford Type 9, five-speed manual

SUSPENSION

Front:	independent by coil springs, MacPherson struts, lower track control arm, anti-roll bar, and telescopic dampers
Rear:	independent, by semi-trailing arms, coil springs, telescopic dampers and anti-roll bar

STEERING

Type:	rack-and-pinion (optional power-assistance)
Lock-to-lock:	4.2 turns

BRAKES

Front:	10.08in (256mm) ventilated discs
Rear:	10.0 x 2.25in (254 x 57mm) drums
System:	hydraulic, with vacuum servo assistance, no ABS

WHEELS & TYRES

Wheels:	eight-perforation cast alloys with four-stud fixing, 5.5J x 14in
Tyres:	195/60VR14in

BODY/CHASSIS

Type:	pressed-steel monocoque, based on conventional Sierra, in three-door hatchback style
Weight:	2,656lb (1,206kg)

PERFORMANCE

Max speed:	128mph (496kph) approx
Acceleration:	0–60mph in 7.7sec

PRICE at LAUNCH

£9,170 in 1983

Sierra (Merkur) XR4Ti

1984–1988

Looking almost exactly like an XR4i, the original Merkur XR4Ti had a different badge, and was assembled by Karmann in Germany

Ford-of-Europe wanted to sell fast Sierras to the USA, but needed to make the cars more attractive to American buyers. One way, they decided, was to use an engine with which the dealer chain was familiar, and another was to use a different name. They would also distance it from the domestic-American Ford, and sell it through Lincoln-Mercury dealerships

The result was a car based on the European XR4i, but badged as a 'Merkur' (which is German for 'Mercury'), and fitted with a turbocharged Ford Mustang Lima four-cylinder engine. Confusing? Indeed it was – and that was one of the impressions given by the North American clientele between 1984 and 1988. The 'Merkur' badge, incidentally, was also applied to the few Granada Scorpio cars which went to North America at the same time.

So, what was a Merkur XR4Ti? Start with a European-style Sierra XR4i and work on from there. It used the XR4i's unique three-door body style (complete with the three-window-glass motif on each side), and the bi-plane rear spoiler which caused so much controversy on the XR4i itself. Except that special eight-spoke alloy wheels were then fitted, it was only the Merkur badges which gave the game away.

Choosing an engine took time. On the one hand, Ford-USA wanted this to be a real performance car, and on the other they needed a unit which would meet their own ever-tightening exhaust emission laws. Several engines were considered, but finally the choice went to the turbocharged Lima unit which was already being used in the latest Mustangs: this was a distant relative of the European Pinto, so there was no difficulty in fitting it into the engine bay. Five-speed manual transmission or (with reduced power and torque) automatic transmission were both available, and the cabin was equipped to the very highest current Sierra standards, although speedometer markings ended at 80mph!

Assembly of such a hybrid machine was allocated away from a mainstream factory, to Karmann of Germany (they were already close to Ford-Germany, with manufacture of Escort Cabriolets), a plant conveniently placed near Germany's transatlantic ports. Previewed in mid-1984, this Merkur went on sale towards the end of the year as a 1985 model. Although intended purely for sale in the USA, it was also sold in Switzerland in small numbers, but officially it was never marketed in any other Ford-of-Europe territory.

In North America this was always an expensive car. Its base-line price in 1985 was $16,503, but many cars were loaded up with options like the glass sunroof, automatic transmission and air conditioning, and stickered at nearer $20,000 (or, £12,500). This was a time when Mustangs with the same engine were cheaper by several thousand dollars.

Amazingly enough, when the Ford-badged Sierra range was face-lifted for 1987 (complete with the more-rounded nose), such changes were never made to the Merkur derivative. The only visual change, made for 1988 models, was to fit a discreet single-plane boot lid spoiler instead of the original type. Even so, the XR4Ti's time was already past, and assembly ended in mid-1988.

Originally, Ford hoped to sell 15,000 cars a year. At peak, 16,842 were sold in 1985, and in total 45,748 were made in four years – only 6,968 in 1988, for instance.

There was one intriguing and gratifying postscript. Many of the body assembly facilities installed at Karmann for XR4Ti assembly would later be modified, and used to build Escort RS Cosworths instead.

In the UK, the only XR4Ti models we ever saw were the race cars prepared by Andy Rouse. Using these 300bhp machines, Andy won the British Touring Car Championship in 1985 and 1986.

Specification	
Sierra (Merkur) XR4Ti	
ENGINE	
Type:	Ford-USA Lima
Capacity:	2,301cc
Bore/stroke:	96.04 x 79.4mm
Compression ratio:	8.0:1
Max power:	177bhp at 5,500rpm (Automatic: 147bhp at 4,400rpm)
Max torque:	200lb ft at 3,000rpm (Automatic: 180lb ft at 3,000rpm)
Cylinders:	four, in-line
Cylinder head:	cast iron
Block:	cast iron
Valve gear:	two valves per cylinder, single overhead camshaft and fingers
Fuelling:	Ford EEC IV engine management fuel injection, and Garrett turbocharger
Installation:	front-mounted, longitudinal
TRANSMISSION	
Type:	front-engine, rear-wheel-drive
Gearbox:	Ford Type 9, five-speed manual (Optional Ford three-speed automatic transmission)
SUSPENSION	
Front:	independent by coil springs, MacPherson struts, lower track control arm, anti-roll bar, and telescopic dampers
Rear:	independent, by semi-trailing arms, coil springs, telescopic dampers and anti-roll bar
STEERING	
Type:	rack-and-pinion (optional power-assistance)
Lock-to-lock:	3.6 turns
BRAKES	
Front:	10.08in (256mm) ventilated discs
Rear:	10.0 x 2.25in (254 x 57mm) drums
System:	Girling hydraulic, with vacuum servo assistance
WHEELS & TYRES	
Wheels:	cast alloys (two styles) with four-stud fixing, 5.5J x 14in
Tyres:	195/60HR14in
BODY/CHASSIS	
Type:	pressed-steel monocoque, based on conventional Sierra, in three-door hatchback style
Weight:	2,922lb (1,325kg)
PERFORMANCE	
Max speed:	120mph (193kph) approx
Acceleration:	0–60mph in 7.9sec
PRICE at LAUNCH	
$16,503 in USA in 1985	
Not officially sold in the UK	

Sierra XR4x4

1982–1992

The Sierra XR4x4 was the first four-wheel-drive Ford passenger car to go on sale. Blending the fuel-injected Ford Cologne V6 engine with four-wheel-drive and more conventional styling helped produce a very capable and appealing motor car.

Little Brother

Between 1990 and 1993, a smaller-engined XR4x4 was also on sale. This was equipped with the 1,998cc eight-valve twin-cam four-cylinder power unit, which produced 125bhp. Although it had all the same traction and handling characteristics as the late-model 2.9-litre type, it was much slower, with a claimed top speed of 116mph. In 1990, when introduced, it cost £16,000.

It was a wet day in Southern England, the roads were slippery, and I couldn't believe what my hands and feet were telling me. I had never driven a big Ford saloon at this pace before. The road ahead was twisting, and bumpy – but the chassis never twitched. I was experiencing the delights of XR4x4 four-wheel-drive for the very first time.

Compared with my XR4i, my new XR4x4 was no faster in a straight line, but it was always quicker on ordinary journeys. That much-overworked word 'poise' had to be used. Nothing, but nothing, seemed to disturb the chassis. Special Vehicle Engineering had a lot to be proud of, for they had nurtured a formidable new Ford feature – four-wheel-drive.

It was the XR4x4's sure-footed traction, not the handling, which made it outstanding. Let me remind you, too, that the Sierra Cosworth 4x4, and the Escort RS Cosworth, both used the same basic system.

Ford had been dabbling with four-wheel-drive since the 1960s. The very first one-off car was a Mustang. Harry Ferguson Research then built a series of Zodiac and Capri projects, including three ferocious Capri 4WD rallycross cars.

Each of them used the archetypal Ferguson/FF system for front-engine cars. Behind the main gearbox a Hy-Vo chain drive moved the engine output sideways to a centre differential which split the drive between front and rear. Rear drive was conventional. Drive to the front was by a propeller shaft running alongside the engine, with a front differential alongside the engine, and with drive shafts pointing to left and right.

It was the glamorous Audi Quattro which changed motor industry attitudes. Even before the Sierra XR4x4 was launched, Ford-of-Europe

chairman, Bob Lutz, began to nag his engineers on the subject. To quote a colleague: 'The great thing about Lutz was that he loved cars. He made engineers go crazy, because he always seemed to want another derivative. He very much wanted Ford to go 4x4.'

Lutz, in fact, wanted Ford to make headlines at the Frankfurt Motor Show, where the launch of the Sierra was due, by exhibiting a prototype four-wheel-drive version. At that juncture there was no definite plan ever to put such a car into production. SVE had six months to produce a show car, which could actually be driven. This started with a 2.3-litre V6 engine: FF Developments designed and built the transmission, which included the advanced new viscous coupling limited-slip device in centre and rear differentials.

Then, in a mid-Summer 1992 flurry, Ford's product planners decided that four-wheel-drive was now important to their long-term plans, the show car was cancelled, and SVE got the job of developing a production car instead! At the time the new car, swiftly dubbed XR4x4, was intended to run alongside the biplane XR4i, rather than replace it. Before the XR4x4 was ready, however, the XR4i's death sentence had been confirmed.

SVE's principals, Rod Mansfield and Ray Diggins, then managed a high-pressure development programme, which not only saw the 2.8-litre engine replace the original 2.3-litre V6, the four-wheel-drive installation refined, but it also saw the development of anti-lock braking (ABS), although this did not even become optional until 1986. Depending on the market served, and the emission regulations being applied, two different types of Bosch fuel injection were employed, but the most important decision of all was to choose a torque split of 34 per cent to the front wheels, and 66 per cent to the rear, which ensured a well-balanced chassis with the minimum of understeer under power.

At the same time, SVE looked at the XR4i's suspension settings, decided

The Sierra XR4x4 used the same basic body shell as all other Sierras. All UK-market cars had this five-door hatchback style, although a three-door version was also available in Continental Europe. The 'Motorsport' wheels looked like those employed on the Escort RS Turbo, and the RS200 of the period, but were unique to this model.

Motorsport

In 1987 and 1988, the 2.8-litre XR4x4 had a brief 'works' fling in world-level rallying as Ford's temporary four-wheel-drive Group A contender. With only 210bhp, Blomqvist's car finished fourth in Monte Carlo 1987 (but was then disqualified on a technicality), sixth in Sweden 1987, and second in Sweden 1988. XR4x4s won snow rallies at European level, but that was that.

The fascia/instrument display of the XR4x4 was different from the XR4i in several detail ways – the wheel had a conventional horn push, and there were no red details, for instance – but the seats were of the same basic type, and the function was not disturbed.

that it could do a lot better, and completely reworked spring, damper and anti-roll bar settings. All this, along with power-assisted steering as standard, four-wheel disc brakes and the use of new seven-spoke cast-alloy road wheels, produced a Sierra with an excellent ride and quite sensational handling.

If prices were not to get out of hand, all this high-technology had to be paid for somehow, so the trim and fittings were simplified considerably (no red piping on the trim, no plastic cladding on the flanks, fewer instruments, the sunroof back as an option instead of standard – and only a single, discreet, rear spoiler.

The new XR4x4 was introduced in March 1985. Although made in three-door and in five-door form at first, the three-door model was never sold in the UK, and soon disappeared. The transmission, though, soon found other uses – under a high-spec version of the Sierra estate, and in the new Granada/Scorpio models which went on sale at the same time.

Within weeks Ford dealers knew that they had a success on their hands. Even though four-wheel-drive, as a feature, was never likely to break many sales records (a five per cent penetration was all that most manufacturers could hope for), the salesmen found the XR4x4 much easier to sell than they had ever done with the XR4i. Here was a discreet, practical, versatile and amazingly capable machine, which could only prove its point on the roads, not in the showrooms.

I suppose I was a typical customer. Having run my black XR4i for two

This up-market derivative of the XR4x4 was the Ghia estate, which combined function with load-carrying ability. This was a very successful model.

years, I readily changed it for a pure-white XR4x4 in 1985. At a stroke, it seemed, my journey times fell away, I stopped worrying about weather conditions, I found that I could cruise easily and securely at 100mph wherever the opportunity arose, and the traffic police ignored me. My insurance company loved me, the family found the car to be just as versatile as before – and I had absolutely no problems with the four-wheel-drive transmission.

In the next eight years, until it disappeared with the death of the entire Sierra range, the XR4x4 was always an important member of that family of cars. Many enthusiasts who could not afford a Sierra RS Cosworth happily settled for XR4x4s, police forces bought them in large numbers, and the four-wheel-drive system was later adopted for use in other Sierras – not only the under-estimated 2-litre versions, but the Sierra Cosworth 4x4.

Facelifted in 1987 like all other Sierras (the more rounded headlamp cowls and the increased window sizes tell their own story), the XR4x4 was then given an important mechanical update for 1989 when the deeper-breathing 2.9-litre V6 engine, allied to the brand-new MT75 gearbox, replaced the old-design units. That was a more important change than you might think. Compared with the old T9 gearbox, the MT75 was a much more pleasant and more reliable unit to use.

A year later, there was a further minor facelift, with the adoption of new-style road wheels, 'black' rear tail lamps and a different type of rear spoiler. There was even a short-lived 'bargain-basement' model, on sale in 1989 for £14,500, which had no alloys, no electric windows, no heated windows, but a substantial price reduction. More than 50,000 had been made when the last cars were produced at Genk at the end of 1992.

This was the four-wheel-drive layout of the original Sierra XR4x4, complete with three differentials. Later models would have a 2.9-litre engine (there was even a two-litre four-cylinder derivative), and a more robust MT75 main gearbox.

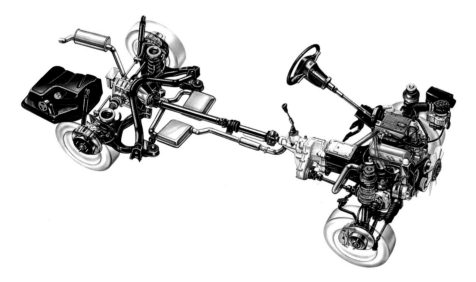

Specification

Sierra XR4x4
(2.9-litre engined car, from 1989, differences in brackets.)

ENGINE

Type:	Ford Cologne V6
Capacity:	2,792cc [2,933cc]
Bore/stroke:	93 x 68.5mm [93 x 72mm]
Compression ratio:	9.2:1 [9.5:1]
Max power:	150bhp at 5,700rpm
Max torque:	161lb ft at 3,800rpm [172lb ft at 3,000rpm]
Cylinders:	six, in 60° vee
Cylinder heads:	cast iron
Block:	cast iron
Valve gear:	two valves per cylinder, single camshaft, pushrods and rockers
Fuelling:	Bosch K-Jetronic fuel injection (Bosch L-Jetronic fuel injection)
Installation:	front-mounted, longitudinal

TRANSMISSION

Type:	front-engine, four-wheel-drive
Gearbox:	Ford Type 9, five-speed manual (Ford MT75)

Four-wheel-drive by FF system, with 34%F/66%R torque split, and viscous coupling centre and rear differentials

SUSPENSION

Front:	independent by coil springs, MacPherson struts, anti-roll bar, and telescopic dampers
Rear:	independent, by semi-trailing arms, coil springs, telescopic dampers and anti-roll bar

STEERING

Type:	rack-and-pinion (power assisted)
Lock-to-lock:	2.9 turns

BRAKES

Front:	10.2in (259mm) ventilated discs
Rear:	9.9in (251mm) solid discs
System:	hydraulic, with vacuum servo assistance; optional anti-lock (ABS) from 1986 (ABS as standard).

WHEELS & TYRES

Wheels:	seven-spoke cast alloys, 5.5J x 14in
Tyres:	195/60VR14in

BODY/CHASSIS

Type:	pressed-steel monocoque, based on conventional Sierra, in five-door hatchback style; some three-door models built in 1985(three-door never sold in UK)
Weight:	2,800lb (1,270kg)

PERFORMANCE

Max speed:	125mph (200kph) approx
Acceleration:	0–60mph in 8.4sec; 50-90 mph (4th gear) 15.7sec; (5th gear) 21.8sec

PRICE at LAUNCH
£11,500 in 1985 [£16,125 in 1989]

Sierra RS Cosworth

1986

The sensational new Sierra RS Cosworth was previewed in 1985, complete with its massive 'whaletail' rear spoiler, special nose, and those unique road wheels.

The story began in 1983 when Stuart Turner took Walter Hayes and their American bosses to watch the Touring Car race at the British GP meeting. Rover Vitesses dominated that race, the best Ford (a Capri) finished ninth, and Turner immediately faced a grilling:

'Is that really the best Ford can do?'

'Yes, we don't have any cars which are fast enough'

'What would you need to win?'

'We don't have a special car – we'd have to design one . . .'

Soon after this, Turner took the same team on a visit to Cosworth Engineering in Northampton, where they just 'happened' to see a 16-valve belt-driven twin-overhead-camshaft conversion on a 2-litre Pinto engine, and Stuart later recalled that the bare bones of the Sierra RS Cosworth were designed over a ploughman's lunch in a local pub: 'I said: "We need a new model for touring car racing, and it will need a lot of power. Why don't we use that Cosworth engine you've just seen, turbocharge it, and put it in a Sierra shell? Special Vehicle Engineering could do the design." After that, we moved swiftly forward.'

But it took time. Before the famous 'whaletail' format was chosen, other options were considered, including the Merkur XR4Ti engine, Ford or proprietary gearboxes, five-door or three-door bodies, and the need for aerodynamic 'add-ons'.

Peter Ashcroft at Boreham made a vital contribution, pointing out that well over 300bhp in race-car form would be needed to make the car competitive, while Lothar Pinske (Ford Cologne) insisted that the new car should be aerodynamically stable at high speeds, preferably with downforce at front and rear.

The Sierra RS Cosworth was originally a three-door car, where all the aerodynamic changes were made to improve stability and provide downforce. Because of the big front spoiler, the three-door always looked as if it was driving along in a nose-down state.

The massive rear spoiler, mounted on a pillar at mid-window level, was a definite aid to high-speed stability.

In March 1985 the prototype was revealed at the Geneva Motor Show. Wind-tunnel testing at MIRA and at Ford-Cologne had produced the correct combination of front and rear spoilers. The famous whale-tail might have been in an awkward position, (halfway up the rear window) but it produced exactly the effect needed, and there was still enough ground-clearance under the deep front spoiler. There was an extra intake in the nose to feed the intercooler, air vents were included in the bonnet panel to cool the engine bay, and of course, the bumpers, wheelarch extensions and sills were all special. The interior was the plushiest of all Sierras so far listed, not only with a very well-equipped fascia/instrument panel (including a 7,000rpm segmental rev counter and a tiny boost gauge), but with a pair of excellent, exclusive-to-Ford reclinable Recaro seats.

The Cossie's real appeal, of course, was hidden away – a 204bhp turbocharged 16-valve twin-cam engine, a sturdy new gearbox, and redeveloped front and rear suspensions. The YBB came complete with convoluted exhaust manifold, a TO3 Garrett turbocharger, and Weber-Marelli fuel injection.

The turbo size was chosen to ensure up to 350bhp in racing form, which meant that it was really too large for road use: indeed, there was noticeable turbo lag on the road car. The standard engine was rated at 204bhp (DIN) at 6,000rpm: not many people remember that this was the world's first road car to be listed with more than 100bhp/litre.

The extra air intake on the Sierra RS Cosworth was to feed cold air to the turbo intercooler and the radiator, the bonnet vents were to get hot air out again, while the big spoiler helped feed air to the radiator and the brakes. Who said that function could not also be attractive?

To keep the inlet charge cool, there was a sizeable air/air intercooler in the nose, mounted above the water radiator itself.

Before settling on a gearbox, Ford engineers had agonised over several alternatives. The old Ford Type 9 Sierra five-speeder was not strong enough, so alternative boxes from Getrag, ZF, and Borg-Warner (of the USA) were all tested. The Borg-Warner, which was already being used in several other Ford-USA models, was eventually chosen because it was quieter and more refined than the German alternatives. Theoretically, it should have been dead reliable – in fact Murphy's Law ensured that it was gearbox development problems which delayed the start-up of Sierra RS Cosworth production by several months in 1986 . . .

Lastly, but vitally, Rod Mansfield's SVE engineers redeveloped the Sierra suspension in every detail. It was a transformation. The media, which had criticised the XR4i's handling, all raved about the Cosworth's behaviour, yet the changes were limited to springs, dampers, anti-roll bars, bushes, mountings, and of course the use of 7.0J wheel rims with 205/50-section tyres.

After the prototype had been unveiled in March 1985, enthusiasts had to wait for more than a year before deliveries began. Job 1 had originally been planned for September 1985, with the 5,000th car scheduled to be built in Summer 1986, but gearbox problems and other development delays pushed the programme back. There was also the problem of how high the price should be, for as ever, Ford was not willing to market a loss-leader: 'Anybody who thinks you can have a loss-leader in the car business,' Walter Hayes once told me, 'is quite securely out of his mind'.

With only three body colours on the agenda – Diamond White, Moonstone Blue and black – the very first pre-production Cosworth was built at the Sierra factory at Genk (in Belgium) in February 1986, a few more followed in April, but series production did not begin properly until May/June 1986. Then the rush to produce 5,000 cars began in earnest. By mid-June 1986 96 cars a week were flowing, but in October and November, 300 cars were being built every week.

Along the way, during November, a further 500 right-hand-drive cars were produced, then stored, so that the RS500 Cosworth programme could be completed in 1987, the 5,000th car was built early in December, and the last of all – the 5,542nd machine – was produced later in the month. No fewer than 2,616 right-hand-drive cars were originally sold in the UK, most of the others (LHD) going to West Germany, France, Italy, Spain and Austria.

British-market deliveries began in July/August 1986, but the entire UK allocation had been sold off by the spring of 1987 – and the records show that Ford dealers received the vast majority of their cars in November and December 1986. For proud Sierra RS Cosworth customers, the problem was that their new toys were extremely visible. Most went straight out to prove that the cars would indeed exceed 140mph, and many were booked when finding out . . .

What happened in the years which followed was good, and bad, for Ford's image. In motorsport, and as an image-builder, the Cosworth was totally successful. Engine tuners discovered how easy it was to 'chip' the engine, and to liberate more power. There were, of course, some very bad conversions, which totally ruined the driveability of the standard car. Unhappily, the criminal fraternity soon discovered that the car's anti-theft measures were puny (don't times change – in those days immobilisers were still extremely rare), so many Cosworths were stolen, joy-ridden, crashed, or stripped down. Have you ever considered why or how there are so many 'Sierra Cosworth specialist parts suppliers' who advertise in some magazines? Some are totally kosher, but others, well . . .

Twenty years on, the mystique of the original three-door Sierra RS Cosworth is as strong as ever. Those cars with standard engines, or with properly developed conversions, and with effective immobilisers, are in great demand, although all the crashes and thefts have reduced numbers considerably. Values, which reached a premium in 1988 and 1989, have now slumped, hit hard by the insurance industry and by the drop from being fashionable. On the other hand, if you can get insurance, and if you can find a fine, straight example, we're sure it will be a great investment in the years to come. If nothing else, you'll be able to pat Escort RS Cosworth owners on the shoulder, and remind them that your car was first – it was the true first-born.

This was the anatomy of the original Sierra RS Cosworth, complete with turbocharged engine, more robust transmission and special suspension.

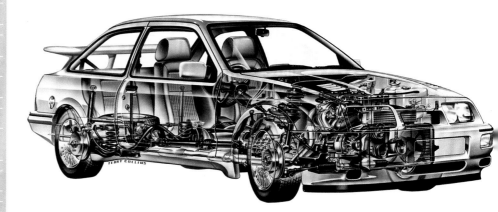

Sierra RS500 Cosworth

1987

Recognition points of the Sierra RS500 Cosworth included the extra splitter/lip on the front spoiler, and the 'flip' on the rear spoiler.

As every Ford enthusiast surely knows, in a few frantic weeks in mid-1987, Aston Martin Tickford of Bedworth, near Coventry, produced 496 RS500 Cosworths, as 'conversions' of existing, brand-new, Sierra RS Cosworths, with completely fresh, big-turbo engines. The other four cars, also from the same batch of 500, had been built earlier, and were development prototypes. The entire road-car development programme was completed in less than six months.

The decision to produce an extra 500 cars at Genk was taken very late. All were built between 13 November and 24 November 1986, shipped to Dagenham, carefully waxed and mothballed and started up regularly, but did no further mileage until mid-1987.

For the RS500 Cosworth (and to make it more suitable as a race car), the engine was changed, but the gearbox and rear axle were not. Except for aerodynamic add-ons, no changes could be made to the car's basic style and structure, or to its interior. Neither could basic changes be made to the suspension layout, nor to the brakes. One further detail, which mystifies any RS500 owner who crawls under his car to look at the rear suspension cross-beam, was the adding of a redundant mounting bracket close to the standard semi-trailing arm. This could be used to support special light-alloy semi-trailing arms on race cars.

Informal approval to build the cars came in October 1986, formal programme approval followed in December, and the projected 'Job 1' date of 18 June 1987 was honoured. The 500th car was completed on 28 July 1987, and sporting homologation followed on 1 August.

The big Garrett AiResearch TO4 turbocharger made it possible for race

The Sierra RS500 Cosworth featured an extra 'flip' on the big rear spoiler. The badge told us what it was – if ever we got the chance to read it, of course!

engines to produce 550bhp/575bhp, but it made the standard road car rather inflexible. Even though 224bhp is claimed (compared with 204bhp) I have yet to see an authentic road test where RS500 acceleration figures are better than those of an RS Cosworth.

RS500 Cosworths – real or fake?

Too many so-called 'RS500 Cosworths' are fake. The authenticated list of real R500s, by VIN number, original engine number, colour and build date is now in the hands of reputable clubs and experts.

Sierra RS500 Cosworths were at their best on the race track. This was one of the phenomenally successful Eggenberger cars, at Monza, in 1988.

This was the basis of the authentic Tickford conversion:

In 1987 every RS500 was given a newly-built engine from Cosworth, in the YBD series. Every one had right-hand-drive. Apart from the four development cars which were white, there were 392 black, 52 Moonstone Blue and 52 Diamond White production cars. The only decorative/badging difference was that slender side stripes were added, while 'RS500' stickers were placed on the front wings above the indicator repeaters, and on the tail below the 'Sierra' badge.

Not only did the YBD engines have the much larger (TO4-type) turbocharger and related trunking, but the inlet manifold/plenum casting featured four extra fuel injectors with an additional fuel rail (which were not originally activated on road-specification cars). YBD-type cylinder blocks were stiffer than YBB types, and there were important visual detail differences which any reputable engine builder can pick out.

RS500s were fitted with an extra-large capacity turbo intercooler (above and behind the enlarged water radiator), whose inlet and outlet passages matched the larger diameter trunking used to plumb connections between the TO4 turbo and the modified inlet manifold.

There was a modified rear suspension cross-beam, which featured two additional simple U-brackets and bolt holes. This had no function on road cars, for they were specifically fitted to allow alternative-type semi-trailing arms to be fitted for racing purposes.

Last, and by no means least, there were three aerodynamic hang ons. At the front there was an extra spoiler at the very bottom of the wrap-around front bumper, which significantly reduced the ground clearance. At the rear, too, the RS500 was given a small extra rear spoiler which fitted below the main whaletail, on the rear corner of the hatchback lid, as well as a small, extra flip-up flap on the rear of the whaletail itself. Ford assured us that it has a useful aerodynamic function at high forward speeds.

The result was a road car that felt no faster than the original three-door RS Cosworth, but which proved capable of phenomenal performance on the race track. And that is what the design of the RS500 was all about. Rare at the time, and always much coveted, the RS500 has become a real sporting icon of the 20th century.

The Sierra RS500 Cosworth's engine, complete with a massive turbocharger, was a snug fit in the Sierra's engine bay.

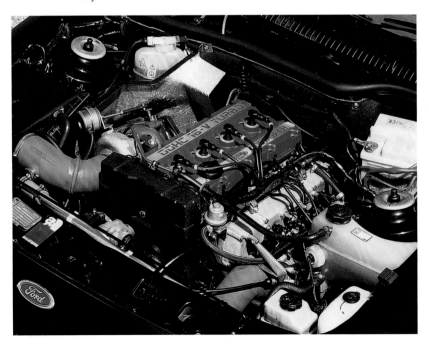

Specification	
Sierra RS500 Cosworth	
ENGINE	
Type:	Ford-Cosworth YB
Capacity:	1,993cc
Bore/stroke:	90.82 x 76.95mm
Compression ratio (nominal):	8.0:1
Max power:	224bhp at 6,000rpm
Max torque:	206lb ft at 4,500rpm
Cylinders:	four, in-line, longitudinally mounted
Cylinder head:	cast aluminium
Block:	cast iron
Valve gear:	four valves per cylinder, twin belt-driven camshafts, hydraulic bucket tappets
Fuelling:	Weber-Marelli fuel injection with Garrett TO3 turbocharger, and intercooling
Installation:	front-mounted, longitudinal
TRANSMISSION	
Type:	front-engine, rear-wheel-drive
Gearbox:	Borg Warner T5, five-speed manual
SUSPENSION	
Front:	independent by coil springs, MacPherson struts, anti-roll bar, and telescopic dampers
Rear:	independent, by semi-trailing arms, coil springs, telescopic dampers and anti-roll bar.
STEERING	
Type:	rack-and-pinion (power-assisted)
Lock-to-lock:	2.4 turns
BRAKES	
Front:	11.1in (282mm) ventilated discs
Rear:	10.8in (274mm) solid discs
System:	hydraulic, with vacuum servo assistance and ABS
WHEELS & TYRES	
Wheels:	lattice-pattern cast alloys, 7.0J x 15in
Tyres:	205/50VR15in
BODY/CHASSIS	
Type:	pressed-steel monocoque, based on conventional Sierra, in three-door hatchback style
Weight:	2,690lb (1,217kg)
PERFORMANCE	
Max speed:	145mph (233kph) approx
Acceleration:	0–60mph in 6.2sec
PRICE at LAUNCH	
£19,950 in July 1987	

Sierra RS Cosworth
(Sapphire)
1988–1989

Executive express, Ford-style – this was the 'Sapphire' RS Cosworth, as launched in 1988, which combined the latest Sierra four-door saloon with the RS Cosworth drive line.

The next time you are at a Ford one-make club meeting, here is a perfect way to start an argument. Suggest that the Sierra Sapphire Cosworth (four-door saloon) is a better car than the original 'whaletail' model . . .

One car is as quick as the other and there are only tiny mechanical differences. The four-door was more practical, but with less aggressive styling. Perhaps the handling of the four-door wasn't quite as 'sharp', but could you really tell the difference?

When the new version of the car, complete with face-lift style four-door Sierra Sapphire body shell was introduced in January 1988, it was almost exactly what had been expected – if not exactly what some people had hoped for. Though not officially known as the 'Sapphire Cosworth' (there were no 'Sapphire' badges on the car, anywhere), since almost everyone calls it that today, the nickname has stuck. Why change a winning formula?

To quote Ford-of-Europe Vice-Chairman Walter Hayes: 'We wanted a car that would sit at traffic lights and look like any other car, except that other drivers would know that it wasn't. You didn't often see BMWs tarted up in strange ways, and the evidence was there to suggest that we were ready to take a share of that BMW market.'

The decision to make a four-door Sierra Cosworth was finally made after Motorsport, at Boreham, said that racing or rallying versions of a car like this would not be needed. There was no need for rear downforce, and large spoilers could be ignored, as could wheelarch extensions: a four-door 'Executive Express' became feasible, and practical.

Visually, the new car looked very similar to the Sierra Sapphire Ghia, plus familiar Cosworth lattice-pattern wheels, an extra chin spoiler, and a nonfunctional rear spoiler. The interior was like that of the three-door types, and those marvellous Recaro seats were retained.

The four-door car was more comfortable, less twitchy, and altogether less 'homologation special' in feel and character than the original three-door car, with stiffer front and rear springs and softer dampers. The front anti-roll bar was the same diameter as before, but the rear roll bar was enlarged, from 14mm diameter to 16mm. This was still a car which would exceed 140mph, and out-accelerate almost anything short of a true Supercar, but it did it more calmly, and in a way that didn't shout its specification to the winds.

In the two years that it was on sale, more than 14,000 were sold – to an entirely different clientele. 'User-Choosers' (don't marketing specialists use awful phrases at times?) who might previously have bought BMWs or smaller Mercedes-Benz types now had an alternative to consider – and many of them chose the new Ford.

If, that is, the thieves didn't take them away first. The four-door, in fairness, had exactly the same type of anti-theft security measures as the original. This, by 1994 standards, can be summarised as 'not much', which many owners found to their cost. The result was heartbreak for hundreds, a ready supply of Sierra Cosworth parts from 'Dodgy Dave' – and a profusion of stolen, then burnt-out body shells. Surviving cars have been treated to a range of anti-theft measures by later owners, which seem to have done the trick . . .

When the car was introduced, Ford stated: 'The average buyer will be earning more than £30,000 a year, will be in a managerial and professional position, and – most important of all – will not be at the far end of a long chain of decision makers.' Where four to six-year-old cars are concerned, that doesn't apply any more. Don't times change?

Because the Sapphire looked so different from the three-door, it has attracted a different type of 'classic' buyer today. As with new car customers, today's owners tend to be less flamboyant, and maybe they need the extra space. They still have potentially very fast transport. Emotion naturally affects rational decisions, and one result of the 'isn't this an anonymous car?' impression is that Sapphire Cosworth values fell further than those of the three-door, even though they cost a lot more when new. Less money buys more car? Do you believe that?

The replacement, with four-wheel-drive, would be even better.

The Sierra 'Sapphire' RS Cosworth four-door was fitted out as a high-speed cruiser, but of course retained those splendid Recaro front seats.

Specification	
Sierra (Sapphire) RS Cosworth (four-door)	
ENGINE	
Type:	Ford-Cosworth YB
Capacity:	1,993cc
Bore/stroke:	90.82 x 76.95mm
Compression ratio (nominal):	8.0:1
Max power:	204bhp at 6,000rpm
Max torque:	203lb ft at 4,500rpm
Cylinders:	four, in-line, longitudinally mounted
Cylinder head:	cast aluminium
Block:	cast iron
Valve gear:	four valves per cylinder, twin belt-driven overhead camshafts, hydraulic bucket tappets
Fuelling:	Weber-Marelli fuel injection with Garrett TO3 turbocharger, and intercooling
Installation:	front-mounted, longitudinal
TRANSMISSION	
Type:	front-engine, rear-wheel-drive
Gearbox:	Borg Warner T5, five-speed manual
SUSPENSION	
Front:	independent by coil springs, MacPherson struts, anti-roll bar, and telescopic dampers
Rear:	independent, by semi-trailing arms, coil springs, telescopic dampers and anti-roll bar
STEERING	
Type:	rack-and-pinion (power-assisted)
Lock-to-lock:	2.4 turns
BRAKES	
Front:	11.1in (282mm) ventilated discs
Rear:	10.8in (274mm) solid discs
System:	hydraulic, with vacuum servo assistance and ABS
WHEELS & TYRES	
Wheels:	lattice-pattern cast alloys, 7.0J x 15in
Tyres:	205/50VR15in
BODY/CHASSIS	
Type:	pressed-steel monocoque, based on conventional Sierra, in four-door saloon style
Weight:	2,660lb (1,206kg)
PERFORMANCE	
Max speed:	142mph (228kph) approx
Acceleration:	0–60mph in 5.8sec
PRICE at LAUNCH	
£19,000 in January 1988	

Sierra Cosworth 4x4

1990–1992

The third-generation Sierra Cosworth – the RS Cosworth 4x4 – combined a four-door saloon shell with an up-rated (220bhp) engine, and permanent four-wheel-drive. The bonnet louvres were a recognition point.

The three-door 'whaletail' Sierra RS Cosworth might be the most famous, but the four-wheel-drive version, which followed in 1990, was certainly the best. The 'whaletail' might have looked the most spectacular, but the four-wheel-drive type was the most capable.

Because the 'whaletail' was originally developed with circuit racing in mind, it was conceived as a rear-wheel-drive car. It was only when Group A rallying became important, even up to World Championship level, that thought turned to four-wheel-drive. Work began on this car in 1987, but it was not until early 1990 that it was introduced, as a direct replacement for the (rear-drive) four-door 'Sapphire' Cosworth saloon.

The mechanical layout was a logical evolution of what had gone before. The same type of 2-litre turbocharged Cosworth YB-type engine was retained, this time in a 'green' tune which could run on unleaded fuel, and there was a similar four-wheel-drive layout as the V6-engined XR4x4. This time, however, the Borg Warner main gearbox of the early models was discarded, replaced by the corporate MT75 five-speed transmission which was also being used in the latest, 2.9-litre, XR4x4. For the first time ever in a Sierra, by the way, there were ventilated front and rear disc brakes.

Compared with the rear-drive 'Sapphire' RS Cosworth, the only obvious outward and visual changes were the addition of cooling louvres in the bonnet panel and discreet 4x4 badges on the front wings, immediately behind the front wheelarch cutouts.

Although the latest engine looked like the original, it was much changed in detail, and Cosworth claimed that 80 per cent of the part numbers were different. The slightly larger turbocharger had been moved on a differently

Motorsport

The Sierra Cosworth 4x4 was nearly, but not quite, a world-class rally car, for that it had great traction and good handling, it was always heavier than its opposition. At World level in 1991 and 1992, 'works' cars set many fastest stage times, but could only notch up two second and five third places. There were many victories at European and national levels.

shaped exhaust manifold, the inlet manifold was altered, and there was a larger inter-cooler ahead of the engine itself.

Ford knew that they could not sell this car on the novelty of its styling (at a distance it was almost impossible to tell it from other up-market four-door Sierras), and it was always marketed on its remarkable handling and traction. The author personally owned two cars in the early 1990s (then changed to Escort RS Cosworth motoring instead!), finding that they had a remarkably supple ride, exceptional grip, and the sort of balance that made it one of the fastest all-purpose road cars that Ford had ever produced.

Like previous Sierra Cosworths, the 4x4 was assembled only at Genk in Belgium. Sales built up rapidly in 1990, and more than 5,000 had already been produced when the car began its international rallying career later that year. If there was a marketing problem, it was caused by the high initial price – in 1990 it retailed at £24,995 (the last 'Sapphire' had cost £21,300), and by the high cost of insurance. In the UK, although not in Germany (which meant that some Ford-of-Europe bosses couldn't understand the situation), the theft problem was serious. All these factors meant that in 1992 sales dropped right back.

There was one little-remembered update to this model, which came in the autumn of 1991 – a time when the car was given a new and more subtly contoured fascia/instrument style, and when more sound-deadening had been added to improve the refinement. This was the point at which a different alloy wheel style was also adopted.

Hundreds, if not thousands, of these cars were treated to tuned-up engines in later life, such that in the late 1990s it was often difficult to find a smart, original and totally reliable unmodified example.

Production of Sierra Cosworth 4x4s closed down towards the end of 1992, when the entire Sierra range gave way to the new front-drive Mondeo, but it was not the end of this mechanical pedigree. By this time the Escort RS Cosworth, which was based on a shortened-wheelbase version of the Cosworth 4x4 platform and running gear, was already on the market.

Specification	
Sierra Cosworth 4x4	
ENGINE	
Type:	Ford-Cosworth YB
Capacity:	1,993cc
Bore/stroke:	90.82 x 76.95mm
Compression ratio (nominal):	8.0:1
Max power:	220bhp at 6,250rpm
Max torque:	214lb ft at 3,500rpm
Cylinders:	four, in-line, longitudinally mounted
Cylinder head:	cast aluminium
Block:	cast iron
Valve gear:	four valves per cylinder, twin belt-driven overhead camshafts, hydraulic bucket tappets
Fuelling:	Weber-Marelli fuel injection with Garrett TO3 turbocharger, and intercooling
Installation:	front-mounted, longitudinal
TRANSMISSION	
Type:	front-engine, four-wheel-drive
Gearbox:	Ford MT75, five-speed manual
SUSPENSION	
Front:	independent by coil springs, MacPherson struts, anti-roll bar, and telescopic dampers
Rear:	independent, by semi-trailing arms, coil springs, telescopic dampers and anti-roll bar.
STEERING	
Type:	rack-and-pinion (power-assisted)
Lock-to-lock:	2.4 turns
BRAKES	
Front:	11.1in (282mm) ventilated discs
Rear:	10.8in (274mm) solid discs
System:	hydraulic, with vacuum servo assistance and ABS
WHEELS & TYRES	
Wheels:	lattice-pattern cast alloys, 7.0J x 15in
Tyres:	205/50 ZR15in
BODY/CHASSIS	
Type:	pressed-steel monocoque, based on conventional Sierra, in four-door saloon style
Weight:	2,870lb (1,305kg)
PERFORMANCE	
Max speed:	144mph (232kph) approx
Acceleration:	0–60mph in 6.6sec
PRICE at LAUNCH	
£24,995 in January 1990	

This graphic shot shows how the power was fed through all four wheels on the Sierra Cosworth 4x4 model, which was built from 1990 to 1992.

RS200

1985–1986

Most RS200s were white, but a handful were painted in Ferrari Rosso Red. The Ghia style looked beautiful from every angle.

RS200s had a Ghia style covering a mid-engined, four-wheel-drive layout. The top-end bulge cowls the engine intercooler.

Too many people have written about the RS200 without ever driving one, and its record as a road car has often been ignored. In my case, the RS200 was part of my every-day life for four years with four different cars. Like Ford's Bob Howe, I had a love-hate relationship with these fascinating machines, which were really competition cars detuned to make them tolerable and practical for road use. Tolerable, mark you – but not ideal.

On the open road – particularly a winding one without too much traffic – nothing was faster, safer or more nimble than an RS200, but in traffic they could be a pain. Long journeys were at first exhilarating because of the car's poise and performance, but the heavy steering, the cockpit noise and the poor rearward visibility all took their toll. Journeys through cities, and times in traffic jams, were best avoided, for it was all too easy to overheat that precious engine or to cook the clutch. There was no power steering, either . . . yet there were hundreds of other occasions when the sheer buzz of handling such a wonderful chassis brought a smile to our faces, and a perilous attitude to traffic laws and speed limits.

In 1983, Ford knew that it had to build 200 RS200s for homologation purposes. They would rather not have made any (the project was a loss-maker), but world-class rally trends forced the issue. The project was inspired by Ford's Director of European Motorsport, Stuart Turner. To beat Group B cars like the Audi Quattro and the Peugeot 205T16, it would need to have four-wheel-drive, and at least 450bhp in 'works' form, and much potential. The first car, completed in March 1984, was mostly designed by F1's Tony Southgate, but the production car had been completely redetailed by John Wheeler and his team.

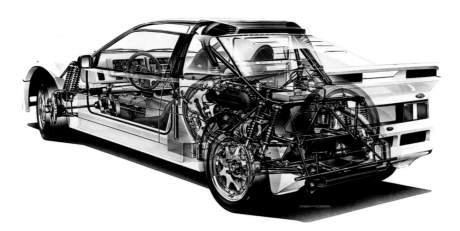

From 1984 to 1986 it was Mike Moreton, more than any other Ford manager, who shepherded the RS200 into production. After the six original prototypes, precisely 194 cars were built at an ex-Reliant factory in Shenstone, Staffordshire, in both right-hand-drive and left-hand-drive. The chassis came from Arch Motors, engines came from Cosworth and JQF Engineering, transmissions from FF Developments, and body panels from Reliant.

It was never meant to be a cost-effective design. The 'chassis' was actually a built-up central monocoque, with Sierra windscreen and side glass, plus many standard-Ford components in the cabin, but the mid-engined/four-wheel-drive layout was unique.

The tub was a complex mixture of steel, carbon-fibre and aluminium composite materials, there were sturdy multi-tube sections at front and rear to support the running gear, the whole being covered by large, sinuous glass-fibre panels.

The engine was a turbocharged version of the familiar Cosworth BDA, while the main transmission was an FF layout incorporating five forward speeds, the front/rear torque split, a central diff and a front-end diff. There was a massive transmission bulge between the seats. The engines had originally been built for the abandoned RS1700T project, and were further modified. The main gearbox components had also been prepared for use in the RS1700T.

Versatile all-independent suspension had two spring/damper units per corner, the wishbones had alternative mounting points on the tub, and the spring platforms were adjustable for height, and there were two fuel tanks (one under and behind each of the seats).

Production cars were fully trimmed with carpets and a full array of instruments. There was space for two passengers, but very little else.

Building the 194 production cars didn't take long – no more than six months in all – but the preparation for this took longer. The last four weeks, after Christmas 1985 and before 31 January 1986, saw Shenstone in a state of controlled bedlam.

Using an RS200 as everyday transport meant adopting special routines. It was not a car which could be neglected or abused: it was really a detuned competition car, which had to be treated as such. In the mornings, when cold, the engine oil pressure was very high, so low rpm was essential at first. At the end of a long run, particularly if the car had been driven hard, one simply did not switch off abruptly: it was best to let the engine idle for a minute or two, to allow the turbocharger to cool down.

Yet it was a comfortable car to drive, with a very supple ride. Most customers used the figure-hugging Sparco seats, although conventional Recaros were optional. It was a well-trimmed and equipped car, with remote-control door mirrors to make rearward visibility practical (the

The RS200's compact two-seater shell was packed with machinery. The engine intercooler was mounted on the roof, and there was a transverse exhaust silencer behind the rear suspension. Note – twin spring/damper units at each corner.

Motorsport

The RS200's career as a Group B rally car lasted only one year – 1986, after which the formula was thrown out by the authorities. Third in its first World rally (Swedish) and leading the Acropolis until a mechanical breakage, it was then rendered ineligible. At European level, however, there were 19 wins in the season, and victory in several National Championships.

In a second career, characters like Martin Schanche and Mark Rennison made the RS200 unbeatable in rallycross for several seasons.

The RS200's unique layout featured an engine behind the two-seater cabin, with the main gearbox and centre differential up front, between the passenger's legs.

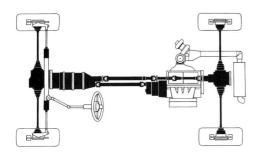

central rear-view mirror was useless!), while electric window lifts, radio-cassette units, and full Tickford trimming were all optional.

All 200 cars were originally painted in Diamond White, although many subsequently had motorsport diagonal striping, and a select few were painted Ferrari Rosso Red.

To reach the fuel filler cap (which was behind the left-side door) you had to lift up the rear section. About 16-18mpg seemed to be normal on 250bhp cars (but much worse on modified examples), and it was wise to check the oil level in the dry sump tank every time one added petrol. Most owners learned to travel light, as the only stowage space was a spare-wheel-shaped box up front. The heater/ventilator system was very poor, and most owners tended to run, if possible, with one of the side windows cracked open.

Most RS200 owners kept down to 4,000rpm in fifth gear on motorways (that was only 80mph – but an RS200 was very visible . . .), but most enjoyed the 5,000–7,000rpm punch of the engine in the intermediates. When the gearbox oil had warmed up the change was slick and positive, but in truth, it was very hard work to use the stubby gearstick on cold mornings.

In town, the steering on those 225-section Pirelli P700 tyres and 8in rims was heavy, and bigger tyres/wider rims made it even more difficult to manoeuvre at parking speeds. A power-steering conversion was available from specialists, but that was very expensive indeed. Even so, if the turbo was on song, and the driver was wide awake, he never needed to make a decision about overtaking slower traffic on the open road – there was always space.

Although Ford originally laid down ample spare parts in the mid-1980s (dismantled/unsold cars at the end of the run provided most of them), they soon disappeared, although most breakages can be made good by the specialists. Less than 100 RS200s now remain, about half of them being in Britain, but only a handful of those cars are in regular use. You won't find people driving them to and from work, but you do still see them turning up at major Ford or Group B Car Club meetings. Values may have fallen a lot since the heady days of 1988/89, but an RS200 still costs more than any other 'classic' Ford I can think of.

Just 20 of the 200 RS200s were fitted with this amazing 2.1-litre BDT-E engine, which had been designed by Brian Hart. In full race-tune, it developed more than 600bhp.

RS200
Note: 'Standard' specification is detailed. In addition, 300bhp and 350bhp engine tunes were also available with alternative gearbox and final drive ratios, and wider-rim wheels. Later a 2.1-litre 550bhp+ BDT-E engine was also made available.

ENGINE

Type:	Ford-Cosworth BDT
Capacity:	1,804cc
Bore/stroke:	86 x 77.6mm
Compression ratio:	8.2:1 (nominal), plus turbocharging to 11.0psi/0.75 bar.
Max power:	250bhp (DIN) at 6,500–7,000rpm
Max torque:	215lb ft at 4,500–5,000rpm
Cylinders:	four, in line, longitudinally mounted
Cylinder head:	cast aluminium
Block:	cast aluminium
Valve gear:	four valves per cylinder, belt-driven twin overhead camshafts bucket tappets
Fuelling:	EECIV engine management, Garrett turbocharger and air/air intercooling.
Installation:	mid/rear-mounted, longitudinal, driving all four wheels

TRANSMISSION

Type:	mid/rear-engine, four-wheel-drive
Gearbox:	Ford/FF, five-speed manual, all-synchromesh

SUSPENSION

Front:	independent by twin coil springs, wishbones, anti-roll bar and telescopic dampers
Rear:	independent, by twin coil springs, wishbones, anti-roll bar and telescopic dampers

STEERING

Type:	rack-and-pinion, no power assistance
Lock-to-lock:	3.0 turns

BRAKES

Front:	11.2in (285mm) ventilated discs
Rear:	11.2in (285mm) ventilated discs
System:	hydraulic, but without vacuum servo assistance, and no ABS

WHEELS & TYRES

Wheels:	seven-spoke cast aluminium, 8.0J x 16in
Tyres:	225/50VR16in

BODY/CHASSIS

Type:	lightweight composite steel/aluminium/honeycomb tub with built-in roll-cage. Bolt-on tubular steel front and rear subframes. Glass-fibre body panels, with carbon/aramid stiffening.
Weight:	2,602lb (1,180kg)

PERFORMANCE :
Standard-spec, 250bhp version:

Max speed:	140mph (225kph) approx
Acceleration:	0–60mph in 6.1sec
Standing start ¼-mile:	15.0sec

PRICE at LAUNCH
£49,995 in late-1985

Fiesta XR2i

1990–1994

The first Fiesta XR2i was given four extra low-mounted driving lamps, and a blue waist-level rubbing strip.

The original Fiesta XR2i had sill extensions, and the badge on the hatch lid told its own story.

In the 1990s, Ford's problem was how to follow up one good idea with a better one. Although the XR2i was never as fashionable as the earlier-shape XR2, it was a better car – and sold well. In a four-year life, it had two entirely different engines, was given a suspension makeover after less than a year, and came in for detail improvements along the way. Unhappily, it was the insurance industry, which killed it off.

The old-type CVH-engined XR2 had been good for 112mph, with the 0–60mph sprint in 9.3sec, whereas the new 1990-model XR2i could reach 118mph and reach 60mph in 8.9sec. Wasn't that a very significant improvement, especially at a price of £9,995? In fact, the fuel-injected 110bhp CVH engine of the new car was a real advance. Gearing was higher, wheels were larger, and the equipment (which included optional anti-lock brakes for £400, and alloy wheels for £200) was more complete.

This time, too, the cabin was more spacious than before and the seats slid back a long way; only very tall drivers couldn't get comfortable. I was happy with the straight-line performance, but I didn't like the low-geared steering, and I thought the handling was too soft. Ford's response to this was

Specification

Fiesta XR2i

(Basic details for original CVH-engined car. 16-valve Zetec engined car, details in brackets.)

ENGINE

Type:	CVH [16-valve Zetec]
Capacity:	1,596cc [1,796cc]
Bore/stroke:	80 x 79.5mm [80.6 x 88mm]
Compression ratio:	9.75:1 [10.0:1]
Max power:	110bhp at 6,000rpm [105bhp at 5,500rpm]
Max torque:	102lb ft at 2,800rpm [113lb ft at 4,000rpm]
Cylinders:	four, in-line, transversely mounted
Cylinder head:	cast aluminium
Block:	cast iron
Valve gear:	two valves per cylinder, belt-driven single overhead camshaft, rockers, and hydraulic tappets [four valves per cylinder, twin belt-driven overhead camshafts, hydraulic bucket tappets]
Fuelling:	Ford EEC IV fuel injection
Installation:	front-mounted, transverse

TRANSMISSION

Type:	front-engine, front-wheel-drive
Gearbox:	Ford, five-speed manual

SUSPENSION

Front:	independent by coil springs, MacPherson struts, anti-roll bar, and telescopic dampers
Rear:	independent, by trailing arms, torsion beam, coil springs/struts, telescopic dampers and anti-roll bar

STEERING

Type:	rack-and-pinion
Lock-to-lock:	4.2 turns [4.5 turns]

BRAKES

Front:	9.4in (240mm) ventilated discs
Rear:	8.0in (203mm) drums
System:	hydraulic, with vacuum servo assistance, and optional ABS anti-lock

WHEELS & TYRES

Wheels:	pressed steel disc/optional alloys, 5.5J x 13in [5.5J x 14in]
Tyres:	185/60HR13in [185/55HR14in]

BODY/CHASSIS

Type:	pressed-steel monocoque, based on conventional Fiesta, in three-door hatchback style
Weight:	2,024lb (918kg) [2,148lb (974kg)]

PERFORMANCE

Max speed:	118mph (190kph) approx [116mph (187kph) approx]
Acceleration:	0–60mph in 8.9sec [9.4sec]

PRICE at LAUNCH

£9,995 in October 1989
[£11,533 in Summer 1992]

interesting. Their engineers had given the XR2i a softer ride, and less razor-sharp steering responses – they thought that was what you, Mr Customer, would appreciate . . .

All the press comments about XR2i steering and handling must have struck home, because Ford then used the Fiesta RS Turbo's handling package complete, making it standard on the XR2i from the winter of 1990/91. Some people then thought the ride too hard....

It was only two years before the next big change. From May 1992 both CVH-engined hot Fiestas (XR2i and the RS Turbo) were dropped – and two new 1.8-litre 16-valve Zetec-engined cars took their place. Although the new version cost £11,533, it was a much better car: cast alloys cost an extra £245, and anti-lock brakes £481.

The improvements didn't end there, for the revised XR2i looked more purposeful, yet at the same time more discreet, than before. First of all, the thin blue decorative line around the flanks had gone, and there was only a discreet '16V' badge on the tail to give the game away. Secondly the cast alloys had more simple styling, but were now of 14in diameter, and the tyres had a chunky 185/55 low-profile section. Inside the cabin there were new profiles to the well-bolstered front seats (but they were still not Recaros . . .), and there was a new three-spoke steering wheel. Unhappily, the steering was as low-geared as ever, and the ride just as hard. Few cars, though, could match the XR2i's grip on smooth tarmac.

All in all this was a more appealing car than the CVH-powered version which it replaced, yet Ford seemed to make little effort to flaunt its merits, and it was rarely promoted. Only those people who read magazine road tests (reports which included many telling phrases such as: 'sweeter engine', 'more flexible', 'better handling' and 'good sporting value') got the message, and you rarely found XR2i-16V cars on show in Ford dealerships. Stuart McCrudden's Fiesta one-make championship did its best, by offering conversion kits to turn obsolete-models into new types.

In the end, this spacious and effective little car died of neglect, the unfair attentions of the insurance companies hastening its end. There would not be a better small Ford package as good as this for several years to come.

From 1992 the Fiesta XR2i was given a 1.8-litre Zetec 16-valve engine, and the blue waist line was abandoned.

Fiesta RS Turbo

1990–1992

The original Fiesta RS Turbo had a green stripe all around the waist line, and these unique three-spoke wheels. It was the smallest car ever to be turbocharged by Ford.

After the second-generation Fiesta was introduced in April 1989, there was a gap before high-performance derivatives were added to the range. However, in the following year (by which time the XR2i was well-established), Ford also unveiled the Fiesta RS Turbo.

Although this was a short-lived model (it would be replaced by the Fiesta RS1800 after only two years) it was the fastest-ever Fiesta (the RS1800 would not be quite as powerful), and the only one to carry both the 'RS' and 'Turbo' badges.

The facile way to describe this car would be as a second-generation Fiesta, with a 1980s-style Escort RS Turbo engine, and all the XR2i trimmings – but that would over-simplify a speedily developed, and rather more focussed, model. Although the engine was based on that of the Escort RS Turbo, it had been provided with a smaller, Garrett TO2 turbocharger, and there was Ford EEC IV engine management control. Not only that but the inlet and exhaust manifolding had changed, and there was a new type of air/air inter-cooler. Clever electronic control meant that the torque curve was claimed to be essentially flat, from 2,400–5,000rpm.

Special Vehicle Engineering had also worked on the steering/suspension package – and on this occasion there were complaints that they might have erred on the side of making it all too stiff. Certainly this was the hardest-riding Fiesta ever, which was sometimes nicknamed the turbo-roller-skate, and gained a street-racer's reputation almost at once. Spring and damper settings were firmer than on any other Fiesta, the steering was higher geared (although still not power assisted), and there was now an anti-roll bar at the rear.

It was the equipment and style package which made this performance all look right. Inside the car, Recaro front seats made all the difference, along with a special steering wheel, electric windows, central locking and a sunroof feature. The way to 'pick' an RS Turbo from the outside was not only the four low-mounted driving lamps, the three-spoke alloy wheels, and the green stripe around the car at mid-door level, but the inclusion of cooling louvres in the bonnet panel.

If the economic times had been different, the RS Turbo would certainly have sold better, but the UK market was already beginning to sink towards recession, the climate against frivolous hatchbacks was fading, and the ever-cautious Ford company was not confident about promoting this model too obviously. Enthusiasts expecting champagne performance for beer money were no doubt disappointed by the price – £11,950 – which was £1,100 more than that of the XR2i.

Yet it was genuinely a very rapid little machine, whose overall appeal was only blunted by the rock-hard ride, and by the rather unexplained 'dead' feeling of the steering. Its top speed – 129mph, according to independent tests, and no less than 11mph faster than the XR2i – made it the second fastest car in the current Ford range (only the Sierra Cosworth 4x4 was quicker!), and it was more than competitive with any hot hatchback in its class.

Not only that, but it could reach 108mph in fourth gear, it could sprint to a quarter mile in only 16.1sec, all at a 24–26mpg everyday fuel consumption figure. If you didn't mind the ride, it was an absolute hoot to drive, for there was nothing better than those Recaro seats to give great car control. And, more than some of its rivals, it was still a genuine four-seater hatchback with plenty of stowage space.

Like other Performance Fords of the period, the RS Turbo suffered from the insurance industry's contemporary vendetta against high-performance cars (and hot hatchbacks in particular), but there is also no doubt that its hard-riding reputation did not help either. Although its replacement, the RS1800, would still have that 'RS' badge, it promised to be more refined in some respects.

There was just – and only just – enough space under the Fiesta bonnet for a turbocharged CVH engine to be installed. Both the turbo, and its intercooler, were in the nose, where they benefited from cooling air.

Specification	
Fiesta RS Turbo	
ENGINE	
Type:	CVH
Capacity:	1,596cc
Bore/stroke:	80 x 79.5mm
Compression ratio:	8.2:1 (nominal)
Max power:	133bhp at 5,500rpm
Max torque:	135lb ft at 2,400rpm
Cylinders:	four, in-line, transversely mounted
Cylinder head:	cast aluminium
Block:	cast iron
Valve gear:	two valves per cylinder, belt-driven single overhead camshaft, rockers, and hydraulic tappets
Fuelling:	Ford EEC IV engine management, Garrett turbocharger and intercooling
Installation:	front-mounted, transverse
TRANSMISSION	
Type:	front-engine, front-wheel-drive
Gearbox:	Ford, five-speed manual
SUSPENSION	
Front:	independent by coil springs, MacPherson struts, anti-roll bar, and telescopic dampers
Rear:	independent, by trailing arms, torsion beam, coil springs/struts, telescopic dampers and anti-roll bar
STEERING	
Type:	rack-and-pinion, no power assistance
Lock-to-lock:	3.75 turns
BRAKES	
Front:	9.4in (240mm) ventilated discs
Rear:	8.0in (203mm) drums
System:	hydraulic, with vacuum servo assistance, and ABS
WHEELS & TYRES	
Wheels:	three-spoke cast alloys, 5.5J x 14in
Tyres:	185/55VR14in
BODY/CHASSIS	
Type:	pressed-steel monocoque, based on conventional Fiesta, in three-door hatchback style
Weight:	2,004lb (910kg)
PERFORMANCE	
Max speed:	129mph (208kph) approx
Acceleration:	0–60mph in 7.9sec
PRICE at LAUNCH	
£11,950 in Summer 1990	

Fiesta RS1800

1992–1995

Although the Fiesta RS1800 shared a model name with the legendary Escort of the 1970s, there were no technical connections. The RS1800 had a 1.8-litre Zetec engine, and was a direct replacement for the RS Turbo.

Launched in 1992, improved considerably in 1994, but never marketed or publicised with any conviction, the Fiesta RS1800 was always a rather unknown high-performance Ford. It was killed off for one compelling reason – that only 493 RS1800s had been registered in the UK between May 1992 and the end of 1995. One reason for this was that British insurance companies had come to hate the 'RS' badge.

In May 1992, Ford launched two, new 16-valve 1.8-litre twin-cam Zetec-engined versions of the Fiesta, one being badged RS1800. Clearly this was an evolution of the RS Turbo, with an engine transplant. Even so, nothing could make up for the turbocharger boost: the RS1800's engine was less powerful less torquey. Yet the Zetec engine was more flexible, civilised and quieter, with far lower exhaust emissions. It used the same B5 five-speed gearbox.

The RS1800 had a very similar chassis to the ousted RS Turbo, but somehow it all felt rather more civilised. Compared with the original rock-solid ride of the turbocharged car, it was a dramatic improvement, but there was still no power-assisted steering.

Compared with the RS Turbo, the RS1800 had no bonnet louvres (the engine bay didn't need extra cooling) and no green stripe around the car. The RS1800 looked positively anonymous although it had smart new five-spoke alloys which looked like those of the latest RS2000, but weren't the same.

Anti-lock braking (SCS) was optional (£481 at first), but this really wasn't a patch on the Mondeo/Scorpio type of ABS brakes, and I don't think it was worth the money. Even so, some dealers included SCS in their package offer, without raising the prices – make up your own mind when you've tried it. The reclining Recaros were still standard.

There was a package of structural improvements in 1994, including new anti-side-intrusion beams in the doors and a great deal of extra work on the shell. From this point the RS1800 had high-ratio power-assisted steering as standard (this made a pleasant car so much easier to drive around town), and by this time the air-bag-equipped steering wheel and the latest immobiliser kit had also been standardised.

With its 1.8-litre 16-valve engine it was more flexible where it mattered in traffic (low down), and the chassis was better-developed. Some say that the Zetec engine still isn't as smooth as a 16-valver should be, but in the RS1800 that didn't matter, and I was always tempted to use fourth gear up to more than 6,500rpm (nearly 100mph) just for the fun of it.

It was no less 'visible' than the RS Turbo (unless, that is, you could spot the RS Turbo's bonnet vents from 100 paces . . .), so there was really nothing to choose between the styling details of the two cars.

But since the RS1800 was about 100lb heavier than the RS Turbo (catalytic converters and various extra structural safety members all saw to that), had five bhp less, and a lot less peak torque (119lb ft vs 135lb ft) a slight drop in performance was actually inevitable.

I've driven both cars, hard and fast, gently and slowly, so my own view is clear. You might notice a difference on the track (or in the bar, where the

Fiesta RS1800s were easily recognised by the new-style five-spoke alloy wheels, which resembled those of the Escort RS2000. The engine was a 16-valve 1.8-litre Zetec.

boasting starts), but in normal traffic, on public roads, you rarely noticed – and because of the way you had to plan around the RS Turbo's turbo lag behaviour, as a lazy driver I would always choose the RS1800 as an everyday car.

In case of argument, let me quote comparative performance figures:

	Fiesta RS1800	Fiesta RS Turbo
Top speed (mph)	123	129
0–60mph (sec)	8.3	7.9
0–100mph (sec)	24.2	20.2
50–90mph through gears* (sec)	12.3	10.5
Standing ¼-mile (sec)	16.5	16.1
Typical fuel consumption (mpg)	25–30	22–30
Unladen weight (lb)	2,105	2,005

*This is the sort of figure that matters when you are overtaking a line of traffic – both cars are quick!

So why didn't you buy one, while it was in production? Now, of course, it's all too late, and you'll have to beat off your rivals in the classic market. Don't all push at once . . .

From 1992 to 1995 the two 'hot' little Fiestas were the 16-valve XR2i and RS1800 types. From this angle it was quite impossible to tell them apart.

Specification	
Fiesta RS1800	
ENGINE	
Type:	Ford Zetec
Capacity:	1,796cc
Bore/stroke:	80.6 x 88mm
Compression ratio:	10.0:1
Max power:	128bhp at 6,250rpm
Max torque:	119lb ft at 4,500rpm
Cylinders:	four, in-line, transversely mounted
Cylinder head:	cast aluminium
Block:	cast iron
Valve gear:	four valves per cylinder, twin belt-driven overhead camshafts, hydraulic bucket tappets
Fuelling:	Ford EEV IV engine management
Installation:	front-mounted, transverse
TRANSMISSION	
Type:	front-engine, front-wheel-drive
Gearbox:	Ford, five-speed manual
SUSPENSION	
Front:	independent by coil springs, MacPherson struts, anti-roll bar, and telescopic dampers
Rear:	independent, by trailing arms, torsion beam, coil springs/struts, telescopic dampers and anti-roll bar
STEERING	
Type:	rack-and-pinion (power-assisted from early 1994)
Lock-to-lock:	3.75 turns or (from early 1994) 2.8 turns with PAS
BRAKES	
Front:	9.4in (240mm) ventilated discs
Rear:	8.0in (203mm) drums
System:	hydraulic, with vacuum servo assistance, and optional ABS anti-lock
WHEELS & TYRES	
Wheels:	cast-alloy, 5.5J x 14in
Tyres:	185/55VR14in
BODY/CHASSIS	
Type:	pressed-steel monocoque, based on conventional Fiesta, in three-door hatchback style
Weight:	2,104lb (954kg)
PERFORMANCE	
Max speed:	127mph (204kph) approx
Acceleration:	0–60mph in 8.1sec
PRICE at LAUNCH	
£12,712 in May 1992	

Scorpio 24V

1991–1998

The Scorpio 24V was, spacious, capable – and very fast with its 195bhp Cosworth-evolved twin-cam V6 2.9-litre engine.

As someone who always loved to drive fast and compact sports saloons, I never thought I would enjoy using a big Scorpio. But in 1991 and 1992 I did just that – in a 24V hatchback. The secret, of course, is that Cosworth had finalised the engine, and that this was much faster than all the other push-rod engined Scorpios of the day.

Originally launched in 1985, the Granada/Scorpio line was a well-respected, although not outstanding five-door hatchback, let down by the use of rather anaemic pushrod overhead-valve engines. Not even the enlarging of those engines (to 2.4-litre and 2.9-litre, in 1987), or the addition of a four-door notchback style (in 1990) could solve the image problem. Yet the rest of the chassis (which, in some ways, was an enlarged derivative of the Sierra type, complete with independent rear suspension) was capable and appealing, for it included four-wheel-disc brakes and ABS anti-lock braking as standard.

In 1991, though, the arrival of the Cosworth-engined 24V model changed all that. Not only was the 2.9-litre engine considerably more powerful – it offered a totally civilised 195bhp instead of the pushrod-engined car's 150bhp – but this was a truly sophisticated new engine, with four-valves-per-cylinder and chain driven twin-overhead-cam cylinder heads per bank. It could run on unleaded fuel, and in this Scorpio installation it was always linked to Ford's latest four-speed automatic transmission.

The engine design itself had started life as a conversion of the Ford-Cologne V6, engineered by Brian Hart Ltd. After Cosworth absorbed the Hart business, the layout was finalised, and put into production at Cosworth's own engine factory at Wellingborough.

As re-engineered by Cosworth, the Ford-Cologne engine of the Scorpio 24V was fitted with twin-cam cylinder heads.

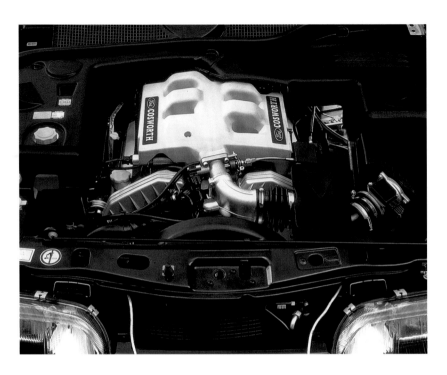

Complete with its leather interior, the driving compartment of the Scorpio 24V was the most luxurious fitted to any early-1990s Ford. Notice the 170mph speedometer!

Naturally, this engine/transmission combination was only applied to the most luxurious big-Ford trim/equipment package, and was allied to a revised suspension kit which included wider-rimmed alloy wheels, firmer suspension, a rear anti-roll bar, and a limited-slip differential. Not only that, but it was allied to Sierra Cosworth 4x4 front and rear disc brakes while ABS anti-lock braking was standard.

Ford never meant the 24V to be a sports saloon – although at 136mph it was a very fast executive model. This explains why the interior was laid out like a top-line model should be, with air conditioning, electrically adjustable front and rear seat adjustment, cruise control, a trip computer, a CD player, an alarm system, and the choice of cloth or leather trim, all as standard. As high-speed, no-fuss, day-in, day-out transport, it was a big success, and after the estate car version arrived for 1993 there seemed to be a derivative for everyone. It was not cheap, of course – hatch or saloon both cost £27,091 in 1991 – which made it the most expensive Ford in the range, but Cosworth soon found themselves using all the capacity of their 7,000/year factory to service customer demand.

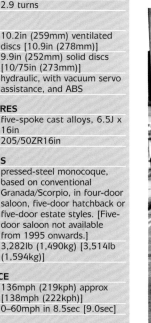

Scorpio 24V
[Changes made for 1995 and subsequent models in brackets.]

ENGINE

Type:	Ford-Cosworth FB
Capacity:	2,935cc
Bore/stroke:	93 x 72mm
Compression ratio:	9.7:1
Max power:	195bhp at 5,750rpm [204bhp at 6,000rpm]
Max torque:	203lb ft at 4,500rpm [207lb ft at 4,200rpm]
Cylinders:	six, in 60° vee, longitudinally mounted
Cylinder heads:	cast aluminium
Block:	cast iron
Valve gear:	four valves per cylinder, twin chain-driven overhead camshafts, hydraulic bucket tappets
Fuelling:	Ford EECIV engine management
Installation:	front-mounted, longitudinal

TRANSMISSION

Type:	front-engine, rear-wheel-drive
Gearbox:	Ford, four-speed automatic transmission.

SUSPENSION

Front:	independent by coil springs, MacPherson struts, anti-roll bar, and telescopic dampers
Rear:	independent, by semi-trailing arms, coil springs, telescopic dampers and anti-roll bar

STEERING

Type:	rack-and-pinion (power-assisted)
Lock-to-lock:	2.9 turns

BRAKES

Front:	10.2in (259mm) ventilated discs [10.9in (278mm)]
Rear:	9.9in (252mm) solid discs [10/75in (273mm)]
System:	hydraulic, with vacuum servo assistance, and ABS

WHEELS & TYRES

Wheels:	five-spoke cast alloys, 6.5J x 16in
Tyres:	205/50ZR16in

BODY/CHASSIS

Type:	pressed-steel monocoque, based on conventional Granada/Scorpio, in four-door saloon, five-door hatchback or five-door estate styles. [Five-door saloon not available from 1995 onwards.]
Weight:	3,282lb (1,490kg) [3,514lb (1,594kg)]

PERFORMANCE

Max speed:	136mph (219kph) approx [138mph (222kph)]
Acceleration:	0–60mph in 8.5sec [9.0sec]

PRICE WHEN NEW

£27,091 in 1991
£24,895 in 1995 for facelift model

I enjoyed my car in so many different ways – but most notably because it was totally invisible to the spoilsports (some in blue, some just obstructive drivers), and because at the end of a long journey I would honestly feel almost as fresh as when I started out. It wasn't very fuel efficient of course – mine averaged about 20mpg – but I didn't complain. The luxury-versus-performance trade-off was worth it.

Although the facelift model which followed in 1994/95 was mechanically improved, with better handling and electronic traction control, and with an all-round better package, it was not a success. Not even a more powerful engine, and a further improved interior specification could save it. The reason, quite simply, was that the styling was heartily disliked. How on earth could management ever have approved of a front and rear 'update' which destroyed the crisp lines of the original? How on earth could they have approved a front-end where the headlamps appeared to be so misshapen, and which more than one motoring writer described as looking like a mournful guppy fish? There wasn't a hatchback any more either, and I would have preferred one of those.

Even so, the 24-valve twin-cam outlived the push-rod V6 engine, which died in 1996. It was not used in any other Ford model.

From 1995, the last of the Scorpio 24Vs had this controversial front-end style, although with more than 200bhp on tap, most people enjoyed the performance anyway!

Escort RS2000 (FWD)

1991–1996

The Escort RS2000 model was reborn in 1991, in the shape of a front-wheel-drive car with a 16-valve, 150bhp, 2-litre engine.

Although a range of new-generation Escorts was launched in the autumn of 1990, initially there were no sporting derivatives, and no RS derivatives either. It was always made clear, however, that a third-generation RS2000 would go on sale before the end of 1991.

In the meantime, the mainstream range got off to a terrible start. It was not that these were bad cars, but apart from being larger and heavier than the 1980–1990 family, they were really not much better. The engineering was fine, but uninspired, and all-in-all they seemed to be rather lacking in character.

In the meantime, a new high-performance derivative of this front-wheel-drive 'Mk V' Escort was on the way, but at first it seemed to evolve without passion. Originally the SVE department was not involved, and neither did it carry an 'RS' badge. Prototypes tested at Boreham (by coincidence, on days when I happened to be there) were apparently not outstanding: in particular, the handling was distinctly stodgy.

Happily, a rethink then followed, SVE was hastily drafted in to add a bit of Fairy Dust, and some unheralded marketing genius decided to resurrect the title 'RS2000'. A decade after the RS2000 MkII dropped out of the charts, the model name was reborn. When the first TV commercials were made for the new car, no wonder the backing music was from one of the Rocky movies: *The Champ is Back*.

Although the formula for the new RS2000 was much like that of its predecessors – an up-market version of an existing range, but fitted with a bigger and better engine, top-of-the-range equipment, and an improved suspension/steering package – there was a new flavour to this machine.

This time round, the secret was in the engine. When the bonnet of the new-generation RS2000 was opened, the engine bay was dominated by a new red-painted cam cover, which topped a brand-new 16-valve twin-cam power unit. With 150bhp and a very broad torque curve, this 2.0-litre engine was a remarkable addition to Ford's long list of sporty products.

So, where had it come from? In 1989, Ford introduced a new iron-blocked range of engines, as a direct replacement for the long-running Pinto power units. This was

The front-wheel-drive RS2000 was only sold as a three-door hatchback, and could be identified by these five-spoke wheels – and the badge on the hatch itself.

a shorter, squatter and more rigid design, with an aluminium cylinder head. Importantly, it was so well packaged that it could be used either in-line, or mounted transversely.

The original engines, used in Sierras and Granada/Scorpios had an eight-valve chain-driven twin-cam layout, of which the fuel-injection version produced 125bhp.

An evolution, complete with a narrow-angle 16-valve twin-cam cylinder head, followed almost at once, and would make its debut in the RS2000. Long-planned, this was a completely 'in-house' Ford design, for Cosworth had not even been consulted. At first it was solely used by the RS2000: later, in further refined and slightly detuned form, at 2.3-litres and with twin balancer shafts mounted in the sump, it also found a home in Scorpios (to 1998) and Galaxy MPVs and was still in evidence in the early 2000s.

By comparison with RS-style engines of the 1970s and 1980s, this was a much more environmentally friendly engine, for it could meet all known, and threatened, exhaust emissions tests, there was an exhaust catalyst in the system, and its exhaust was quieter than before.

Not only was it a remarkably successful road-car engine, but 'F2' rally experience showed that it could be power tuned to produce at least

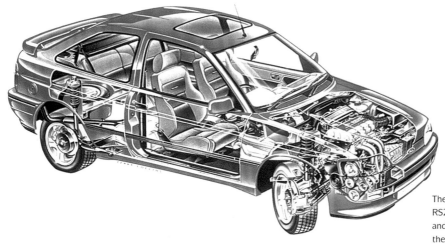

The front-wheel-drive Escort RS2000 was a more complex, and more capable, car than the early 1970s types.

The 1991-type Escort RS2000 featured this type of instrument layout – plus Recaro front seats, of course.

The third nose style to appear on the front-wheel-drive Escort RS2000 was introduced in 1995, and matched to new-style wheels and a different rear spoiler.

282bhp in normally aspirated form: that was more than the Cosworth BDG engines had ever achieved . . .

In the RS2000, it was linked to the brand-new MTX75 five-speed manual transmission, which Ford had evolved for large-scale use in its 1990s range of Mondeos. By comparison with the 'B5' of the earlier front-wheel-drive RS Turbos, this was a more robust design, with a more satisfactory change.

The rest of the chassis, as expected, was merely an up-grade of that already specified for the mainstream Escorts, although it featured up-rated suspensions settings and more direct steering with power assistance. This was the first time that PAS had been standard on a newly launched RS Escort and the use of four-wheel disc brakes was a novelty, as were the newly styled five-spoke alloy wheels.

The three-door body style had been derived from that of other Escorts, with twin 'power bulges' in the bonnet (one real, to clear the I4 engine, the other a visual balancing feature), a deep front spoiler, and a simple hatchback lid rear spoiler. A tilt-and-slide sunroof was also standard equipment, and there were neat wheelarch flares at front and rear.

The interior was well-equipped, with more features than other front-drive Escorts, the ensemble being set off by a pair of those excellent tilt/recline Recaro front seats that no other rival manufacturer has ever managed to beat,

It was, in other words, a genuine successor to earlier-generation RS2000s – yet it did not sell well. At first sight, this was an insoluble puzzle, for it was fast (more than 130mph, flat out), capable, well-equipped, comfortable and (as usual with a series-production Ford car) easy to service and maintain. Was the lack-lustre image of other Escorts to blame?

It was not this, as looking back, it seems that there were two major problems. One was that all such cars were expensive to insure in the early 1990s, but the other was that this new-type RS2000 was seen as expensive to buy.

The insurance problem was serious. At the time the British insurance industry was reacting badly to two trends – one was the accident risk and record of the hatchback market sector in general, and the other was that they had somehow taken against Performance Fords in particular. According to their spokesmen, it was OK to own an equivalent Peugeot or VW 'hot hatch', but not a Ford. And for why? This was never explained.

Since the last of the Escort RS Turbos had sold for only £13,985, the RS2000's original selling price of £15,995, was undoubtedly an obstacle, although if UK cost inflation was taken into account (and the new car's capabilities) it was not excessive. Not that this helped, for although costs then rose, they were reduced sharply in 1993, then rose again, and were reduced yet again in 1995, but this was always a sticking point.

Technically, there were two

important sets of improvements. Along with every other car in this Escort range, in October 1992 the RS2000 was given a new front-end style, complete with a new 'smiley face' oval front grille (and a reshaped bonnet which eliminated the 'power bulges'), plus modified headlamps. At the rear there was a different-shaped hatchback with a large glass area, a new spoiler and bigger tail lamps, while plastic sill extensions now featured under the doors. Hidden away was a stiffened-up shell structure.

Finally, in early 1995, came another package of improvements. The Escort was now given yet another type of nose – this time with a 'slitty-mouth' grille, and a third-style of headlamp, yet more body stiffening, and a revised instrument package that definitely leaned towards that of the charismatic Escort RS Cosworth. The handling had been further improved and – most importantly – the price actually fell – to £14,605.

There was no question that this was the best of all the 1990s-generation RS2000s, but since Ford shortly announced that it would be dropping the car at the end of 1996, it never really had time to make its mark. The cull, it was claimed, was due to the cost of meeting new and arduous exhaust emission and noise regulations, but no-one was fooled: for the time being, it seemed, Ford had fallen out of love with the 'RS' concept.

From 1993/94, of course, there was also a four-wheel-drive version of this much under-estimated car, which had so many technical novelties that it deserves analysis on its own.

The last of the Escort RS2000s was built in 1995 and 1996, still with 150bhp, and now with a choice of front or four-wheel-drive.

Specification	
Escort RS2000 (FWD)	
ENGINE	
Type:	Ford-UK (Dagenham-built)
Capacity:	1,998cc
Bore/stroke:	86 x 86mm
Compression ratio:	10.3:1
Max power:	150bhp at 6,000rpm
Max torque:	140lb ft at 4,500rpm
Cylinders:	four, in line, transversely mounted
Cylinder head:	cast aluminium
Block:	cast iron
Valve gear:	four valves per cylinder, chain-driven twin overhead camshafts, bucket tappets
Fuelling:	Ford EECIV engine management
Installation:	front-mounted, transverse, driving front wheels
TRANSMISSION	
Type:	front-engine, front-wheel-drive
Gearbox:	five-speed manual
SUSPENSION	
Front:	independent by coil springs, MacPherson struts, anti-roll bar and telescopic dampers
Rear:	independent, by coil springs, trailing arms, twist beam, anti-roll bar and telescopic dampers
STEERING	
Type:	rack-and-pinion (power-assisted)
Lock-to-lock:	2.9 turns
BRAKES	
Front:	10.2in (260mm) ventilated discs
Rear:	10.6in (270mm) discs
System:	hydraulic, with vacuum servo assistance and ABS
WHEELS & TYRES	
Wheels:	five-spoke cast alloys, 6.0J x 15in
Tyres:	195/50VR15in
BODY/CHASSIS	
Type:	pressed-steel monocoque, based on conventional Escort, in three-door hatchback style
Weight:	2,477lb (1,125kg)
PERFORMANCE	
Max speed:	131mph (211kph) approx
Acceleration:	0–60mph in 8.3sec
PRICE at LAUNCH	
£15,995	

Escort RS2000 4x4

1993–1996

Deliveries of the Escort RS2000 4x4 began in 1994. Visually, the only difference from the front-wheel-drive car was that 4x4 badges were fitted to the flanks.

The four-wheel-drive Escort RS2000 4x4 was, and remains, one of Ford's least-known hot hatches. Although forecast in 1991 and officially previewed in 1993, it did not actually go on sale until mid-1994. Thereafter it led a shadowy existence, rarely promoted, rarely found in stock at a Ford showroom, and was finally discontinued at the end of 1996.

Yet here was an extremely capable performance Ford, which did everything that an Escort RS Cosworth ever could, except not go quite as fast. It was one of several model derivatives built around the same four-wheel-installation (the Mondeo was another) which died of neglect, and lack of promotion.

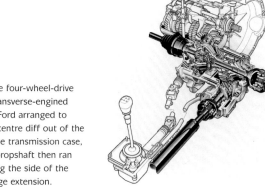

To provide four-wheel-drive on the transverse-engined Escorts, Ford arranged to 'grow' a centre diff out of the side of the transmission case, and the propshaft then ran back along the side of the gearchange extension.

That the RS2000 4x4 had to wait for its launch until 1993/94 became clear when the all-new Mondeo was finally introduced. There was also to be a Mondeo 4x4, which would use the same basic gearbox, 4x4 centre differential and transfer box, rear differential and rear suspension type. Ford also admit, by the way, that the Mondeo 4x4 was another unknown warrior, for these were only built in 1995 and 1996, and were then withdrawn without fuss! At one time Ford fans were also promised a four-wheel-drive derivative of the new-generation XR3i. Although cutaway drawings of this installation exist in Ford's photographic archive to this day, such a car was never put on to the market. So, how could Audi make so much of their four-wheel-drive 'quattro' system, where Ford failed? We were never told.

In the Escort RS2000 4x4, the basic front-mounted, transversely positioned, 16-valve engine and MTX75 main gearbox of the front-wheel-drive car were retained. A torque-splitting centre differential was grafted alongside that transmission, and a propeller shaft then led back to the rear differential, which was mounted to the body shell in an aluminium sub-frame. A new type of independent rear suspension was needed to accommodate the drive shafts, and a new under-seat petrol tank was needed to give clearance for the propshaft.

Except for the fitment of small '4x4' badges on the front wings, close to the front door panel joints, there was no external evidence of all this engineering change, which may be one reason why customers were reluctant to pay an extra £1,025 – £16,675 against £15,650 in mid-1994.

In many ways the RS2000 4x4 was always an unknown car, with unknown habits. Like the Escort RS Cosworth, but with an entirely different mechanical installation, the torque split was arranged to send 60 per cent of the torque to the rear wheels leaving only 40 per cent for the front. When this was weighed against the rather front-heavy weight distribution, the result was a nicely balanced car which handled as well as any Escort had ever done.

The result was a fast, capable and well-balanced Escort 4x4 which was at once simpler and rather cheaper to own than the Escort RS Cosworth. Because it was rather heavier than the front-wheel-drive car – by approximately 150lb – and there were unavoidable powertrain losses in the extra transmission, the 4x4 was slightly slower than the front-wheel-drive variety – but only just. Top speed was marginally down – from 131mph to 128mph – while it took 9.4sec to accelerate to 60mph instead of 8.3sec, but when balanced against the utterly secure feel of four-wheel-drive handling this was absolutely no loss.

To quote one *Autocar* tester: 'Enter a corner slightly too fast in the 4x4 and squeezing on the power in mid-bend merely tightens your chosen cornering line. Do the same in the front-wheel-drive car and you would have to come off the power to adjust your cornering line.

Quite simply, the RS2000 4x4 is more efficient than its front-drive sibling . . .' Which is a perfect way to sum up this appealing package.

Specification	
Escort RS2000 4x4	
ENGINE	
Type:	Ford-UK I4
Capacity:	1,998cc
Bore/stroke:	86 x 86mm
Compression ratio:	10.3:1
Max power:	150bhp at 6,000rpm
Max torque:	140lb ft at 4,500rpm
Cylinders:	four, in line, transversely mounted
Cylinder head:	cast aluminium
Block:	cast iron
Valve gear:	four valves per cylinder, chain-driven twin overhead camshafts, bucket tappets
Fuelling:	Ford EECIV engine management
Installation:	front-mounted, transverse, driving all four wheels
TRANSMISSION	
Type:	front-engine, four-wheel-drive
Gearbox:	five-speed manual
SUSPENSION	
Front:	independent by coil springs, MacPherson struts, anti-roll bar and telescopic dampers
Rear:	independent, by coil springs, MacPherson struts, anti-roll bar and telescopic dampers
STEERING	
Type:	rack-and-pinion (power-assisted)
Lock-to-lock:	2.9 turns
BRAKES	
Front:	10.2in (260mm) ventilated discs
Rear:	10.6in (270mm) discs
System:	hydraulic, with vacuum servo assistance and ABS
WHEELS & TYRES	
Wheels:	five-spoke cast alloys, 6.0J x 15in
Tyres:	195/50VR15in
BODY/CHASSIS	
Type:	pressed-steel monocoque, based on conventional Escort, in three-door hatchback style
Weight:	2,756lb (1,250kg)
PERFORMANCE	
Max speed:	128mph (206kph) approx
Acceleration:	0–60mph in 9.4sec
PRICE at LAUNCH	
£16,675	

Compared with the front-drive car, the RS2000 4x4 had a totally different type of rear suspension, and of course a propeller shaft and rear differential.

Escort XR3i (16-valve)

1992–1994

The 1990s-generation of XR3i went on sale in 1992, with the original 'MkV' style, but this would change within the year.

Except that the 1992 XR3i had plain-spoked alloy wheels, and a different tailgate badge, it was almost impossible to pick it from the current RS2000.

Here's an unanswerable question? Why was the 1980s-style XR3i such a towering success, and the 1990s-style 'Mk V' model a commercial failure? How could hundreds of thousands be sold in the 1980s, but so few in the 1992/94 period? The sad answer is – the British insurance industry, and changing fashions.

In spite of an excellent 16-valve twin-cam engine, the final XR3i was a lot heavier than before, so it was really no faster, no more economical, and certainly no more capable, than its ancestors of ten years previously.

Two years after the old-style XR3i disappeared, the new XR3i hatchback arrived in February 1992. It shared the RS2000's rear spoiler, the same basic front style (but there were no bonnet bulges), and the alloy wheels were similar, but without the radial slots. Not only was there a three-door hatchback, but a smart two-door Cabriolet too – this type of Escort being assembled by Karmann at Osnabruck, in Germany.

There was a new Zetec engine, the robust MTX-75 gearbox, power-assisted steering, and the RS2000 suspension package. With four-wheel disc brakes, and a choice of engines, this was obviously a very serious attempt to produce a 1990s-style XR3i.

Ford originally intended all XR3is

to have 130bhp engines, but a 105bhp version was added before sales began. Insurance pressure hit the 130bhp model, this being dropped by 1993, only a year after it had been launched.

Although everyone gave the XR3i a friendly reception – even the most cynical journalists, those recently weaned on Peugeot 205GTis and Renault Clio 16Vs, described the XR3i as a car which Ford engineers could be proud of – the new car sold very slowly.

This was so unfortunate. I have already sketched out the reasons, and there's no doubt that this was a fine car produced at the wrong time. It wasn't as fast as the RS2000, it didn't really look any different from the other Escorts – yet it had a great chassis, and was as fast as any other modern-breed of European hatchback, all of which were encumbered by catalytic converters, crash-protection pressings, and loads of sound-deadening equipment.

Only eight months after it went on sale, the XR3i received the same structural and style up-date as every other front-wheel-drive Escort. Ford, in fact, claimed that 792 parts were new. The most obvious change was that there was a front-end facelift which gave the car a more obvious front grille opening (some people call it the 'nostril nose', others the 'smiling face'). The tailgate glass area was enlarged by 11 per cent, there were new tail lamps, new rear spoilers and modified bumpers on XR3is, plus a stiffened body shell, and side-impact protection door beams.

All in all, this made the cars better – but heavier. There was still no sign of a steering wheel air bag at that stage, but this became available a year later, from the autumn of 1993. All this meant a shake-up in prices (Ford prices yo-yo'd at this period, to milk every possible sale out of recession-hit British motorists). The late 1992 105bhp model was priced at £12,578 – and the 130bhp version was virtually non-existent!

This well-thought-out package did nothing for the XR3i, which carried on as the forgotten car in the Escort range. By the end of 1993, with the insurance companies piling on the pressure (I once asked for proof of the Escort's so-called poor record, but was told that it was 'not available' – make up your own minds . . .), Ford decided to kill off the famous old badge, and when the Escort Si was launched in the spring of 1994 the XR3i breathed its last.

It was a great shame. I'm willing to bet that their rarity value will make them prized cars among club members in future years. Do you want to take bets?

As with the mid-1980s variety of the XR3i, in the 1990s there was a cabriolet version of this model.

Specification	
Escort XR3i	
(Details of optional 130bhp version in brackets.)	
ENGINE	
Type:	Ford Zetec
Capacity:	1,796cc
Bore/stroke:	80.6 x 88mm
Compression ratio:	10.0:1
Max power:	105bhp at 5,500rpm [130bhp at 6,250rpm]
Max torque:	113lb ft at 4,000rpm [119lb ft at 4,500rpm]
Cylinders:	four, in-line, transversely mounted
Cylinder head:	cast aluminium
Block:	cast iron
Valve gear:	four valves per cylinder, twin belt-driven overhead camshafts, bucket tappets
Fuelling:	Ford EECIV engine management system
Installation:	front-mounted, transverse
TRANSMISSION	
Type:	front-engine, front-wheel-drive
Gearbox:	Ford MTX-75, five-speed manual
SUSPENSION	
Front:	independent by coil springs, MacPherson struts, anti-roll bar, and telescopic dampers
Rear:	independent, by trailing arms, torsion beam, coil springs, telescopic dampers and anti-roll bar.
STEERING	
Type:	rack-and-pinion (power-assisted)
Lock-to-lock:	3.0 turns
BRAKES	
Front:	10.2in (260mm) ventilated discs
Rear:	10.6in (270mm) solid discs
System:	hydraulic, with vacuum servo assistance – optional ABS
WHEELS & TYRES	
Wheels:	cast alloys (extra cost on 105bhp version), 6.0J x 14in
Tyres:	185/60HR14in
BODY/CHASSIS	
Type:	pressed-steel monocoque, based on MkV Escort, in three-door hatchback or cabriolet style
Weight:	2,492lb (1,130kg)
PERFORMANCE	
(105bhp version)	
Max speed:	118mph approx
Acceleration:	0–60mph in 9.9sec
PRICE at LAUNCH	
(105bhp version) £14,245 in February 1992	
(130bhp version) £14,995 in February 1992	
Alloy wheels (on 105bhp version) £314	

Escort RS Cosworth

1992–1996

The majority of Escort RS Cosworths were fitted with the high rear spoiler. This was the Acropolis limited edition.

The Escort RS Cosworth was a flamboyantly styled car, with its high rear spoiler and those aggressive-looking five-spoke wheels.

Even though it is 16 years since John Wheeler had the bright idea, and 14 years since the world had its first look at a prototype, the Escort RS Cosworth is still a head turner.

Why did Ford drop it from production when they did? There were official reasons, and real reasons. Officially, there was talk about new or pending EC legislation, emission rules, and details you and I don't want to understand. Actually, the Escort RS Cosworth had just about stopped selling, and Ford could see no reason why they should continue supporting expensive facilities at Karmann which were only working for one day a week.

It's sad, but it was true. There was only ever a limited market for a car like this one, and by the end of 1995 it had filled up. Price, running costs, insurance companies' attitudes, and dealer indifference all had much to do with this. Incidentally, although insurance companies hated the Escort RS Cosworth, thieves hated it even more, for the Vecta immobiliser system seemed to be foolproof: I had experience of this, for low-life once tried to take away my car – and failed . . .

That showroom record is nothing new, by the way – the same applied to the original Sierra RS Cosworth, to the Escort RS1600i, and to the Escort RS1600 in the 1970s. What was great as a basic competition car was not always the easiest road car to own.

Origins

The Big Idea was hatched by Boreham's chief engineer, John Wheeler, in 1988, but the first true prototype wasn't even built until 1990. By that time Wheeler was convinced that all future World Championship-winning rally cars needed four-wheel-drive – and that he knew just how to design one.

Designing a competitive car was going to be demanding, but forcing it through Ford's management labyrinths was going to be very difficult indeed. That's why Wheeler and planner Mike Moreton took so long to urge the Escort RS Cosworth into the showroom.

There were three obvious constraints – 5,000 identical four-seater cars would have to be built to gain homologation, the new car would have to be based on a lot of existing Ford hardware – and the sales force would have to be happy with what they were offered.

In 'works' form it would have to be able to beat everybody, on snow, gravel, tarmac, and in searing heat. In basic form, too, it had to be a practical road car – in 1988/89 Ford was not about to approve the production of 5,000 identical production cars if these could not be sold, and not make a profit.

According to every technical analysis, an in-line engine, with a gearbox behind it, offered more, not only in terms of accessibility, but to make the weight distribution as near to ideal as possible. For such a new car, developed versions of the Sierra Cosworth 4x4 hardware looked to be ideal. Was it coincidence, or was it the sort of divine fortune that gifted designers always need, that the Sierra running gear fitted so well, and allowed development time to be telescoped dramatically?

But doesn't it take a long time to turn a Good Idea into a production car? Although the Escort RS Cosworth rally car was previewed in September 1990, when Mia Bardolet won the Spanish Talavera Rally on its World debut, production cars did not go on sale until May 1992.

In any case, this wasn't a straight engine/transplant project. The finalised Escort RS Cosworth used a much-modified, shortened Sierra Cosworth 4x4 platform and running gear, the basics of a current Escort three-door shell – and a whole lot more! Special Vehicle Engineering developed a hugely effective aerodynamic package ('I knew we needed a rear wing as big as that,' Wheeler recalls,' but I wasn't sure management would "buy" it at first . . .'), chose the 16in road wheels and produced a remarkably successful ride and handling package. Along the way, they also oversaw the

If you asked nicely, it was possible to have an Escort RS Cosworth without the high rear spoiler. The proportion of such sales was limited.

121

From 1992, original-specification Escort RS Cosworths had YB engines with blue-painted cylinder heads. This was a very neat engine bay installation.

The Escort RS Cosworth's fascia panel was very striking, and featured back-lit white instrument dials.

development of a more powerful version of the famous engine, and chose those unique instruments.

During this period there was another stroke of luck, when FISA reduced the production numbers for Group A homologation from 5,000 to a mere 2,500 cars. The big breakthrough, though, came when Karmann of Germany got the job of tooling the new structure, and manufacturing the production cars. Preparations were completed in record time, using old Merkur XR4Ti facilities, and once the team began building road cars early in 1992 the production rate built up rapidly.

Production cars

Karmann built the first few cars early in 1992, but series production did not start until the spring of that year. The road car's specification, in any case, had already been publicised by that time, and customers were already waiting to take delivery.

Motoring magazines – *Fast Ford* being at the very head of the queue – first got their hands on the launch cars in March 1992, when Ford revealed two distinctly different specifications – the fully equipped 'Luxury' version for £23,495, and the rather stripped-out 'Road Sport' type for £21,380.

Mechanically, there was no difference between the two types – both of which had the 227bhp/2-litre turbocharged YBT engine, the four-wheel-drive, the ABS braking, the new-style white-faced instruments, the 8 x 16in alloy wheels, and the sensational handling/traction balance.

'Road Luxury' types, however, were completely kitted out for fast road use, complete with sunroof, electric window lifts, top-line stereo/cassette, opening rearquarter windows, heated screen and mirrors and extra driving lamps: 'Road Sport' types were much cheaper, and intended for stripping out for conversion into motorsport cars, lacked all those items. Both types, though, were fitted with a Vecta engine immobiliser as standard.

'Sport' types were only supplied in Diamond White (once again, it was thought that private owners could then build up a sponsor's motorsport scheme on that basis), while 'Luxury' models came in a full range of colours, including the unique Mallard Green which was introduced on that model.

Incidentally, if you think that the Escort RS Cosworth used mostly Sierra Cosworth 4x4 running gear under the skin, think again. It might have started out like that, but SVE's development produced many special differences. The engine, for instance, had a different (larger) turbo, springs and dampers had different settings, there was a complex and different type of intercooler, while new types of suspension bushes were evolved to suit the latest car's chassis.

New-technology tyres – Pirelli P-Zeros of 245/45-16in size – had never been seen on earlier Fords, and neither had the wheels. Long-term users like myself soon found that the penalty of ultimate grip from the P-Zeros was rapid wear. If you got much more than 10,000 miles out of a set, then you weren't trying very hard . . .

A four-year life

In 1992, there was a great rush of activity at Karmann, to make sure that more than 2,500 cars were made to achieve homologation, with UK deliveries starting during the spring of the year. To help Ford Motorsport achieve its best possible homologation, a rudimentary intercooler water-injection system was supplied, provided loose, in the boot! Even when fitted, that didn't work, by the way – not until the appropriate motorsport ECU was installed as well.

Way back in 1992, Ford suggested that the original package – big turbo, Weber-Marelli injection, whaletail aerodynamics and a very basic 'Standard' specification – might be changed for 1993, but in the event none of these changes was made until June 1994. By mid-1993 an electric sun-roof had taken over from the manual variety for 'Road Luxury' versions, and the expected airbag-equipped steering wheel followed early in 1994. By this time, if you asked nicely, it was possible to take delivery without the big rear spoiler (which was allied to the front splitter): in the UK, at least, few did this.

Sales had already dropped off considerably by the end of 1993, and because the appropriate motorsport specification had been achieved, a small-turbo version was standardised. This, the 'MkII' version, went on sale in May 1994, had a more flexible version of the engine, complete with a smaller (T25) turbocharger, Ford EEC 1V electronics, revised throttle body, exhaust manifold, new HT coil arrangements, new-style camshaft covers and more hidden details. As before, you could delete the big rear spoiler if you wanted to be anonymous.

According to official figures, the latest engine was marginally less powerful than before (224bhp vs 227bhp), but mid-range engine response was much better than before. On the original car, nothing much happened below 3,000rpm, after which the turbo woke up, and was singing strongly from 4,000rpm. On the latest car, there was sturdy turbo boost from 2,500rpm upwards – and the temporary overboost which kicked on with full throttle lasted a few seconds longer than before.

Unhappily, it didn't help Escort RS Cosworth sales, which were at a very low level in later years. Ford tells us that Karmann built a total of about 7,000 cars from 1992 to January 1996, of which about 2,000 were originally sold in the UK.

A great day-to-day car

I was very lucky. I used two Escort RS Cosworths as my normal, day-to-day, business cars throughout 1994 and 1995. Like BBC *Top Gear's* Jeremy Clarkson, once smitten, I never recovered, for I loved them like my own children. Although they were no faster than my previous Sierra Cosworth 4x4s, they were smaller, felt smaller, were a lot more nimble, and had the most astonishingly pliable ride, and inch-accurate steering.

Both my cars had the original large-turbo specification, so I soon learned to keep the engine revs singing away about 3,500rpm. With the first cars, in fact, if you drove them with low revs – 'old man' fashion – they actually felt quite sluggish, and could be humiliated around town. There were times when my other car – a front-drive RS2000 – felt more snappy.

With both types of Escort Cosworth, though, once you woke up and concentrated, using the gear lever to keep the revs of that 16-valve YBT engine in the right place (around 4,400rpm felt great!) there was very little which could keep up on an ordinary main road.

Specification

Escort RS Cosworth
Main spec for original model, (mid-1994 model onwards, details in brackets).

ENGINE

Type:	Ford-Cosworth YB
Capacity:	1,993cc
Bore/stroke:	90.82 x 76.95mm
Compression ratio (nominal):	8.0:1
Max power:	227bhp at 6,250rpm [224bhp at 5,750rpm]
Max torque:	224lb ft at 3,500rpm [220lb ft at 2,500rpm]
Specific output:	114bhp per litre [112bhp per litre]
Power/weight ratio:	181bhp/tonne [174bhp/tonne]
Cylinders:	four, in-line, longitudinally mounted
Cylinder head:	cast aluminium
Block:	cast iron
Valve gear:	four valves per cylinder, twin belt-driven overhead camshafts, hydraulic bucket tappets
Fuel and ignition:	Weber-Marelli fuel injection with Garrett TO3/TOI4B turbocharger, and intercooling (Ford EECIV, with T25)
Installation:	front-mounted, longitudinal

TRANSMISSION

Type:	front-engine, four-wheel-drive, with 34%/66% front/rear torque split
Gearbox:	Ford MT75, five-speed manual

SUSPENSION

Front:	independent by coil springs, MacPherson struts, anti-roll bar, and telescopic dampers
Rear:	independent, by semi-trailing arms, coil springs, telescopic dampers and anti-roll bar.

STEERING

Type:	rack-and-pinion (power-assisted)
Lock-to-lock:	2.45 turns

BRAKES

Front:	10.9in (278mm) ventilated discs
Rear:	10.8in (273mm) solid discs
System:	hydraulic, with vacuum servo assistance, and Teves ABS anti-lock.

WHEELS & TYRES

Wheels:	five-spoke cast alloys, 8.0J x 16in
Tyres:	225/45ZR16in

BODY/CHASSIS

Type:	pressed-steel monocoque, based on Sierra Cosworth 4x4 floor pan, in three-door hatchback style, with high rear spoiler
Weight:	2,811lb (1,275kg) [2,882lb (1307kg)]

PERFORMANCE

Max speed:	137mph (220kph) approx
Acceleration:	0–60mph in 6.2sec [6.3sec]

PRICE at LAUNCH
Road Standard £21,380 in May 1992 (£22,535 for small-turbo car in June 1994)
Road Luxury £23,495 in May 1992 (£25,825 for small-turbo car in June 1994)

Escort World Rally Car

1997–1998

Compared with the Escort RS Cosworth, the World Rally Car had a vast front lower moulding, which hid bigger radiator and intercooler elements.

For the Escort WRC, Boreham developed a new type of rear spoiler, which not only complied with new regulations, but provided more down-force at higher speeds.

Maybe the four-wheel-drive Escort World Rally Car doesn't really count as a road car, but they were used on public roads, and if you were rich enough you could have persuaded M-Sport to sell one to you. This, in fact, was the last of the front-line rally cars to carry the famous 'Escort' badge. Used in 1997 and 1998 by the 'works' team (which was run by the M-Sport organisation), such cars were eventually provided to private owners, either as used machines, or as kits to convert Escort RS Cosworths.

To meet the regulations, the Escort WRC was really an Escort RS Cosworth with most of the rallying shortcomings eliminated. Because this was an 'interim' car intended to keep Ford in the sport, regulations requiring the car from which it was derived to be made at 25,000 cars/year, were waived.

The turbocharged YB engine was modified, with an IHI turbocharger, a different exhaust manifold and eight (instead of four) fuel injectors. Behind the new nose, there were relocated water radiator and intercooler blocks. The rear suspension was new – being a MacPherson strut conversion, eliminating the semi-trailing arm layout which had served the Escort RS Cosworth so long.

To match this there was a modified front end, which channelled much more cold air into the radiators and the brakes, a new front bumper profile, and a new-type single-plane rear spoiler.

Twenty such cars were built up rapidly in 1996 and 1997, with more cars following in 1998. In the years which followed, more and more Escort RS Cosworths were converted to WRC standard with the use of mechanical and aerodynamic kits.

As a rally car this was a very successful, although interim model, for it met a new set of regulations, and bridged an otherwise yawning gap between the end of the Escort RS Cosworth, and the fact that a new Focus rally car could not be ready until 1999. Visually, of course, it looked rather different from the RS Cosworth – the use of a single-plane rear spoiler made sure of that.

Functionally, it was an improvement over the Escort RS Cosworth because it had a more precisely controlled rear suspension geometry – the camber change which was in-built to the Sierra-type semi-trailing arm layout had always been a problem – and the use of the smaller, higher-revving, Japanese IHI turbocharger (plus the ear-drum bursting anti-lag fuel injection add-ons) meant that there was very little turbo lag.

As a rally car, the WRC was effective but not earth-shattering – in 1997 it notched up two victories and four second places in World Championship events, all by Carlos Sainz, while in 1998 there were three third places, all for Juha Kankkunen.

No, of course, this could never be a satisfactory road car, for the interior was completely gutted, there was a massive roll cage, there were only two hard seats, and of course the ride and noise levels were shattering. Amazingly, though, Ford's press department built up a 'replica' which was almost as fast, and much more civilised. This gave a lot of fun to a few selected journalists, magazines and national newspapers, and in the high street its posing value was supreme.

Even in their old age, although it isn't likely that any of these cars will ever be turned into a fully trimmed and furnished road-going WRCs, the production figures should be made known. If we include the original development cars built at Boreham, in 1997 no fewer than 29 WRCs were produced at M-Sport, and a further 15 were built in 1998. Adding in all the later kit-built cars means that at least 70, and maybe even up to 100, different cars were eventually produced.

One important new World Rally Car regulation, by the way, was that if a body shell had to be written off after a crash, then the identity had to go with it. Unless someone is really up to no good, therefore, there should be no chance of any extra machines now being produced.

This is what the Escort WRC was really for – winning World rallies. Left to right: Luis Moya, Malcolm Wilson and Carlos Sainz, the team having just won the 1997 Acropolis Rally.

Specification	
Escort World Rally Car	
ENGINE	
Type:	Ford-Cosworth YB
Capacity:	1,993cc
Bore/stroke:	90.82 x 76.95mm
Compression ratio (nominal):	9.6:1
Max power:	300bhp at 5,500rpm
Max torque:	434lb ft at 4,000rpm
Cylinders:	four, in-line, longitudinally mounted
Cylinder head:	cast aluminium
Block:	cast iron
Valve gear:	four valves per cylinder, twin cogged-belt driven overhead camshafts, bucket tappets
Fuelling:	Ford F8 engine management system, IHI turbocharger, with air/air intercooler
Installation:	front-mounted, longitudinal
TRANSMISSION	
Type:	front-engine, four-wheel-drive, three differentials
Gearbox:	Ford/M-Sport six-speed sequential manual
SUSPENSION	
Front:	independent by coil springs, MacPherson struts, anti-roll bar, and telescopic dampers
Rear:	independent, by coil springs, MacPherson struts, telescopic dampers and anti-roll bar
STEERING	
Type:	rack-and-pinion (power-assisted)
Lock-to-lock:	2.4 turns
BRAKES	
Front:	(tarmac) 14.9in (378mm), (gravel) 12.4in (315mm) ventilated discs
Rear:	(tarmac) 12.3in (313mm), (gravel) 12.4in (315mm) ventilated discs
System:	hydraulic, with vacuum servo assistance, no ABS
WHEELS & TYRES	
Wheels:	cast alloys – 15in to 18in, depending on application
BODY/CHASSIS	
Type:	pressed-steel monocoque, based on Escort RS Cosworth shell, in three-door hatchback style, with different aerodynamic features
Weight:	2,712lb (1,230kg)
PERFORMANCE	
Never accurately measured	
PRICE at LAUNCH	
Subject to specification and spares package	

Mondeo ST24

1996–1999

The ST24 was the first of the truly high-spec Mondeos, combining V6 power with a top-of-the-line equipment package, firmer suspension and modified styling.

This was the fascia of the Mondeo ST24, well set off by the Recaro front seats.

When Ford introduced the new front-wheel-drive Mondeo in 1993, there was no obvious intention to develop any truly 'Performance Fords' from the new layout. On the other hand, one of the engine options was an all-new 60° twin-overhead-camshaft V6 (from Ford-USA), and on another a handful of very special Mondeo race cars began winning Supertouring car races all round the world . . .

Since the V6 engine was known to have much development and 'stretch' already built in (the same basic power unit, with new cylinder heads and many other novel details, would eventually be taken up by Jaguar for its X-type saloon) all the ingredients were present. In the beginning, though, Ford preferred to leave its engine alone, rated at 168bhp, and the Mondeo sold on its merits as an all-round family car.

A change in marketing strategy then followed. When the mid-life facelift of the Mondeo came on stream in Autumn 1996 (this was mainly concerned with a different front and rear style, plus thorough redevelopment of many chassis details), a new derivative of the V6 engined car, titled Mondeo ST24, was put on sale. 'ST' presumably stood for 'Specially Tuned', and the '24' obviously referred to the use of the 24-valve V6 engine.

Ford, however, had deliberately restrained itself in the power stakes, for there was no change to the 168bhp/2,544cc V6 engine. This, in fact, was the same engine as fitted to original-style Mondeos (the writer ran one of these cars for two years and more than 40,000 miles in the mid-1990s), and was already known to be rock-solid, dead-reliable, and high-revving. At this stage, Ford was automatically limiting these capabilities by fitting hydraulic pivots to the fingers which were interspersed between the camshafts and the valve stems.

The Mondeo's style, chassis and equipment merits were already well-known. The rounded monocoque body shell covered a transverse-engined front-wheel-drive chassis in which several different petrol and diesel four-cylinder engines were topped off by the Ford-USA V6. All petrol engines had catalytic converters in the exhaust system. Not only was there independent suspension at front and rear, but there were disc brakes all round, ABS braking as standard, multiple airbags, and an impressive line up of safety features in the structure itself. V6 engined cars also had traction control as standard equipment.

For the ST24 model package, both four-door notchback or five-door hatchback types were on offer, although it was the saloon which came on stream first, in February 1997. The ST24, therefore, combined the normal package, but with the firmed up Si-type specification, air conditioning and all the toys, and it had its own stiffened chassis/suspension settings.

The main, and obvious changes, though, were visual, for the ST24 five-door (hatchback) had a more bulbous and altogether more sexy front and rear bumpers, side skirts, a mesh front grille, and part-leather covered seats. RS-type alloy road wheels with 205/50-16 tyres were standard. In early 1997, when the cars were first price listed, the four-door cost £19,980, while the more extrovert five-door was £21,500.

Purists may sneer at the ST24, pointing out that it should not be called a 'Performance Ford' unless it was very different from its relatives. Although it is true that other V6 engined Mondeos were just as fast in a straight line – and we are talking about a near-140mph top speed here – the more extrovert looks of the car, its crisper handling, and those unique-style RS wheels all have to be considered.

The ST24, in fact, made its own name in a modest way between 1997 and 1999, but as soon as the more specialised ST200 came along its time was over.

The Mondeo ST24 was a full five-seater, with extra aerodynamic fittings, front and rear spoiler changes, and different sills, plus modified suspension.

Specification

Mondeo ST24

ENGINE

Type:	Ford-USA Duratec
Capacity:	2,544cc
Bore/stroke:	82.4 x 79.5mm
Compression ratio:	9.7:1
Max power:	168bhp at 6,250rpm
Max torque:	162lb ft at 4,250rpm
Cylinders:	six, in 60° vee, transversely mounted
Cylinder head:	cast aluminium
Block:	cast iron
Valve gear:	four valves per cylinder, chain-driven twin overhead camshafts, fingers and hydraulic limiters
Fuelling:	Ford EECIV engine management system
Installation:	front-mounted, transverse

TRANSMISSION

Type:	front-engine, front-drive
Gearbox:	Ford MTX-75, five-speed manual

[Optional four-speed automatic transmission]

SUSPENSION

Front:	independent by coil springs, MacPherson struts, anti-roll bar, and telescopic dampers
Rear:	independent, by multiple links, coil springs, telescopic dampers and anti-roll bar

STEERING

Type: rack-and-pinion (power-assisted)
Lock-to-lock: 2.8 turns

BRAKES

Front:	10.9in (278mm) ventilated discs
Rear:	10.0in (253mm) solid discs
System:	hydraulic, with vacuum servo assistance and ABS

WHEELS & TYRES

Wheels:	five-spoke cast alloys, 6.0J x 16in
Tyres:	205/50VR16in

BODY/CHASSIS

Type:	pressed-steel monocoque, in five-door hatchback, four-door saloon or five-door estate car styles
Weight:	2,994lb (1,358kg)

PERFORMANCE

Max speed:	139mph (224kph) approx
Acceleration:	0–60mph in 7.9sec
Standing-start ¼-mile:	16.1sec

PRICE at LAUNCH

£19,980 in October 1996

Mondeo ST200

1999–2000

The Mondeo ST200 was only on sale in 1999 and 2000, and was much faster than the ST24 which it replaced.

Except for the two-tone Recaro front seats, the interior of the ST200 was much the same as that of other high-spec Mondeos.

The Mondeo ST200, which was announced in October 1998, went on sale in April 1999, and was then only available until 2000, and was a much better car than the ST24 which it replaced. Not only was it much more powerful – it had 202bhp instead of the ST24's 168bhp – but its chassis had also been modified and made much more sporting.

It was the first and only Mondeo in which the 2.5-litre V6 engine was given the tune-up treatment, and the general marketing approach was to build on the reputation of the Supertouring race cars. This, no doubt, explains the use of Ford Racing Blue, and the sexy new style of alloy wheels.

Although it was assembled in Belgium, the ST200 was a model designed solely for the British market, and not sold elsewhere in Europe. It evolved because Ford realised that they had to improve on the ST24 which had looked better than the original Mondeo, but had not gone any faster: the ST200 was meant to be a more capable package – faster, more nimble, and more specialised.

The US-built engine was reworked in detail, not only with different cam profiles, but with changes to the cylinder head porting, with different air-cleaner arrangements, and with dual exhaust pipes. The result was 34 extra bhp with no loss of torque – and a top speed of 135mph, with 0–60mph acceleration in just 7.5 seconds.

The chassis was also reworked – not only with revised springs, dampers, anti-roll bars and bushes, but with some changes to the power-assisted steering response. The most obvious upgrade, though, was a new type of 17in cast-alloy wheel, which had a 7.0in rim, and 215/45-section Pirelli tyres. Even though this was still only a front-wheel-drive (Ford had abandoned all ideas of marketing four-wheel-drive versions of this model), it had most impressive traction and roadholding balance.

Compared with the ST24 there were new front and rear bumpers, while the special side skirts were retained and the accent was on the five-door style (to reinforce links with the BTCC car). It was inside the car that enthusiasts could drool a little – Recaro front seats were standard, these still being the standard by which all other sporty-car seating had to be judged. Carbon-fibre look-alike finish was applied to the dash panel, and to the gear-lever knob itself and the instrument dials were white-on-blue (once again emphasising the Ford Racing Blue angle).

All in all, this was Ford's first serious attempt to upgrade the Mondeo. Previous models had all shared the same very capable front-wheel-drive platform, but needed more power to make them special. Now that extra power was present – and it showed. Compared with the ST24, the extra urge was felt at higher engine revs – this was a very free-revving engine, at least up to the limits of the hydraulic pivots – for the red-line was set at 6,800rpm. It is worth remembering that the ST200 was good for 127mph in fourth gear, and a spirited 90mph in third!

Although this was never meant to be a bargain-price car – the original five-door hatch cost £23,000, for which air conditioning and leather-trimmed upholstery was standard – it seemed to have a lot to offer. No wonder that in 1999 Britain's *Autocar* magazine praised it so highly in an independent road test. Comparing it with its rivals, they wrote: 'The ST200 would walk away with first prize today without even breaking into a sweat . . . What is most impressive about this car is its completeness as a package . . . Arguably the most satisfying thing about the ST200 is, simply, the way it goes down the road . . . The suspension engineers in particular deserve praise for creating a car that is so relaxing and so rewarding to drive in equal measure . . .'

Yet the ST200 had only a short career, as a new-generation Mondeo was already on the way.

If you could ever get close enough to the rear panel to read the badging, the 'ST200' labelling gave the game away that this was no ordinary Mondeo.

Specification	
Mondeo ST200	
ENGINE	
Type:	Ford-USA Duratec
Capacity:	2,544cc
Bore/stroke:	82.4 x 79.5mm
Compression ratio:	10.3:1
Max power:	202bhp at 6,500rpm
Max torque:	173lb ft at 5,500rpm
Cylinders:	six, in 60° vee, transversely mounted
Cylinder head:	cast aluminium
Block:	cast iron
Valve gear:	four valves per cylinder, chain-driven twin overhead camshafts, fingers and hydraulic limiters
Fuelling:	Ford EECV engine management system
Installation:	front-mounted, transverse
TRANSMISSION	
Type:	front-engine, front-drive
Gearbox:	Ford MTX-75, five-speed manual
SUSPENSION	
Front:	independent by coil springs, MacPherson struts, anti-roll bar, and telescopic dampers
Rear:	independent, by multiple links, coil springs, telescopic dampers and anti-roll bar
STEERING	
Type:	rack-and-pinion (power-assisted)
Lock-to-lock:	2.8 turns
BRAKES	
Front:	10.9in (278mm) ventilated discs
Rear:	10.0in (253mm) solid discs
System:	hydraulic, with vacuum servo assistance and ABS
WHEELS & TYRES	
Wheels:	14-spoke cast alloys, 7.0J x 17in
Tyres:	215/45ZR17in
BODY/CHASSIS	
Type:	pressed-steel monocoque, in five-door hatchback, four-door saloon or five-door estate style
Weight:	3,109lb (1,410kg)
PERFORMANCE	
Max speed:	135mph (217kph) approx
Acceleration:	0–60mph in 7.5sec
Standing-start ¼-mile:	15.9sec
PRICE at LAUNCH	
£23,000 in Spring 1999	

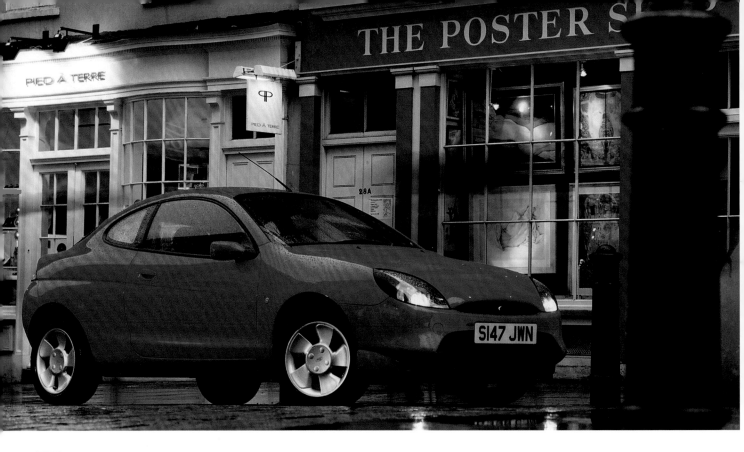

Puma

1997–2002

It is difficult to see how anyone could produce such an attractive little coupé on the basis of the Fiesta platform – but the Puma (announced in 1997) managed it.

Not only did the Puma look good, but it also handled extremely well – in fact, it was difficult for a driver to persuade himself to drive slowly!

Puma! Now there's a name to conjure with. It is one of those generic Ford-worldwide project codes and model names which seems to have been around for decades – yet its use on a road car was delayed until the 1990s.

Even today, the Puma is still under-appreciated. Maybe it was because it never carried an 'RS' or an 'ST' badge, and maybe it was because it was never actively promoted in motorsport. This didn't worry Ford, for they were always happy with the way it sold – up to 200 cars a day were being produced at one point. The fact is that this Fiesta-based coupé was a great little car, which was also built to the limit of its tooling capability, but that when the 1990s-generation of Fiesta died away, so did the Puma.

Like many Performance Fords of earlier years, the Puma owed its life to more mundane machinery. Although the 2+2-seater style was unique, the platform, the 16-valve Zetec SE engines, and the front-wheel-drive engines were all lifted from the contemporary Fiesta family car, but with a difference. Compared with the Fiesta, the SE engine was enlarged, power-tuned and its character changed, while the body style was as sporty as could be achieved on that stubby 96.3in wheelbase platform.

The Puma, therefore, had an appealing 2+2 coupé body style (although most customers, to be fair, treated it purely as a two-seater with loads of stowage space), very rounded, and in many ways carrying the same design 'cues' as other new Fords of this period. Because both front and rear tracks were wider than those of the Fiesta, the wheelarches were rounded – and at the rear flared too – while new-type five-spoke alloy wheels were standard. Were there any complaints? Two – one being that the Puma seemed to sit up rather high at the rear (this impression may have been due

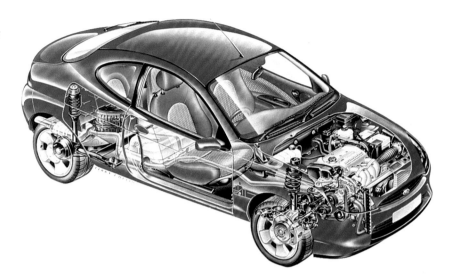

Under the skin of the Puma was a front-wheel-drive engine package, with power by the neat little Zetec SE 16-valve engine.

to the style), the other being that the boot was both tiny, and had a high rear loading sill.

No matter. By any standards this was a pretty little coupé (it made rivals like the Vauxhall Tigra look truly gawky), and the nicely laid out interior, complete with unique fascia/instrument panel, and that magic little alloy-knobbed gear lever, set it off very well indeed.

The Puma was a stylish package from any angle.

It was the running gear of the new car which made so many friends. The platform itself, with MacPherson strut front suspension, twist-beam rear end, power-assisted rack-and-pinion steering and five-speed gearbox, was all based very closely on that of the latest Fiesta (on which Richard Parry-Jones's team had worked their magic in 1995). According to Ford claims, Special Vehicle Engineering had revisited and modified every feature of that layout – and it certainly felt like it. The result was a taut-handling little front-wheel-drive car – not the fastest car in the world, but one which seemed to get a smile on to the driver's face within minutes of him getting behind the wheel.

The secret was in the engine. Originally coded 'Sigma', this lightweight engine (aluminium block and cylinder head) was partly designed and developed by Yamaha of Japan, and was a family designed for the 1.2-litre–1.7-litre bracket. Ford's family name was Zetec SE, and it was one full size/class smaller and lighter than the beefier Zetecs used in Escorts and Mondeos. As expected, it had 16-valves and cogged-belt-driven twin overhead camshafts, and was a high-revving little jewel.

For use in the Puma the capacity of this Spanish-built engine was somehow enlarged to 1,679cc (apparently this was the absolute limit of its 'stretch'), which explains why it was slightly under (not over) square. To achieve this, the cylinder walls needed a special nickel/silicon plating process, which was actually applied by Yamaha in Japan – blocks were flown to/from Spain for this to be carried out. For Puma use, it was also given electronically sensed VCT (variable camshaft timing) on the inlet side. In absolute terms, maybe the 123bhp output was little more than the 1.6-litre BDA of 1970 – but this was a far lighter, more sophisticated, and more environmentally friendly power unit.

No sooner had it gone on sale than the Puma was bumping up against the limits of its production capacity. Originally it had been hoped to build 160 cars a day in Cologne, but that soon had to be raised to 195 cars a day: this was done to reduce six-month waiting lists, and a third shift was needed to make it happen. It was amazingly popular all over Europe, especially after a package of improvements, including a lowered driving seat position, and revised instrumentation was introduced in 1999: the Puma continued selling well until the last cars were assembled in 2002.

Although it was the 1.7-litre car which captured most of the headlines, there were two other versions of the Puma which sold healthily too. From February 1998, Ford introduced a 1.4-litre version, this having an 88bhp power output, but this car was never really fast enough, so from late 2000 it was replaced by a 1.6-litre car with 103bhp, which gave a more acceptable performance.

Because the Puma was based on the platform and running gear of the faster-selling Fiesta, it could only survive while that hatchback did so. Accordingly, when that generation of Fiesta disappeared in 2002, so did the much-loved Puma. Its spiritual, although not its actual, replacement, was the appealing little Streetka roadster of 2003.

Although based on the fascia of the Fiesta, the Puma driving compartment was neat, compact, and packed with dials and switches.

Specification

Puma
(Main spec for 1.7-litre type. Differences for 1.4-litre and 1.6-litre types in brackets.)

ENGINE

Type:	Zetec-SE
Capacity:	1,679cc [1,388cc, 1,596cc]
Bore/stroke:	80 x 83.5mm [76 x 77mm, 79 x 81.4mm]
Compression ratio:	10.3:1 [10.3:1, 11.0;1]
Max power:	123bhp at 6,300rpm [88bhp at 5,600rpm, 103bhp at 6,000rpm]
Max torque:	116lb ft at 4,500rpm [92lbft at 4,500rpm, 107lb ft at 4,000rpm]
Cylinders:	four, in line, transversely mounted
Cylinder head:	cast aluminium
Block:	cast aluminium
Valve gear:	four valves per cylinder, cogged-belt-driven twin overhead camshafts, hydraulic bucket tappets
Fuelling:	Ford EEC-V engine management
Installation:	front, transversely mounted, driving front wheels

TRANSMISSION

Type:	front-engine, front-wheel-drive
Gearbox:	five-speed manual

SUSPENSION

Front:	independent by coil springs, MacPherson struts, anti-roll bar and telescopic dampers
Rear:	independent, by coil springs, trailing links, twist beam, anti-roll bar and telescopic dampers

STEERING

Type:	rack-and-pinion (power-assisted)
Lock-to-lock:	2.9 turns

BRAKES

Front:	9.45in (240mm) ventilated discs
Rear:	7.1in (180mm) drums
System:	hydraulic, with vacuum servo assistance, and ABS [Optional ABS]

WHEELS & TYRES

Wheels:	five-spoke cast alloys, 6.0J x 15in
Tyres:	195/50R15in

BODY/CHASSIS

Type:	pressed-steel monocoque, based on conventional Fiesta platform, in three-door coupé style
Weight:	2,291lb (1,039kg) [2,229lb (1,011kg), 2,282lb (1,035kg)]

PERFORMANCE

Max speed:	123mph (198kph) approx [111mph (179kph), 118mph (190kph)]
Acceleration:	0–60mph in 8.6sec [10.6sec, 10.0sec]

PRICE at LAUNCH
£14,550 [£13,200, £12,280]

Wider, closer to the ground and with special wheels, the Puma Racing was a very fast, specialised, version of the standard Puma: only 500 were made, every one of them in this shade of blue.

Specification

Puma Racing

ENGINE

Type:	Zetec-SE
Capacity:	1,679cc
Bore/stroke:	80 x 83.5mm
Compression ratio:	10.3:1
Max power:	153bhp at 7,000rpm
Max torque:	119lb ft at 4,500rpm
Cylinders:	four, in line, transversely mounted
Cylinder head:	cast aluminium
Block:	cast aluminium
Valve gear:	four valves per cylinder, belt-driven twin overhead camshafts, hydraulic bucket tappets
Fuelling:	Ford EEC-V fuel injection and engine management
Installation:	front-mounted, transverse, driving front wheels

TRANSMISSION

Type:	front-engine, front-wheel-drive
Gearbox:	five-speed manual

SUSPENSION

Front:	independent by coil springs, MacPherson struts, anti-roll bar and telescopic dampers
Rear:	independent, by coil springs, trailing links, twist beam, anti-roll bar and telescopic dampers

STEERING

Type:	rack-and-pinion (power-assisted)
Lock-to-lock:	2.9 turns

BRAKES

Front:	11.6in (295mm) ventilated discs
Rear:	10.6in (270mm) discs
System:	hydraulic, with vacuum servo assistance, and ABS

WHEELS & TYRES

Wheels:	14-spoke cast alloys, 7.5J x 17in
Tyres:	215/40VR17in

BODY/CHASSIS

Type:	pressed-steel monocoque, based on conventional Fiesta platform, in three-door coupé style
Weight:	2,589lb (1,174kg)

PERFORMANCE

Max speed:	121mph (195kph) approx
Acceleration:	0–60mph in 7.4sec

PRICE at LAUNCH

£22,750

Puma Racing

1999–2000

Here's a mystery. Why did the Puma Racing not sell better than it did? How could it be that Ford produced such a sparkling limited-production version of an already well-loved little coupé, stated that it would only build 1,000 (all for sale in the UK), and eventually found that sales were limited to a mere 500? Was it the high price? Was it the hard ride? Was it because it was only available in one colour – Ford Racing Blue? No, the problem was a lack of facilities.

Once the Boreham Motorsport department had stopped building rally cars, the team turned to development projects instead. First, there was the Puma Evolution, then the ST-160 concept, but it was not until August 1999 that the definitive Puma Racing appeared. The objective had been to evolve the ultimate road-car derivative of the appealing 1.7-litre Puma, and to turn it into a potential 'Junior' series rally car. Functionally and visually, this was achieved – but at a cost. Whereas series-production Pumas all took shape in Germany, the Puma racing would be built, as a conversion, at Tickford, in the British Midlands.

The tune-up job had been comprehensive. Not only had the 1.7-litre engine been boosted to 153bhp, but the suspension had been reworked, with a much wider front and rear track, with 7.5in rim, 17in alloy wheels, and grippy 215/40-section Pirelli tyres, plus enlarged four-wheel disc brakes. Apart from those big wheels and tyres, the most obvious changes were that the 'Racing' had big, bulbous, flared front and rear wheelarches, along with a front splitter.

Because of the blue-trimmed interior, with blue-rimmed steering wheel, alloy-trimmed fascia, and those amazing 'Ford Racing' logo'd seats, the inside of the cabin looked almost pure 'racing' too.

Although the performance was excellent – the 'Racing' could beat 120mph, and felt like it – the exhaust note was obvious, and the ride was extremely hard. It was not to everyone's taste. In the end, there's no doubt that it was the cost of the Puma Racing which killed it off: it was launched at £22,750, when a German-built Puma 1.7 retailed for just £14,995, that was a £7,755 premium. Put it another way, the extra power, the hunky style, and the extra 'bells and whistles' cost an additional 52 per cent.

Focus World Rally Car

Introduced 1999

You rarely find a Focus WRC in a dealer's showroom – more likely at a major show, like the NEC. The Martini livery changed subtly from season to season.

Like the Escort World Car, the Focus WRC only counts as a performance Ford road car because the company says so. Designed and developed solely to meet World Championship Rally regulations, the Focus WRC was almost entirely different from the other hatchbacks on which it was theoretically based.

Because the Focus would be on sale by 1999, Ford wanted a new World-level rally car to reflect the new style. Work on a new Focus WRC began early in 1998, the new car was previewed in October 1998, and the first actual rally start was in Monte Carlo, in January 1999. In the next five seasons it would be steadily refined, improved, and made faster, and an impressive number of machines was built, all of them at the M-Sport motorsport facility in Cumbria.

The Focus WRC engine was based on that of the Zetec fitted to normal 2-litre Focus cars, but was turbocharged and much modified.

There was no problem in meeting regulations which stated that a new-generation WRC had to be based on a car being built at a rate of more than 25,000 per year, for almost every other technical feature could be new. However, there was precious commonality between a true series-production Focus (such as the RS) and the World Rally Car. The basic body lines were retained, as were the glass outlines, and some of the skin panels, but everything else (which included the entire engine, drive line, chassis, suspension, and floorpan pressings) was new.

Although the engine itself was broadly based on the 2-litre 16-valve Zetec power unit of the Focus road car, and was still transversely mounted at the front of the car, it was turbocharged, laid back towards the bulkhead, and was different in almost every other detail. The main six-speed gearbox of the four-wheel-drive transmission was longitudinally positioned between the passenger's feet, and of course, there was drive to a rear bodyshell-mounted rear axle.

New all-independent suspension, wheels and brakes, specially placed and developed radiator and oil coolers, and a much modified bodyshell profile which not only provided positive down-force at speed (which explains the use of a rear, roof-mounted spoiler), but also enveloped the larger, fatter, wheels and tyres was all especially designed for this Focus, and this Focus alone.

The interior trim was non-existent, for apart from the two bucket seats and the massively strong roll cage, there was a multitude of controls, switches and safety features. Not wood, and certainly not leather, but carbon-fibre, was predominant here!

As with the Escort WRC, but to an even higher degree, the Focus WRC was designed for only one purpose, which was to provide Ford with a World Championship-winning machine. It was not meant to be quiet, refined, or flexible – and it was none of those.

It was, on the other hand, extremely effective. Colin McRae drove the Martini-liveried car to outright victory in only its third event – the Safari Rally of 1999. In the months and years which followed, the Focus WRC was always 'on the pace' (as usual with a Ford, more competitive on rough events than on tarmac). Crashes, breakdowns of highly stressed components and victories seemed to be equally spaced – almost all the victories going to Colin McRae or Carlos Sainz.

As with the Escort WRC, the number of new Focus WRCs actually built in the first few years is impressive. M-Sport alone used nine cars in 1999, ten new ones in 2000, 12 more in 2001 and a further ten in 2002 – which makes 41 cars. To add to this total there were new cars built for well-financed private teams in Europe and the Middle East, so the total was already over 50 cars by the time this section was originally compiled.

Although many of those cars have already been retired from competition, they are not likely to be converted to normal road use.

Once the Zetec engine of the Focus WRC had been turbocharged, leaned back towards the bulkhead, and the radiator and inter-cooler blocks squeezed in ahead of it, the engine bay was full!

Specification	
Focus World Rally Car	
ENGINE	
Type:	Ford-Cosworth Zetec-M (later known as Duratec-R), based on Zetec
Capacity:	1,988cc (later 1,998cc, with 85mm bore)
Bore/stroke:	84.8 x 88mm
Compression ratio (nominal):	9.0:1
Max power:	300bhp at 6,500rpm
Max torque:	405lb ft at 4,000rpm
Cylinders:	four, in-line, longitudinally mounted
Cylinder head:	cast aluminium
Block:	cast iron
Valve gear:	four valves per cylinder, twin chain-driven overhead camshafts, bucket tappets
Fuelling:	Ford/Pi engine management system, and Garrett turbocharger, with air/air intercooler
Installation:	front-mounted, transverse
TRANSMISSION	
Type:	front-engine, four-wheel-drive, three differentials
Gearbox:	M-Sport/X-Trac six-speed sequential manual
SUSPENSION	
Front:	independent by coil springs, MacPherson struts, anti-roll bar, and telescopic dampers
Rear:	independent, by coil springs, MacPherson struts, telescopic dampers and anti-roll bar
STEERING	
Type:	rack-and-pinion (power-assisted)
Lock-to-lock:	2.0 turns
BRAKES	
Front:	(tarmac) 14.6in (370mm), (gravel) 11.8in (300mm) ventilated discs
Rear:	(tarmac) 14.6in (370mm), (gravel) 11.8in (300mm) ventilated discs
System:	hydraulic, with vacuum servo assistance, no ABS
WHEELS & TYRES	
Wheels:	cast alloys – 7.0J x 15in (gravel), 8.0J x 18in (tarmac), depending on application
BODY/CHASSIS	
Type:	pressed-steel monocoque, based on Focus three-door shell, in three-door hatchback style, with high-mounted rear spoiler
Weight:	2,712lb (1,230kg)
PERFORMANCE	
Never accurately measured	
PRICE at LAUNCH	
Subject to specification and spares package	

Mondeo ST220

Introduced 2002

The Mondeo ST220 was the first high-performance version of the new-generation model. Announced in 2001, it replaced the old-type ST200.

By the early 21st century, there was no doubt that Ford was still reluctant to use the 'RS' badge on any but the most outstandingly-fast products. After the Escort RS Cosworth died in 1996, there were tentative stabs at producing high-performance cars under other names, and 'ST' (for 'Special Tuning') was most popular.

This explains why there was never a straight replacement for the Sierra RS Cosworth pedigree. First-generation fast Mondeos had been ST200s – and now the new, second-generation car to replace this model was to be called ST220.

Although this was yet another front-wheel-drive car (no matter how many traditional-minded Ford fanatics kept asking for a front-engine/rear-drive

Six-speeds clearly indicated on the gear-lever knob – this was a 'first' for a genuine Ford performance car in 2003.

136

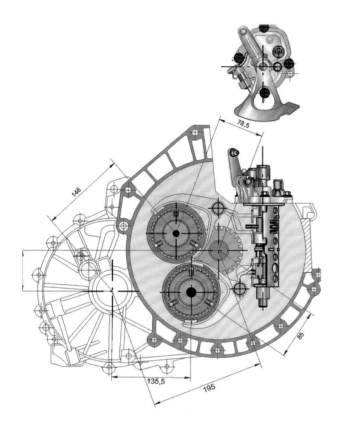

car, Ford was not about to give it to them), the specification of the ST220, at least, looked promising. With 217bhp from a normally aspirated V6 engine, and a probable top speed of 151mph, it was set to be the fastest Mondeo of all – and Ford insisted that there would not be a more powerful version in the future.

Ford made it clear that this car had a purpose. It was not meant to be a performance flagship. It was not meant to be used in motorsport. It was not meant to have extrovert styling. It was meant to be the best-possible fast Mondeo that could be offered at a sensible price. So – no big spoilers, no turbocharged engines, no saloon car race programmes in prospect – for this was just a car meant to go anywhere a lot faster than any other Mondeo in the range. Since the most powerful 'other Mondeo' only had 168bhp, that was easy enough.

More than just a high-performance straight-line car, this was meant to be an all-round rapid package. The V6 engine, therefore, was not as highly tuned as that of the early ST200, basically because it was in 3.0-litre instead of 2.5-litre size. Even so, it peaked at 6,150rpm, and revved very freely. The original transmission was the familiar MTX75 type which Ford had first seen in the RS2000 of 1991, and which had been refined and made more capable ever since then – in this application, the ratios were closer together and the final drive was a touch shorter, to match the new rolling radius of the large tyres.

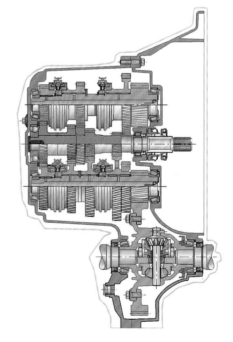

Apart from the high-performance engine, from mid-2003 the most significant ST220 technical feature was its new-type six-speed gearbox.

Mondeo suspension was already very well-matched to this performance, but for the ST220 Ford also added a set of impressive multi-spoke 18in alloys with 225/40-section tyres. Front and rear springs and dampers were all stiffened up, the power-assisted steering was revalved to aid the 'feel', and the whole car was lowered by 0.6in.

Visually, you picked an ST220 not only by its fat new wheels and tyres, but by the new front spoiler and flared arches, and the mesh front grilles, and the very macho control layout, which included a four-spoke silver steering wheel and silver-backed dials. (Naturally, too, there were leather-covered Recaro seats. Naturally – is there really any such thing as a real performance Ford which doesn't have Recaros?)

Once again this was a new high performance Ford which wasn't cheap – it went on sale at £21,745 in the spring of 2002, but Ford's attitude to such cars had hardened as the new century opened. Cheap and cheerful was one thing – an approach which appeared to have been abandoned. In future, fast, competent and carefully built was likely to take over as the modern philosophy.

This, in fact, was a rather different type of Performance Ford – and if the 'ST' philosophy took off, it was likely to be repeated in other models. A new type of six-speed transmission was introduced in mid-2003.

What a difference a set of wheels makes! Apart from the special styling features, and the obvious straight-line performance, the ST220 of 2001 had a massive and aggressive presence on the road.

Specification	
Mondeo ST220	
ENGINE	
Type:	Ford-USA Duratec
Capacity:	2,967cc
Bore/stroke:	89.0 x 79.5mm
Compression ratio:	10.0:1
Max power:	217bhp at 6,150rpm
Max torque:	207lb ft at 4,900rpm
Cylinders:	six, in 60° vee, transversely mounted
Cylinder head:	cast aluminium
Block:	cast iron
Valve gear:	four valves per cylinder, twin chain-driven overhead camshafts, fingers and hydraulic limiters
Fuelling:	Ford EECV engine management
Installation:	front-mounted, transverse
TRANSMISSION	
Type:	front-engine, front-drive
Gearbox:	Ford MTX-75, five-speed manual; six speed from mid-2003
SUSPENSION	
Front:	independent by coil springs, MacPherson struts, anti-roll bar, and telescopic dampers
Rear:	independent, by multiple links, coil springs, telescopic dampers and anti-roll bar
STEERING	
Type:	rack-and-pinion (power-assisted)
Lock-to-lock:	2.8 turns
BRAKES	
Front:	11.8in (300mm) ventilated discs
Rear:	11.0in (280mm) solid discs
System:	hydraulic, with vacuum servo assistance and ABS
WHEELS & TYRES	
Wheels:	16-spoke cast alloys, 7.0J x 18in
Tyres:	225/40ZR18in
BODY/CHASSIS	
Type:	pressed-steel monocoque, in five-door hatchback, four-door saloon or five-door estate car style
Weight:	3,215lb (1,458kg)
PERFORMANCE	
Max speed:	151mph (243kph) approx
Acceleration:	0–60mph in 7.1sec
Standing-start ¼-mile:	15.7sec
PRICE at LAUNCH	
£21,745 in Spring 2002	

Focus RS

2002–2003

Compared with the mainstream Focus, the RS had a vastly larger front-end air intake, and chunky wheels. With only front-wheel-drive, this was a more powerful car than the Sierra RS Cosworth of 1986.

Many of us were relieved when the Focus RS actually made it into the showrooms, for its launch had been delayed for ages – for even longer than many other recent sporting Fords. Originally previewed in October 2000, it was promised for sale in June 2001. That date was missed, and even though the full spec was published in July 2002, the first deliveries did not follow until October 2002.

The delays were not only practical ones – these included ushering the new car through a multitude of crash, noise and exhaust emission tests – but because Special Vehicle Engineering was not about to pass this one off easily, without first making sure that it was the best that the package, and a budget, would allow. Although SVE's reputation had been secure for some time, the Focus RS would be yet another outstanding product to add to their illustrious CV.

Ford, however, was always relaxed about the delays. Having decided, right from the start, that only 4,500 such cars would ever be made (all at Saarlouis), at a maximum rate of 30 cars a day, there was little likelihood of any unsold stocks remaining. That figure, incidentally, should be compared with the overall capacity at Saarlouis, which approached 2,000 cars a day . . .

Ever since the Escort RS Cosworth had been withdrawn from production in 1996, Ford fanatics had been waiting for a successor, but as engineering guru Richard Parry-Jones had commented that there would be 'no more RS-badged Fords for some time to come', they looked like being disappointed. For years, in any case, Ford promoted the ST label instead – but kept on getting a message from the clientele that this was not enough.

The instrument display of the Focus RS included a boost gauge, a speedometer calibrated to 260kph (160mph), with an engine red-lined at 6,500rpm.

The Focus RS engine was well-filled, because there was a turbocharger, and a big intercooler, all extra to the normal kit in a 2-litre Focus.

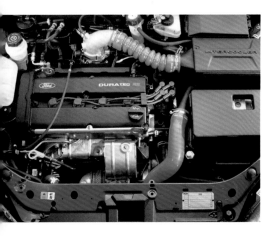

The arrival of the very capable front-wheel-drive Focus, and the huge publicity successes gained by the Focus WRC rally cars, soon changed all that. Ford decided that the RS badge would have to be revived. With the Focus 2-litre hatchback (130bhp) in full production, and with the more powerful Focus ST170 on the way, the decision was taken to provide a 'flagship'.

It would not be the base from which competition cars could evolve – the Focus WRC was already doing that job, superbly and successfully – but it would be the best derivative that SVE could produce. When the mock-up appeared in October 2000, this was supposed to be the ultimate Focus – although, to be more accurate, this probably meant that it would be the ultimate front-wheel-drive Focus. One day, the rumour mill suggested, there would be a Cosworth-badged four-wheel-drive Focus too.

The Focus RS took shape around the three-door hatchback body shell of the mass-production Focus cars which were in production at Saarlouis, but almost every feature of the car – in styling and in engineering – was revisited, and up-rated. The transformation was so complete that when it eventually went on sale in the UK, at an RRP of £19,995 – which was £6,750, or 51 per cent, more than that of the ordinary 2-litre – there were very few complaints. Demand was brisk, waiting lists soon grew, and the UK allocation was apparently sold out before the production run had ended.

The basis of the Focus RS was a much more powerful, turbocharged, version of the transversely mounted four-cylinder engine, allied to much-modified transmission, suspension and braking installations. Although the same basic body shell was retained, it was much-changed in detail. All in all, Ford claimed that there were 385 new parts in the car.

At the front end of the shell, there was a vast new lower front moulding, with a mesh-grilled gaping hole to channel air into the radiator and charge cooler cores, and the rear moulding was also enlarged to match. The wheelarch flares looked the same as ever, although front and rear wings were both subtly flared, and there was a nicely integrated (but not very noticeable) rear roof-corner spoiler, and once again it was only available in one colour – Ford Racing Blue.

The new, 18in five-spoke alloy wheels were a real talking point. Inside the car, naturally, there was a very sporty-looking interior, complete with metal gear knob and pedals, and body-enveloping Sparco front seats. The neatest, and most functional, gimmick of all was that the carbon-fibre centre console included a green starter button – very 'racer'.

Most of the mechanical innovation was under the bonnet. The 2.0-litre engine itself produced no less than 212bhp – and if you're not very impressed with this, remember that this was achieved on a Focus-based engine, and was a higher figure than Cosworth rated the sensational Sierra RS Cosworth in 1986! The torque increase, incidentally, was colossal, for at 229lb ft it was 75 per cent higher than for the standard 2-litre type.

The miracle is that an uprated derivative of the well-known MTX75 five-speed gearbox (you have seen that acronym applied to many front-wheel-drive Fords of the 1990s and 2000s) could cope with the increased power and torque – but Ford had one major advance to add. To help transmit all this power through the 225/40-18in front tyres, a Quaife torque-sensing limited-slip differential was standardised, a device which (Ford claimed) eliminated torque steer under hard acceleration. Even so, electronic traction control was not available.

The chassis was well-and-truly reworked, with widened tracks, front and rear, with a 1.5° increase in negative camber at the wheels. Springs, dampers and roll bar settings were all firmed up, which gave the RS a hard, but not bone-shattering, ride, and Ford also proudly pointed out the huge size of the disc brakes – 12.8in (325mm) at the front, and 11.0in (280mm) at the rear

Those who assess a car only by its paper specification might think that this was quite ordinary, predictable even, for a 'Performance Ford' layout. According to the figures, that was indeed so – but the actual driving experience was extraordinary. According to my tester friends on *Autocar* magazine:

'But it's the way the RS handles – and stops and steers – that really makes your eyes water. In short, we've never driven a front-drive car with so much grip, composure or basic point-to-point speed.'

The fact is that the Focus RS was such a hoot to drive, so compact and at once so capable, that it put almost every driver's licence instantly at risk. Those of you who believe that no speed limit should ever be ignored, and that speed cameras save lives instead of merely raising revenue, might not approve – but Ford, and thousands of Ford enthusiasts, simply didn't care.

What was most outstanding about the Focus RS was that its performance, its balance and its sheer extrovert character were all achieved by SVE at their very first attempt on this platform. Ford fanatics were intrigued, and Ford's rivals must have been terrified at the thought that further, faster and even more capable 'fast Focus' models might follow. Focus RS Cosworth, anyone . . .?

From the tail, the Focus RS could be identified by the big five-spoke wheels, the massive exhaust pipe, and the tailgate-located spoiler.

Specification	
Focus RS	
ENGINE	
Type:	Duratec
Capacity:	1,998cc
Bore/stroke:	84.88 x 88mm
Compression ratio:	8.0:1
Max power:	212bhp at 5,500rpm
Max torque:	229lb ft at 3,500rpm
Cylinders:	four, in line, transversely mounted
Cylinder head:	cast aluminium
Block:	cast aluminium
Valve gear:	four valves per cylinder, twin overhead camshafts, rockers, and hydraulic tappets
Fuelling:	Ford EEC-V engine management, Garrett turbocharger
Installation:	front-mounted, transverse, driving front wheels
TRANSMISSION	
Type:	front-engine, front-wheel-drive
Gearbox:	five-speed manual
SUSPENSION	
Front:	independent by coil springs, MacPherson struts, anti-roll bar and telescopic dampers
Rear:	independent, by coil springs, multi-link location, anti-roll bar and telescopic dampers
STEERING	
Type:	rack-and-pinion (power-assisted)
Lock-to-lock:	2.9 turns
BRAKES	
Front:	12.8in (325mm) ventilated discs
Rear:	11.0in (280mm) solid discs
System:	hydraulic, with vacuum servo assistance, and ABS
WHEELS & TYRES	
Wheels:	five-spoke cast alloys, 8.0J x 18in
Tyres:	225/40ZR18in
BODY/CHASSIS	
Type:	pressed-steel monocoque, based on conventional Focus, in three-door hatchback style
Weight:	2,818lb (1,278kg)
PERFORMANCE	
Max speed:	143mph (230kph) approx
Acceleration:	0–60mph in 6.3sec
PRICE at LAUNCH	
£19,995	

Streetka

Introduced 2003

The Streetka of 2003 was Ford-of-Europe's first-ever open-two-seater model. Based on the platform of the Ka hatchback, it had front-wheel-drive and a 1.6-litre overhead-cam engine.

The Streetka was different. Not just in its name, but in its character. And its market, and its style, And its aspirations. For Ford, it also broke new ground – it was the first two-seater open sports car the company had ever put on sale in Europe, and the very first to be assembled on their behalf at the Pininfarina factories in Turin, Italy.

So, where to start? How on earth could Ford-of-Europe, so often accused of being staid, and not in tune with modern youth, produce a car like this, at such a reasonable price? There was no single answer, but there were a number of influences. Two of them, no question, were that Ford was hurt by the number of people who were buying two-seaters like the Mazda MX-5, and another was that Pininfarina of Italy had made it clear that they could – and wanted to – make cars on Ford's behalf.

Next there were the technical opportunities. Not only was there the availability of an excellent, compact, chassis platform (that of the Ka hatchback, itself a derivative of the Fiesta), there was also the promise of a new 1.6-litre single-overhead-camshaft engine. Ten or even five years earlier, neither would have been available.

The Duratec Ro-Cam engine, in fact, was still little known in Europe when it was previewed in the Streetka. Although it had been designed at Ford's technical centre at Dunton in the late 1990s, it was originally intended for use only in small Fords to be built in Brazil, Argentina, and India. All of these cars would be based on European Ka, Fiesta and old-style Escort models. It was, in fact, a lineal though not-obvious descendant of the long-running overhead-valve Ka unit (the Endura-E – which was itself a descendant of the truly ancient 1970s design first seen in the original Fiesta!), but re-engineered with an aluminium cylinder head and single overhead camshaft. All this, along with Siemens fuel injection, meant that 95bhp was available from 1.6-litres. This is exactly the same rating as the RS Mexico had enjoyed in 1976, incidentally, but Ford does not like to be reminded of this!

The major impulse, though, came from a marketing breakthrough, and public response to a show car. In the beginning, and among many other 'wouldn't-it-be-interesting . . .?' one-offs built by the Ghia design house in Turin, in 2000 Ford built a transverse-engined, front-wheel-drive, two-seater roadster prototype, and exhibited it the Turin Motor Show, where it caused something of a sensation. At the time it was suggested that it might sell for only £10,500 (high hopes!), but at that time there was no place for it in Ford's product plan, and no engine, or final assembly location, had been chosen. Fortunately, at that time Ford-of-Europe's chairman was Sir Nick Scheele, a great automotive enthusiast (and an ex-chairman of Jaguar), so there was no surprise when Ford eventually let it be known that it would go on sale, after all.

But not in any hurry. The big decisions which had to be made were – which of Ford's many small four-cylinder engines should be used, and where would such a car (which, by definition, would not sell in millions) be made? Both these were serious considerations.

When choosing an engine, product planners work backwards from the performance they need from a car, and the power output the engineers tell them will be needed to deliver it. At that point they have to start juggling engine costs, and specifications.

Needing between 90bhp and 100bhp, therefore, they could have chosen

Some of the Streetka's styling cues were lifted from the Ka hatchback, but this was an entirely different type of Ford. The roll-hoops were there for very practical safety reasons.

Ford really hit the jackpot when it persuaded pop Superstar Kylie Minogue to be associated with the Streetka during her 2002 European Tour.

a Puma-type Zetec SE (too complex and costly, perhaps), or a Focus/Mondeo type Zetec (too big and too heavy). The existing Ka engine (60bhp/1.3-litres, very old-fashioned design) was never even considered. In the end, the new-type 1.6-litre 'third world' Ro-Cam power unit almost chose itself, especially as the same engine could then be fitted to a lively little Sportka hatchback. As expected, this engine was then mated to the latest B5 type of five-speed transmission, whose roots were way back in the 1980s, where earlier varieties had been fitted to Escort XR3s and their successors.

But where should this new type of car be assembled? This exercised Ford planners for some time. As they were hoping to produce up to 18,000 Streetkas a year, experience at the Cologne plant with the Puma had shown that such limited-production cars often interfered with the mass-production of Fiestas which were all around them. Other Ford 'satellite' factories were not suitable – Tickford, for instance, was not only small, but old fashioned, while Karmann had not worked with Ford since the Escort Cabriolet had died off.

At this time, fortunately, Pininfarina of Italy made a very strong case. Not only could they cope, admirably, in modern surroundings, but were capable of building up to 25,000 Streetkas a year. Not only was Pininfarina a well-respected styling house, but it was independent of any other manufacturer, and had been assembling cars under contract – for customers such as Alfa Romeo, Fiat and Peugeot – for many years.

The deal, therefore, was done. Ford would supply standard Ka hatchback front, rear and centre floor pressing assemblies from Valencia (in Spain) to Pininfarina in Turin, other major components (such as engines and transmissions) would follow, and the Italians would do the rest.

It was Ford, not Pininfarina, who had styled and engineered the car. Although there were obvious family links with the Ka, whose platform and Fiesta/Puma-like suspension, steering and braking installations were all used, almost every panel was unique, there were chunky front and rear wheelarch extensions, and the 5.5J x 16in six-spoke alloy wheels told their own story. Thanks to the inclusion of long, swoopy, tail lamp clusters which followed the rear wing profile, and the fitment of twin, separate, roll over hoops as standard, no-one was ever likely to mistake a Streetka for its rivals. Amazingly, although the seats were special, and the manual fold-back soft-top was engineered in conjunction with Pininfarina, the Ka hatchback's bulkhead and fascia layout were retained.

Here was a fascinating mixture of cute styling, youth appeal, brisk performance, and the sort of sports car handling which could only be assured by a combination of fat tyres, firm suspension and front-wheel-drive. Like the Puma which it effectively (but not directly) replaced, the Streetka promised to deliver what none of its obvious rivals could approach.

Even before it was officially launched, Ford started the drip-feed of publicity which would build an image. One real coup was to attract the pop superstar Kylie Minogue to associate herself with the Streetka during a 2002 tour – the day on which she took part in a photographic session at Ford's studio will no doubt live for ever – and the pictures were stunning!

Officially previewed in September 2002 (when the UK price was expected to be around £14,000), the Streetka actually went on sale in March 2003 at a considerably lower price level. Everyone hoped that it was just the start of a burgeoning new model line.

Except for the steering wheel, and the seats, the fascia/instrument display of the Streetka was almost like that of the Ka hatchback. It was not the fastest Ford, by any means, but it certainly offered a great deal of fun.

Specification	
Streetka	
ENGINE	
Type:	Duratec Ro-Cam, OHC
Capacity:	1,597cc
Bore/stroke:	82.1 x 75.4mm
Compression ratio:	9.5:1
Max power:	94bhp at 5,500rpm
Max torque:	99lb ft at 4,500rpm
Cylinders:	four, in line, transversely mounted
Cylinder head:	cast aluminium
Block:	cast iron
Valve gear:	two valves per cylinder, chain-driven single overhead camshaft, roller rockers, and hydraulic tappets
Fuelling:	Siemens engine management
Installation:	front-mounted, transverse, driving front wheels
TRANSMISSION	
Type:	front-engine, front-wheel-drive
Gearbox:	five-speed manual
SUSPENSION	
Front:	independent by coil springs, MacPherson struts, anti-roll bar and telescopic dampers
Rear:	independent, by coil springs, trailing links, twist beam, and telescopic dampers
STEERING	
Type:	rack-and-pinion (power-assisted)
BRAKES	
Front:	10.15in (258mm) ventilated discs
Rear:	8.0in x 1.4in (203mm x 36mm) drums
System:	hydraulic, with vacuum servo assistance, and ABS
WHEELS & TYRES	
Wheels:	five-spoke cast alloys, 5.5J x 16in
Tyres:	195/45R16in
BODY/CHASSIS	
Type:	pressed-steel monocoque, based on conventional Ka/Fiesta platform, in two-door sports car style
Weight:	2,340lb (1,061kg)
PERFORMANCE	
Max speed:	108mph (174kph) approx
Acceleration:	0–60mph in 10.8sec
PRICE at LAUNCH	
£12,495 in March 2003	

Appendix A
Ford's factories

Over the years, Performance Fords have been assembled in a whole variety of factories. This is the complete listing of plants, and the cars they have built:

Bedworth (Tickford)
 Capri Tickford
 Sierra RS500 Cosworth (completion from RS Cosworth)
 RS200 (refurbishment, and preparation for delivery)

Cheshunt (Lotus)
 Lotus-Cortina MkI

Daventry (Tickford)
 Puma Racing

Dovenby Hall, Cockermouth (M-Sport)
 Escort WRC & Focus WRC

Cologne (Germany)
 Capri 2300GT/RS
 Capri RS2600
 Capri 3-litre 2
 Capri 3-litre 3
 Capri 2.8 Injection
 Capri 2.8 Turbo
 Scorpio 24V
 Puma

Dagenham
 Cortina GT MkI
 Cortina GT MkII
 Cortina 1600E
 Corsair 2000E
 Lotus-Cortina MkII
 Fiesta XR2
 Fiesta XR2 (Facelift)
 Sierra XR4x4
 Fiesta XR2i
 Fiesta RS Turbo
 Fiesta RS1800

Dagenham was the centre of Ford-UK's assembly operations from 1932 until 2002. Dagenham has now been converted to a massive centre of diesel engine assembly.

Ford-UK's massive design, engineering and development centre at Dunton was the original home of many high-performance Fords. It has expanded even further since this 1980s photo.

Genk (Belgium)
Sierra XR4i
Sierra XR4x4
Sierra RS Cosworth (three-door)
Sierra 'Sapphire' RS Cosworth
Sierra Cosworth 4x4
Mondeo ST24
Mondeo ST200
Mondeo ST220

Halewood
Corsair 2000E
Escort Twin-Cam
Escort RS1600
Capri 3-litre MkI
Capri RS3100
Capri 3-litre MkII
Escort XR3
Escort XR3i
Escort RS2000 (1990s)
Escort RS2000 4x4
Escort XR3i (1990s)

Osnabruck (Germany)
(Karmann)
Sierra (Merkur) XR4Ti
Escort RS Cosworth

Saarlouis (Germany)
Escort RS2000 MkII
Escort RS Mexico MkII
Escort RS1600i
Escort RS Turbo MkI
Escort RS Turbo MkII
Focus RS

Shenstone
(leased from Reliant)
RS200

Slough (FAVO)
GT40

South Ockendon (AVO)
Escort RS1600
Escort Mexico
Escort RS2000 MkI
Escort RS1800

Turin (Italy) (Pininfarina)
Streetka

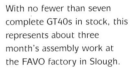

Dagenham in 1967, with a very early example of the Lotus-Cortina MkII being checked off before delivery.

With no fewer than seven complete GT40s in stock, this represents about three month's assembly work at the FAVO factory in Slough.

Even before it was launched in 1969, the Capri was already into series production at Halewood, on Merseyside.

Assembly line shots of the legendary AVO 'Merry-go-Round' facility at South Ockendon are rare – this being a peaceful weekend study. That day, clearly, was good for red cars!

All 500 Sierra RS500 Cosworths were first built in Belgium as RS Cosworths, then stored on this site in Essex, near the Dagenham factory, until conversion took place at the Tickford plant. There are about 200 well-protected cars in this single shot!

By the 1980s, Dagenham's body plant was heavily robotised – this being the Sierra line where 4x4s were produced in some numbers.

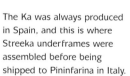

Before RS200s were delivered for use as road cars, they were carefully refurbished, and sometimes customised, at the Tickford factory near Coventry. Sierra RS500 Cosworths had been produced in the same facilities only a year earlier. There are 11 RS200s in this 1988 view.

Body shell assembly of Fiestas at Dagenham in the early 1990s.

The Ka was always produced in Spain, and this is where Streeka underframes were assembled before being shipped to Pininfarina in Italy.

Appendix B
The engines
40 years of performance Ford power

It is no good producing a new car for a sporty market if the engine doesn't match up. Ford took this on board right from the start, and made sure that there was always enough power – and enough tuning potential – to do the job. This was not just with one or two different engines either. Looking down the list, it is fascinating to see how many different types of engine have been used since the first Performance Fords appeared in 1963.

In line or transversely mounted, ahead or behind the seats, four-cylinder and six-cylinder, straight or V formation, overhead valve, single or twin overhead cam, two-valve or four-valve, belt-driven or chain-driven cams, designed 'in house' or by consultants, it is a fascinating line up.

In each case, I have listed the models in which a particular engine has been used:

Kent – OHV, 4-cylinder (1963–1983)
Cortina GT – 1,498cc (pre-cross-flow)
Cortina GT/Cortina 1600E/Escort Mexico/Fiesta XR2 –
1,599cc (cross-flow)
Built in millions, this was one of Ford's most versatile 'building blocks', for in a career spanning more than twenty years, one or other type powered vehicles as different as the Anglia and the Capri, the Fiesta and the Transit van. Complete with a cast iron block, head and (most types) crankshaft, this was a totally conventional power unit.

It had two features which made it ideal for sporty-car use. One was that each and every version was over-square (the cylinder bore was larger than the stroke), which allowed it to rev freely, and the other was that careful and experienced design produced engines that seemed to be rock solid and unburstable.

The original engines (1959–1967) used a conventional cylinder head layout, with inlet and exhaust ports all on the same side of the casting, but from that point an efficient cross-flow head design was adopted.

For many years after 1967, the Kent engine, in 'blueprinted' form, was the specified engine for use in all Formula Ford single-seater racing cars.

When you read catalogues or homologation forms, don't be fooled because the Mexico was quoted at 1,601cc. Like others of this type, Mexico engines were actually 1,599cc units, but the top-tolerance stroke dimensions were quoted to allow it to fit into a capacity just over the 1.6-litre sporting class limit! Where the regulations allowed, engines could therefore be enlarged!

Early in the 1960s, this was the engine that started it all. Shown in its 1.5-litre Cortina Super form, this was the over-square four-cylinder engine, with five-bearing crankshaft, from which the Cortina GT and the Lotus twin-cam were both evolved.

From late 1967, the definitive Kent engine emerged, complete with cross-flow cylinder head breathing. This was the GT derivative, with twin-choke Weber carburettor.

In all its forms, the Kent cross-flow engine was rock-solid, and extremely tuneable.

Lotus evolved a twin-cam engine in the early 1960s, using a Cortina 1500 cast-iron cylinder block as the basis.

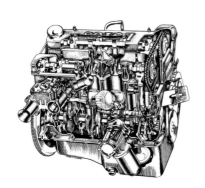

By early 1960s standards, the eight-valve Lotus Twin-Cam was a complicated piece of kit. For Ford, it powered the Lotus-Cortina and Escort Twin-Cam models.

In standard form, the Ford-USA V8 engine of the early 1960s was a compact 90° power unit. Installed in millions of Ford-USA products, in highly tuned form it was also used in the GT40.

Incidentally, the pre-cross-flow 1,498cc engine formed the basis of the bottom end of the Lotus-Ford twin-cam engine, while the cross-flow engine formed the basis of the original Cosworth-Ford BDA.

Lotus-Ford Twin-Cam – DOHC, 4-cylinder (1963–1971)

(Derived from pre-cross-flow 'Kent' OHV)

Lotus-Cortina MkI/Lotus-Cortina MkII/Escort Twin-Cam – 1,558cc

Originally designed as a private venture by Lotus for its own use, the Lotus-Ford Twin-Cam was then used in three different Ford models – the Lotus-Cortinas and the Escort Twin-Cam. It was used in greater numbers in three Lotus model families of the 1960s and 1970s – Elan, Elan Plus Two, and Europa Twin-Cam/Special.

Because Lotus could not afford to design an all-new engine, this power unit was effectively a twin-cam conversion of the pre-cross-flow Ford pushrod engine, using a unique aluminium eight-valve cylinder head and chain-driven camshafts. Originally previewed in 1962 as a 1,498cc engine, by the time that volume production began, it had been enlarged (by increasing the cylinder bore), to 1,558cc.

Race-tuned 1.6-litre engines with fuel injection could produce up to 175bhp.

These engines were never assembled/manufactured by Ford. In the early years, this was done by the proprietary engine specialists JAP in London, but by the late 1960s, Lotus took over assembly at its Hethel factory, in Norfolk.

Ford-USA V8 – OHV, V8-cylinder (1964–1969)
GT40 – 4,727cc

Ford-USA introduced a new 'small block' V8 (it all depends on what you mean by 'small'!) in 1961, when it was built as a 3.62-litre or 4.2-litre. Only one year later the now-legendary 289cu in/4.7-litre derivative was introduced. This family of engines, more and more developed (and enlarged) over the years, went on to have a phenomenally long life.

In the beginning this all-iron V8 was seen as a strictly workaday power unit, but it was relatively light and sturdy, and the Hot Rod fraternity soon discovered that it could produce a great deal of power.

When Ford became involved in the Indianapolis 500 race of 1963, and when it decided to evolve the GT40 racing sports car, the original choice was of aluminium block/head versions of the 4.2-litre, but by the time the GT40 was made reliable the iron block/head 4.7-litre had been chosen instead.

Strictly conventional in all but its sheer tuneability, in Endurance racing form this Ford-USA V8 was good for at least 340/350bhp at 6,500rpm. Some GT40s, especially those theoretically intended for road-car use, were tuned more lightly than this, while the last race cars of all (with 5.0-litre dimensions and special Gurney-Weslake heads) used 440–460bhp.

As mass-production units, these engines eventually grew to 5.75-litres/351cu in, and lineal evolutions were still being used in NASCAR saloons in the early 2000s.

Essex – OHV, V4-cylinder (1967–1970)
Corsair 2000E – 1,996cc

Ford-UK developed a completely new family of V-layout engines in the mid-1960s, these being intended as 'fit-anywhere' building blocks for cars as small as the Capri, and lightweight trucks as large as the Transit. Designed as a family, these were 60° V4 and V6 types, whose cast iron cylinder blocks and heads were machined on the same transfer machinery at Dagenham.

The V4 engines (of 1.7-litre or 2.0-litres) were eventually used in four different Ford private car ranges – the Corsair of 1965-1970, the Zephyr/Zodiac MkIV of 1966–1972, the Consul/Granada of 1972-1974, and the Capri of 1969–1974. Because their V-angle was not ideal for dynamic balance purposes, these V4 engines featured a counter-rotating balancing shaft, but even so, these were never the smoothest of engines.

Amazingly, the 2.0-litre variety fitted to the Corsair GT (and to the Capri 2000GT which followed it) were not only more powerful than the originals, but had also been smoothed out somewhat.

Cosworth-Ford BDA family – DOHC, 4-cylinder (1970–1986)
Escort RS1600 – 1,601cc (really 1,599cc)
Escort RS1800 – 1,835cc
RS200 – 1,803cc

The Cosworth-designed 16-valve, twin-cam BDA (belt-driven, Series A) was evolved to meet a Ford requirement. At first, the company considered producing a top-of-the-line Capri with BDA power, but soon abandoned that idea. Instead, the engine was adopted to fit the Escort, which therefore became the RS1600 as a direct replacement for the Escort Twin-Cam.

Originally based on the iron-cylinder block of the cross-flow Kent engine, the rest of the BDA engine, especially its aluminium cylinder head, was almost entirely special. Not only was it the first 16-valve engine ever to power a Ford road car, but it was also the first to have its overhead camshafts driven by an internally cogged belt.

For sporting homologation reasons, the size of the RS1600 engine was quoted as 1,601cc, although in fact, all engines were nominally 1,599cc units. The 1,601cc capacity was 'achieved', not mechanically, but by quoting the maximum dimension tolerance of the stroke! If suitable Dagenham cast-iron cylinder blocks were available, the capacity could therefore be pushed out to 1.8-litres, and well over 200bhp was available in super-tuned rally guise.

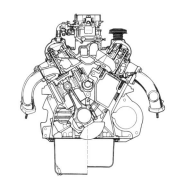

Launched in 1965, the Essex V4 was the first of the vee-engine family which would be used in Corsair, Capri. Zephyr/Zodiac and Granada models in the next decade.

The Essex V4 was shaped on the same transfer machinery as the V6 which would soon follow it.

The legendary BDA power unit was put on sale in 1970, in the Escort RS1600. From late 1972, it would have a light-alloy cylinder block.

The BDA engine, as fitted to several Performance Fords in the 1970s and 1980s, was Ford's very first four-valves-per-cylinder power unit.

The Pinto power unit was launched in 1970, and featured this belt-driven single-overhead-camshaft type of valve gear.

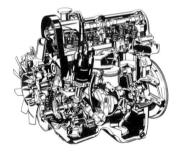

Like its ancestors, the Pinto engine had a very solid bottom end and crankshaft. This was the original 2-litre variety, as fitted to the Escort RS2000.

The Pinto featured belt-drive to its overhead camshaft.

To increase the capacity to a full two litres (and the class limit, not only for rallying, but for Formula Two racing) Brian Hart designed a new aluminium cylinder block with revised, siamesed, cylinder walls. This was previewed early in 1972, and went into production in the summer of that year. All subsequent RS1600s, and of course RS1800s and RS200s, had aluminium blocks.

For motorsport derivatives, the 2-litre types were usually known as BDGs (although this was not strictly accurate in every case), and fuel injection was a popular fitment.

At the very end of the life of this engine, a larger and different-in-every detail BDT-E (belt-driven, turbocharged, evolution) was designed for RS200 rallycross cars. This was a 2.1-litre unit which could produce up to 650bhp!

Neither Ford nor Cosworth ever undertook series manufacture or assembly of BD-type engines, although many of the special components – such as camshafts and valve gear, came from Cosworth. Over the years this was carried out in a variety of locations, originally at Harpers of Letchworth, sometimes at Brian Hart Ltd, and finally at JQF Engineering of Towcester.

Pinto – OHC, 4-cylinder (1973–1980)
Escort RS Mexico MkII – 1,593cc
Escort RS2000 MkI/RS2000 MkII – 1,993cc

Ford's first single-overhead-camshaft engine design, the four-cylinder 'Pinto', was meant to power many different Ford products – cars and light trucks – in the 1.3-litre to 2.0-litre form. It was an engine designed in conjunction with Ford-USA, who would use a near-identical engine for its own Pinto family car – which explains its generic name.

All Pintos had cast-iron blocks and cast-iron cylinder heads. Although the camshaft was in the head, above the line of the valves to reduce the loadings there were fingers between the cam lobes and the heads of the valves. Camshaft drive was by internally cogged belt, this being new, modern and very fashionable at the time.

Although the 1.3-litre engine was never used in a Performance Ford, both the 1.6-litre (MkII RS Mexico) and the 2.0-litre (RS2000s, both models) were used in such cars.

In 1974, incidentally, a revised version of the 2.0-litre engine was homologated, with twin downdraught dual-choke carburettors and approximately 140bhp. In later years, where homologation did not apply, this engine was often enlarged to no less than 2.4-litres, and could produce excellent power outputs.

Essex – OHV, V6-cylinder (1970–1981)
Capri 3-litre – 2,994cc
Capri RS3100 – 3,091cc

This V6 was the 'big brother' blood relation of the V4 Essex which has already been described. It was always machined and assembled on the same production lines at Dagenham. Like the V4, it had cast iron cylinder heads and cylinder block, although the V6 layout was inherently better for balancing purposes, and a counter-rotating balancer shaft was therefore not needed.

Early engines were apparently not very robust (Boreham's mechanics were very rude about them . . .), but this failing was rectified, and from late

1971 they were made more powerful, and more torquey too. In road-car form they were known as extremely tough, simple and reliable power units. Like the V4s, they were used in all manner of Ford cars and small commercial vehicles, from 1966 to 1981 inclusive.

For 'Group 1½' Touring Car racing, this big 3-litre Essex was eventually power-tuned to give 255bhp at 7,500rpm.

The 3.1-litre engine used in the Capri RS3100 was another homologation special, made larger by using an already approved service-overbore piston dimension. This size increase, on its own, was not significant – but it placed the RS3100 in the 'Over 3.0-litre' class. Cosworth designed GAA V6s, using an enlarged version of the RS3100 block, and with aluminium twin-cam four-valve cylinder heads, were 3.4-litre/450bhp monsters which turned this into a race-winning European Touring Car machine.

Note that although this engine had the same basic 60° vee formation as the Ford Cologne engines used in cars like the Capri 2.8 Injection, and the Sierra XR4i and XR4x4, the two power units were completely different.

Cologne – OHV, V6-cylinder (1970–1992)
Capri 2300GT/RS – 2,294cc
Capri RS2600 – 2,637cc
Capri 2.8 Injection/Capri 2.8 Turbo/Capri Tickford/Sierra XR4i/
Sierra XR4x4 – 2,792cc
Sierra XR4x4 – 2,935cc

In the 1960s, Ford-Germany and Ford-UK operated as separate, competing businesses. Although both were 'encouraged' (which really means directed) to produce V4/V6 engine families, this explains why the two ranges had nothing at all in common.

The Ford Cologne V6 was unveiled as early as 1964, when it found a home in new-type Taunus 20M models. Like its Dagenham cousin (the Essex) it had cast-iron cylinder heads, and a cast-iron cylinder block, although it was always slightly smaller, being built in 2.0, 2.3 and 2.6-litre capacities. The 2.8-litre capacity followed during the 1970s.

Race-engine derivatives of the Capri RS2600 were eventually enlarged to almost 3.0-litres, and with entirely different cylinder heads and fuel injection produced well over 300bhp, but this knowledge was never applied to road-car engines.

Bosch fuel injection suited this engine very well, being applied to Granada-type 2.8-litre units from 1977, and to Capris and Sierras which followed.

Because some of the exhaust ports were siamesed, this was not an engine which breathed very deeply, and improvements were made in the late 1980s: at the same time as new six-port heads were included, the capacity crept up to 2.9-litres. It was that definitive power unit which was used as the basis of the Cosworth-evolved Scorpio 24V which followed.

Cosworth actually took over the manufacture of the 2.9-litre

Even in 3-litre form, the Essex V6 power unit was compact, if somewhat heavy. This is an early Capri installation.

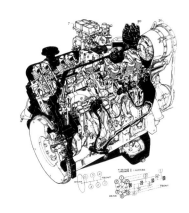

The Essex V6 was the 'Big Brother' derivative of the earlier V4 type, and commercially much more successful.

From 1977, Ford-of-Germany's Cologne V6 engine took over from the Essex in British Performance Fords. Although similar in concept, the two V6s were totally different in detail.

As fitted to cars like the Granada 2.8 Injection, and the Capri 2.8i, the Ford Cologne V6 engine had Bosch fuel injection.

The CVH of 1980 was a brand-new engine family, not only with a belt-driven overhead camshaft, but with a complex combustion chamber/valve gear orientation. This drawing shows a carburetted 1.6-litre version.

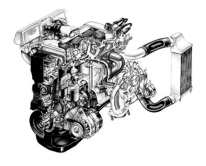

For the Escort RS Turbo of 1984, the CVH engine was given a turbocharger at the side of the cylinder block, and an air/air intercooler close to the front grille.

Late-model 1980s Escort XR3is had the Ford EECIV-managed fuel injection version of the CVH engine.

engines from Cologne in the 1990s, these being built in 12-valve and 24-valve form at Wellingborough for a few years.

CVH – OHC, 4-cylinder (1980–1992)
Escort XR3/XR3i/Fiesta XR2/Escort RS1600i/Escort RS Turbo/ Fiesta XR2i/Fiesta RS Turbo – 1,596cc

For the 1980s and beyond, Ford designed an all-new four-cylinder engine, which was coded CVH, an acronym which stood for compound valve angle, hemispherical head. Dedicated for transverse installation in front-wheel-drive cars, it also took account of the latest exhaust emission rules. In Ford's long-term product planning philosophy, it was a direct replacement for the Kent engine, and would itself gradually be displaced by the Zetec engine in the mid-1990s.

Huge amounts of investment went into this power unit, including a brand-new factory at Bridgend in South Wales where it was to be manufactured. Although it had single overhead camshaft valve gear, this was entirely different in detail from the Pinto. In a life which spanned the 1980s and 1990s, the CVH was used in all manner of Fiestas, Escorts and Sierras.

Not only were the inlet and exhaust valves more steeply opposed to each other in the aluminium cylinder head, but they were also skewed relative to the cylinder bores. Along with the cogged belt drive and hydraulic tappets, this had all been done to make it suitable for meeting modern legislation requirements. The only high-performance derivatives were the 1.6-litre types, and only in the RS1600i were solid valve lifters used.

European CVHs would be built in millions, in 1.3, 1.4 and 1.6-litre sizes (there was a Ford-USA version which was different in every detail), in carburetted, fuel-injected, and injection/turbocharged form. Compared with the legendary Kent engine these were not high-revving, or free-revving, power units.

As fitted to cars like the XR4Ti, Ford-USA's Lima engine showed obvious family resemblances to the European Pinto power unit.

Lima (Ford-USA) – OHC, 4-cylinder (1984–1988)
Sierra (Merkur) XR4Ti – 2,301cc

The simple way to describe the Lima is as an enlarged, improved, development of the original Pinto power units. The main differences were that the Lima was a 2.3-litre 'four', and was built only in North America for use in Ford-USA and Mercury-badged models.

Like the Pinto, it was a single-overhead-cam design, that cam being driven by an internally cogged belt, and hydraulic tappets

Although it could be rated at 175bhp in the Merkur XR4Ti, the Lima engine was a compact power unit.

were fitted. For use in the European Merkur, and in certain versions of the Mustang, it was built in turbocharged form.

Cosworth-Ford YB family – DOHC, 4-cylinder (1986–1998)
(Derived from the Pinto cylinder block)
Sierra RS Cosworth three-door/Sierra RS500 Cosworth
Sierra RS Cosworth four-door/Sierra Cosworth 4x4/Escort RS
Cosworth/Escort WRC – 1,993cc

The engine which started life as a tentative after-market project at Cosworth in the early 1980s become one of the most successful of all 'Performance Ford' engines. At the peak of its race-winning progress in the late 1980s, it was possible to race this 2.0-litre turbo Ford with at least 550bhp!

In the beginning, Cosworth had considered building a normally aspirated 16-valve/twin-cam version of the long-established Pinto engine, and selling it on the after-market. Such engines existed when Ford bosses saw a prototype in 1983: 'If we turbocharged that, and put it in a Sierra', motorsport director, Stuart Turner, commented, 'Rover and BMW would not win another touring car race . . .' Initially for use in the Sierra RS Cosworth model – and later applied to other cars – the Cosworth YB was precisely that. Not only was it a great race engine, but a fabulous road car engine too.

Starting with a Pinto/'Type T88' cast-iron block, Cosworth developed an aluminium 16-valve/twin-cam cylinder head. The valves were opposed at 45°, and were operated directly from the camshafts by inverted bucket tappets. Cam drive was by internally cogged belt.

All road-car derivatives of this mighty engine were turbocharged (the Sierra RS500 had a monstrous Garrett AiResearch T4 turbo, which was far too large for the job – except when it was race tuned! For use in other cars, as after-market conversions, Cosworth eventually made normally aspirated versions available too.

Originally rated at 204bhp in 1985 (this making it the first-ever road-car engine to be listed at more than 100bhp/litre), the same engine was improved to 220bhp by the end of the 1980s, and to 227bhp for the Escort RS Cosworth of 1992.

Every road-car engine – well over 30,000 of them – was built by Cosworth at a factory at Wellingborough, in Northamptonshire.

Zetec family – DOHC, 4-cylinder (introduced in 1992)
Fiesta XR2i/Fiesta RS1800/Escort XR3i (1992 variety) – 1,796cc
Focus WRC/Focus RS – 1,998cc

Like the Kent engine of the 1960s, or the CVH engine of the 1980s, the engine we now know as the Zetec was a massive undertaking, with many applications in mind, and with a projected life of millions of units, over more than a decade. Designed for use in Fords built all round Europe and in the USA, its European manufacturing base was at Bridgend in South Wales, where it gradually displaced the CVH as new model after new model came along.

Originally coded 'Zeta' (until Fiat-Lancia protested that they held a trademark of the same name!), the Zetec was a state-of-the-art mass-production 16-valve twin-cam when designed. First seen, in limited-production form, in the Escort XR3i of 1992, it was nevertheless intended for use in other Escorts, and in Mondeos, and would be produced in 1.6, 1.8, and 2.0-litre forms.

The famous Cosworth YB turbocharged engine powered tens of thousands of Sierra RS Cosworths, and the Escort RS Cosworth. This was the original YBB type of 1986.

The Cosworth YB engine was based on the Pinto cylinder block, and placed its turbocharger to the right side of that block, and the inlet manifold 'log' on the left side.

Late-model YBs, as fitted to the final Escort RS Cosworths, used a smaller turbocharger, and restyled cam drive and camshaft covers.

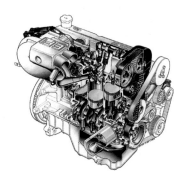

The Zetec engine first appeared in 1992, and became Ford's standard power unit for cars in the Escort, Focus and Mondeo ranges. It featured four valves per cylinder, and twin belt-driven overhead camshafts.

Two views of a Zetec cutaway display engine, showing the four valves per cylinder, and the robust,

compact, layout, which made it suitable for use in a variety of transverse applications.

The cylinder block was in cast iron, the head in aluminium, and the twin overhead camshafts were driven by internally cogged belts. The valves, opposed at 40° and were operated directly from the camshafts by inverted hydraulic tappets.

Zetecs fitted to XR2i, XR3i and Fiesta RS1800 models were in standard, conventional, drop-in-place tune, but as fitted to the more racing Focus WRC and Focus RS types they were utterly non-standard.

Except that the original cylinder block and head castings had to be retained (to meet regulations) the WRC engine, of course, was completely redeveloped, and turbocharged. The Focus RS engine was also turbocharged, but in a different, more civilised manner.

Cosworth-Ford FB – DOHC, V6-cylinder (1991–1998)
Scorpio 24V – 2,935cc

The silky-smooth 2.9-litre V6 'FB' power unit was evolved from the basis of the Ford Cologne 2.9-litre pushrod overhead valve engine, and retained the same bore and stroke dimensions. As so often in the past, this clever conversion was completed for Ford by Cosworth, who also undertook series manufacture at Wellingborough.

Cosworth's FB engine, as used in the Scorpio 24V road car, was one of the very first road-car engines to carry that famous name on the cam covers. Originally this 2.9-litre power unit developed 195bhp.

Cosworth's FB engine of the 1990s was purely intended for 'executive' road car use, which explains the mass of belts, to drive items like power-assisted steering, and air conditioning pumps.

The original conversion was engineered by Brian Hart Ltd, but after that concern was absorbed by Cosworth it became a Cosworth project. As might be expected from such an illustrious beginning, this was a classic case of a cast-iron block bottom end topped by two aluminium cylinder heads, each with twin overhead camshafts, four valves per cylinder opposed at 31.5°. Camshaft drive was by chain, and in view of the 'executive' nature of this power unit, hydraulic tappets were also standard.

In its original state of tune, the FB V6 was ultra-smooth and ultra-refined. Accordingly, when the time came to up-grade the Scorpio in 1994/95, there was no hesitation in up-grading the engine too – its peak power was boosted from 195bhp to 204bhp with no loss of smoothness or purpose.

When the Scorpio dropped out of production in 1998, this engine also died away, for it was always costly to manufacture, and had not found a home in any other Ford model.

Ford-UK (I4) – DOHC, 4-cylinder (1991–1996)
Escort RS2000/Escort RS2000 4x4 (1990s family) – 1,998cc

Since the Pinto engine had been in service since 1970, Ford set about designing a replacement for the entire family in the 1980s. Because it was planned for use in products as diverse as the Sierra, the Scorpio, the Transit van range, and the planned Galaxy MPV 'people carrier', either in-line, or transversely positioned, it had to be more compact than the Pinto – and it was also intended to be 'stretchable' to 2.3-litres. Manufacture was at Dagenham.

All the engines in this family were twin-cams, with aluminium cylinder heads. Most of them were eight-valve units (with carburettors or fuel injection), but the 'Performance Ford' application came in the form of a squat, powerful and purposeful 16-valve derivative.

Previewed in 1990, but in production from late 1991, this 150bhp 2-litre engine was entirely designed by Ford, with no official input from Cosworth. The valves were opposed at 40° and there was direct actuation of inverted bucket-type tappets from the cam lobes. Camshaft drive was by chain.

In standard form, this engine had much mid-range torque, but examples supertuned for motor racing were capable of at least 300bhp in normally aspirated form.

The only 'performance Ford' to use this engine was the Escort RS2000 of 1991–1996, but in enlarged yet slightly detuned form – 145bhp/2,295cc – it was also used in Scorpio and Galaxy models. In this form, it was given a cleverly detailed installation, of twin chain-driven balancer shafts. Engineered by Cosworth, these shafts were very neatly installed in the sump itself, below the line of the crankshaft.

Zetec SE family – DOHC, 4-cylinder (1997–2002)
Puma 1.4 – 1,388cc
Puma 1.6 – 1,596cc
Puma 1.7/Puma Racing – 1,679cc

When the much-revised Fiesta range of 1995 was introduced, it was powered by a brand-new 16-valve engine, which had been coded 'Sigma', but was officially christened as the Zetec SE. This was confusing, for although it carried the same name as the engines used in 16-valve Escorts and Mondeos it was an entirely different, and rather smaller, engine family.

Designed, along with considerable consultancy help from Yamaha of Japan, the Zetec SE was originally to be built, in Spain, in 1.25-litre and 1.4-litre guise. Both the cylinder head and the block were cast in aluminium, and it was immediately admitted that there was a little, though not much more, cylinder capacity to come. The twin overhead camshafts were opposed at 42° (the larger Zetec engine used an angle of 40°), and were driven by internally cogged belt.

For the Puma, this lightweight, high-revving, little engine was stretched

The 60° V6 FB engine fitted very snugly into the Scorpio's engine bay, leaving little space for any other items.

The Escort RS2000 of 1991 used this 150bhp 16-valve 2-litre power unit. Later it would be enlarged to 2.3-litres, for other uses.

The 16-valve engine fitted to the 1990s-type Escort RS2000 could be tuned to more than 280bhp for rally purposes. Cam drive was by chain.

Yamaha of Japan were consulted over the design of the Zetec SE engine, but manufacture was concentrated in Spain. This lightweight 'four' was a typical state-of-the-art 16-valve unit, with belt-driven camshafts.

Made in various sizes from 1.25-litres to 1.7-litres – this particular engine is a 1.4. The Zetec SE was fitted to cars like the Fiesta, the Focus, and the Puma.

The Ford-USA V6, of 2.5 or 3.0 litres, as used in the Mondeo ST24, ST200 and ST220 models, was so compact that it was mounted transversely. Jaguar evolved its own version for use in the S-type and X-type models.

to its ultimate – 1,679cc – where the cylinder bore was 80mm, and uprated to 125bhp at 6,300rpm. Like all Japanese-influenced engines, however, it was so tuneable that when the Puma Racing appeared, it was rated at no less than 153bhp at 7,000rpm.

The Zetec SE was always manufactured in a Spanish Ford factory.

Duratec Ro-Cam single-cam – OHC, 4-cylinder (introduced in Europe in 2002)
Streetka – 1,597cc

Early in the 2000s, Ford began to use a new derivative of the old-design four-cylinder overhead-valve engine which had powered Ka (and earlier-generation Fiesta) economy hatchback models for so long. Although it had been modified, improved and rejigged several times in the 1990s, the roots of that engine dated from the original Fiesta of 1976.

Known also as the Duratec-Ro-Cam, this was an eight-valve single overhead camshaft power unit which had first been seen in Ford-Brazil Kas revealed in 1999, where it was produced in 1.0 and 1.6-litre capacities. Produced in Brazil, it was also used in Ford-Argentina Fords, and in the Indian-built (Fiesta-based) Ford Ikon saloon.

The cylinder block was cast iron, the cylinder head was aluminium, and the valves were located in vee, opposed at 42°, with roller cams operating them, from a single, central, overhead cam, driven by chain. New to Europe in the Streetka, this ohc engine was also due for use in a new hatchback, the Sportka, and other applications would follow in future years.

Duratec Mondeo V6 family – DOHC, V6-cylinder (introduced 1993)
Mondeo ST24/ST200 – 2,544cc
Mondeo ST220 – 2,967cc

When Ford developed what it swore would be a medium-sized 'World' car for the 1990s, there were to be four-cylinder petrol, four-cylinder diesel, and V6 petrol engines. Although the V6 engine would be manufactured on the North American continent, it would also be supplied for fitment to the European version of the car, the new Mondeo.

Although the original engine was a 2.5-litre unit, it was always known to be capable of enlargement to 3.0 litres, and although it was a free-revving unit, it was also always very conservatively rated. Even so, it had aluminium cylinder heads and cylinder block, four valves per cylinder (opposed at 50°), and twin overhead camshafts, driven by chain. In something of a throw back to the Pinto layout of the 1970s, fingers were mounted between the camshafts and the valve stems themselves.

Later in the 1990s, this engine was also used as the starting point for a new range of Jaguar V6s, although there were many differences between the two types. Not only did the Jaguar derivative have different cylinder head castings, but different cylinder bore and overall capacity figures: there was also a smaller, 2.1-litre version not replicated behind a Ford badge. They were also more highly rated.

Incidentally, this was not the V6 engine used in Supertouring racing versions of the Mondeos which won so many events in the 1990s. The regulations allowed alternative Ford engines to be used, and for technical reasons, a Ford-USA/Mazda V6 was used instead.

Index